ARMY OF ROSES

ARMY OF ROSES

INSIDE THE WORLD OF
PALESTINIAN WOMEN
SUICIDE BOMBERS

BARBARA VICTOR

Foreword by Christopher Dickey, Newsweek
Paris bureau chief and Middle East editor

ROBINSON
London

Constable & Robinson Ltd
3 The Lanchesters
162 Fulham Palace Road
London W6 9ER
www.constable.com

First published in the US by Roedale Inc.

First published in the UK by Robinson,
an imprint of Constable & Robinson Ltd, 2004

A copy of the British Library Cataloguing in
Publication data is available from the British Library

ISBN 1-84119-937-0

Printed and bound in the EU

TO GÉRARD

FOREWORD

AT THE VERY BEGINNING of the first Intifada in 1987, when the shock troops of Palestinian resistance in the West Bank and Gaza were still children with stones, and neither the Israeli intelligence services nor exiled Palestinian groups knew quite what to make of these kids, I went to Baghdad to visit Yasser Arafat. The grizzled leader of the Palestinians' "armed struggle" for the previous twenty years was comfortable and secure there, thanks to Saddam Hussein's generous patronage, and when I arrived to meet him he was relaxing with aides in the living room of a luxurious government guest house. Arafat didn't look up to see who'd come into the room. His eyes were fixed on a TV, which showed news footage of the uprising in far-away Gaza. "Look, look!" shouted Arafat suddenly, drawing everyone's attention to the screen. "Look! They're girls!" He just couldn't believe that little Palestinian schoolgirls, just like little Palestinian schoolboys, were taking to the barricades and hurling rocks at the Israeli troops. Few of his men had ever been so brave.

Later, when Palestinian groups like Arafat's Fatah and the Islamic movement Hamas managed to gain control over the insurrection and to organize the violence, little girls were excluded from the front lines. Yet, as Barbara Victor makes clear in this extraordinary chronicle of passion and politics, terror and liberation, Palestinian women have always known that when it comes to suffering and dying, they are the equals of their men. And in the last few years, as they have slung backpacks full of explosives over their shoulders or strapped bombs around their waists—indeed, around their wombs—some have chosen, too, to be killers.

Victor begins this book asking how it can be that women, who are bearers of life, are turned into killing machines. By following that elemental theme she takes us deeper into the minds of suicide bombers, and the world that creates them, than most of us have ever been or imagined we could be. I've known Barbara Victor for years, and I can't think of anyone who could bring more empathy to these tragic stories of terror and loss. Like many of us, journalists who've worked both sides of the conflict, she tries to understand, even to feel, the anger and the grief in order to explain the atrocities and the retributions. And, like the novelist she is, she also searches for human truths even in the most inhumane actions.

Yes, the reasons behind the act of each of these women are social, and religious, and political. But that clearly is not enough to make them make this extraordinary and horrible sacrifice. A suicide bombing is not merely an act of protest, or even of combat. Probably more than any other fighter in any other kind of war, the suicide bomber carrying out an act of terror makes an intensely personal and direct decision. The would-be martyr stands before her victims: soldiers, sometimes, or perhaps other women just shopping for dinner, or maybe a girl very much like herself. And she pushes the button, or does not. She and she alone decides.

By interviewing the mothers and friends of the bombers, their brothers and ex-husbands, their recruiters and "handlers," and some of the girls who have held the button in their hand and refused, in the end, to die or to kill, Victor gives us an extraordinarily intimate sense of their motives. Even as her narrative follows them on the way to their deaths, she tells the stories, as we have never had them before, of their lives.

These are not the first women to embrace terror; not even the first Palestinians. (On the same visit to Baghdad in 1987, Arafat proudly introduced me to a beautiful Palestinian protégée who had lost several fingers on one hand while making a bomb.) And these are not the first women to immolate themselves along with their victims. In Sri Lanka, the Tamil Tigers have trained brigades of young girls ready to kill by dying, including the woman who, bearing flowers and a bomb, assassinated former Indian prime minister Rajiv Gandhi in 1992.

As far back as 1985, Syrian intelligence encouraged and coerced young Lebanese women to blow themselves up in attacks on Israeli troops and the Israel-backed militias of South Lebanon. One, dubbed "the Bride of the South," won such posthumous fame as a symbol of resistance that posters of her were seen even in the back alleys of East Jerusalem. But the Palestinians of the West Bank and Gaza in 1985 were one of the most docile occupied populations in history. They seemed a long way from adopting the bloody and terrifying tactics that had become so common in Lebanon as a response to Israel's invasion three years before.

Victor gives us the history we need to understand how those passive, occupied people in the Palestinian territories could move to popular revolt, and through the tragedy of a failed peace, to the ferocious anger of suicidal bombing campaigns. But she does not claim that history alone can explain what has happened to create this "army of roses," as Arafat called his female followers.

In one of the most striking passages of the book, Victor alludes to the stories she heard from the families of the dead and directly from the mouths of women who tried and failed to become *shahidas*, or martyrs: "It is painful enough in life to be left by a husband; or to find yourself the focus of ridicule and disdain because you fell in love with more than one man; or to be considered damaged because you can't have a child; or to be forced to bear the full responsibility for raising a child as a single mother; or because you crave an education unavailable to you; or to feel the crushing responsibility of saving a beloved male relative from humiliation or death. But when every life opportunity ends with a closed door, when there are no friends who will offer emotional support, no professional fulfillment that could contribute to a sense of pride and independence, and no structure in place within the society to help cope, economically or emotionally, with fatherless children, then it becomes a little less mysterious that some of these vulnerable women could be convinced to end their lives."

But Victor reveals, too, the role of the men who do whatever needs doing to make the suicide happen. They handle the young women quite differently than they do the young men. As one of the many psychologists interviewed by Victor explains, "When an adolescent boy is humiliated at an Israeli checkpoint, from that moment, a suicide bomber is created. At the same time, if a woman becomes a *shahida*, one has to look for deeper, more underlying reasons."

That is just what the men who prepare the women for their deaths know, instinctively perhaps, how to do: "The differences between men and women in a society steeped in fundamentalism and a culture of double standards do not disappear even within that extraordinary concept of martyrdom. Women understand from the beginning that men do not accept them as equals or look upon them as warriors within their ranks until they achieve Paradise and are accepted as such at Allah's table. But by then, they are dead. And, there are no women who can testify to having had those promises fulfilled in another life."

This is an angry book, filled with human emotion, and a frightening one, which is as it should be. This is not a story that will end soon. One child psychologist told Victor that his studies showed, as early as 2001, that among Palestinian school children little girls were just as likely as little boys to say they longed to be suicide bombers. They thought that such a death was the highest honor that life could bring them. Nor is this spreading psychosis of martyrdom, so intimately tied to the humiliations of occupation and the hopelessness of deeply stagnant societies, limited to the West Bank or Gaza. Among men, and among women, it is spreading throughout the Arab and Muslim world, and not least in Iraq. Here America's ostensible war of liberation has turned very quickly into a thankless and seemingly endless confrontation with hopeless and hostile people. Saddam is gone. Someday soon, Arafat will be, too. But the cult of death that they helped create lives on. And so do the occupations.

—**Christopher Dickey**
Baghdad, June
2003

INTRODUCTION

THERE ARE CERTAIN MONUMENTAL EVENTS in life that mark us forever, when we remember time, place, and person so vividly that our own actions or thoughts at that moment replace the enormity of the event itself. For each generation the references are different: the attack on Pearl Harbor, the assassination of John F. Kennedy, and, of course, September 11, 2001.

Then there are other events that, because we happen to find ourselves in the middle of the fray, touch us more personally; pivotal moments that take a permanent place in our memories. Many of these moments happened for me while I was working as a journalist in the Middle East. The first was in 1982, during the war in Lebanon, when I arrived in Beirut just in time to witness the massacre at the Sabra and Shatilla refugee camps. When the press was finally allowed into the camps to record the horrors there, after we had digested the visual shock of bloated bodies and houses reduced to rubble intermingled with an occasional sign of life—a twisted plastic doll, or a broken plate—an incident transpired that has remained with me throughout the years.

A Palestinian woman was sitting on the ground, cradling a lifeless child in her arms, while all around her was the stench of death that lingered after two days and nights of unrelenting carnage. Kneeling down next to her, I asked her the prerequisite media questions: how she felt when she found herself the sole survivor in her family and, more crucial, how she would manage to live the rest of her life with those memories constantly there to torture her. She knew immediately that I was an American, and without any hesitation she looked up at me and said, in surprisingly good English, "You American women talk constantly of equality. Well, you can take a lesson from us Palestinian women. We die in equal numbers to the men." This tragic concept of women's liberation stayed with me.

In one of those horrific ironies that occur more frequently than anyone could imagine unless one is familiar with that part of the world, the other moment that has remained with me forever happened while I was in Ramallah in November 2001, accompanying a French journalist who was filming a report about the Palestinian Red Crescent. My friend was doing a story on these young volunteers as they rode in ambulances, tending to the dead and dying after violent clashes with Israeli soldiers.

The Red Crescent office in Ramallah is housed in a three-story white building with a red tile roof, not far from the town's main square. On the first floor of the headquarters, the room where the staff gathered in between emergency calls was furnished sparsely with a wrought-iron sofa and kitchen chairs grouped around a low blond-wood table. In one corner of the room, perched high on a wall, a television set tuned to the Palestinian Authority station monitored all events throughout the West Bank and Gaza and gave hourly news reports.

Waiting for the inevitable call that day were five Red Crescent workers, three men and two women who obviously knew each other well. There was casual banter and a lot of joking, although what struck me was how they each rocked back and forth on their chairs, arms clasped tightly around their chests. Their body language was a sign of the extreme stress that each of them undoubtedly felt, given the daily reality of closures, the possibility of a suicide attack within Israel that would bring military reprisals, and knowledge that at any minute they could be called out in the middle of a confrontation. As my friend's camera panned the group, each one gave his or her name and age, beginning with Tared Abed, twenty-seven years old; Ahlam Nasser, twenty-three; Nassam al-Battouni, twenty-two; Bilal Saleh, twenty-three; and Wafa Idris, who said she was twenty-five. Almost immediately the others teased her, since she had apparently lied about her age, making herself younger than she actually was.

Of all the Red Crescent volunteers, Wafa was the most animated; she played with a big elastic band, aiming it playfully at the others like a slingshot. She was a full-figured young woman with long black hair, tinged with henna, and a round face, made up lightly to accentuate her dark eyes and cupid-bow mouth. On her head was a black velvet cap. It was not surprising, given her

3

cheerful personality and good looks, that I later learned that several Western journalists had asked her out, although, as a good Muslim woman, she had refused their advances.

As I was observing the volunteers, there was a moment when the image on the television showed a man, his head and face wrapped in a checkered red-and-white kaffiyeh to conceal his features, speaking in Arabic, holding a Kalashnikov rifle in one hand and a Koran in the other. While the others continued laughing and talking, I saw Wafa's expression turn suddenly serious as she watched the man on the screen make what was his last speech before he set off to blow himself up in a suicide attack somewhere in Israel. Concentrating on the "martyr's" every word, she sat forward in her chair, her jaw set, her demeanor intense, silent and unmoving until he concluded his videotaped testament to the Palestinian community, his friends, and his family. I remember a gesture Wafa made after the suicide bomber finished his speech; she suddenly raised her right arm and waved.

Two months later, on January 27, 2002, Wafa Idris entered Palestinian infamy when she became the forty-seventh suicide bomber and—more significantly—the first woman kamikaze to blow herself up in the name of the Palestinian struggle. Back in Paris, I would always remember where I was and what I was doing when I heard the news. Several hours later, my journalist friend who had taken me along that November day to the Red Crescent office called to say he had footage of the suicide attack. I rushed over to see it, and while the entire scene was horrifying, the sight of Wafa's body lying in the middle of Jaffa Road in Jerusalem, covered haphazardly with a rubber sheet, was stunning. Even more shocking was the image of an arm, her

4

right arm, which had been ripped from her body, lying bloody and torn several inches away. At that moment something clicked in my head and I recalled her good-bye that day in Ramallah.

Such acts of "martyrdom" perpetrated by Palestinian militants have taken hundreds of Israeli lives and have resulted in reprisals by the Israeli military, where hundreds more lives, namely Palestinian civilians, have been lost as well. But the constant bloodshed broadcast on television or reported in newspapers and magazines reveals only the immediate aftermath of the devastation and destruction, rarely the effect they have weeks and months later, especially on the people who barely survived them or who lost loved ones. We who watch the gruesome images from afar have almost become inured to their horrors. Certain phrases—explosive belts, martyrdom—have become part of our lexicon, although often their terrible significance eludes us. Yet if anything could jar us into facing the cruel reality of these attacks, perhaps that happened when the world learned that a woman had blown herself up in the heart of Jerusalem.

A week after Wafa's suicide blast, I traveled to the al-Amari refugee camp in an attempt to visit with her family. Approaching the house, which is situated on a narrow alley in the camp, I noticed photographs of Wafa displayed on all the buildings. Children carrying toy guns and rifles ran up excitedly to point to Wafa and ask me to take a picture of them with their heroine, the woman who died a martyr's death. "One of us!" they exclaimed with glee. A group of adults lingered near the Idris home, including several shopkeepers who wanted to share personal anecdotes about Wafa so that I would understand how she was revered.

But the Idris home was deserted, the family gone into hiding. Immediately after Wafa's death, the house had been ransacked and partially destroyed by the Israeli military. Pushing aside the remains of a white metal door that had been torn from its hinges and stepping over shards of glass that had once been the living room windows, I entered. Suddenly, a white, old-fashioned dial telephone on a table began to ring and ring into oblivion. The noise startled me, and it took several seconds to regain my composure.

There were bullet holes in the walls, drawers had been tossed, beds turned upside down, and slashed cushions strewn around the floor of the living room. The only intact items were pictures on the walls of Wafa, in various stages of her brief life: in a graduation gown and cap with a diploma in her hand; standing with a group of Red Crescent workers at a reception with Yasser Arafat; and finally, the now-familiar photo of Wafa wearing a black-and-white checkered kaffiyeh, the symbol of the Fatah organization, with a green bandanna around her head on which was written "Allah Akhbar," or "God is greater than all other gods."

It seemed to me that amidst all the destruction and chaos, Wafa's spirit was still strong and very present in her childhood home. It was hard to leave, but since there was no one to talk to, no one to see, I finally walked out into the street. There were more people crowding around the house and they were pushing and shoving to reach me and talk about Wafa. All of them, regardless of age or gender, said the same thing: that one of their own had become a heroine for the Palestinian struggle—a woman, a symbol of the army of women who were ready to die for the cause.

It was then that the journey began that would take me

throughout the Middle East in an effort to understand this misguided feminist movement, which held up Wafa Idris as an example of the new, liberated Palestinian woman.

In the course of my research for this book—and while I simultaneously filmed a documentary on the same subject, which was broadcast on French television in February 2003—three more women strapped on explosive belts, following in Wafa's footsteps, and blew themselves up in the name of Allah. As I traveled throughout Gaza and from one West Bank town to another, interviewing the families and friends of the four women who had succeeded in giving their lives, as well as approximately eighty girls and young women who had tried and failed, I discovered the hard reality that it was never another woman who recruited the suicide bombers. Without exception, these women had been trained by a trusted member of the family—a brother, an uncle—or an esteemed religious leader, teacher, or family friend, all of whom were men. What I also discovered was that all four who died, plus the others who had tried and failed to die a martyr's death, had personal problems that made their lives untenable within their own culture and society.

I found that there were, in fact, very different motives and rewards for the men who died a martyr's death than for the women. Consequently, it became essential for me to understand the reasoning of the men who provide the moral justification for the seduction and indoctrination that eventually convinces a woman or girl that the most valuable thing she can do with her life is end it; at the same time, I saw it was crucial to understand the social environment that pushes these young women over the edge of personal despair.

7

What stunned me as I questioned these men, some of whom were in jail, was that all of them, by virtue of their powerful role in these women's lives, had managed to convince their sisters, daughters, wives, or their charges that given their "moral transgressions" or the errors made by a male family member, the only way to redeem themselves and the family name was to die a martyr's death. Only then would these women enjoy everlasting life filled with happiness, respect, and luxury and finally be elevated to an equal par with men. Only in Paradise, and only if they killed themselves and took Israeli lives with them.

For more than a year I traveled with a cameraman throughout the West Bank, Gaza, and Israel, interviewing people on audiotape and on camera, including members and leaders of Hamas, the Islamic Jihad, and the various factions of Yasser Arafat's Fatah movement, along with Israeli government officials, academics, psychiatrists, medical personnel, intelligence officers, historians, and feminists on both sides of the Green Line. I also spoke with families and friends of the victims of suicide bombings. At the end of my journey, because of the honesty of the many voices of reason on both sides of this struggle, it became obvious that a culture of death had permeated Palestinian society and destroyed the lives of many adults, as well as guaranteed the destruction of future generations.

This book tells the story of the women who died for reasons that go beyond the liberation of Palestine. If nothing else, let it serve as an example of the exploitation of women taken to a cynical and lethal extreme.

CHAPTER ONE

On December 11, 1987, after twenty years of almost passive resignation, the Palestinian population took action to end Israeli occupation. It was on that day that an uprising, or Intifada, erupted throughout the West Bank and Gaza. The image of Palestinian youngsters hurling rocks at Israeli soldiers and armored vehicles—a reenactment of the David and Goliath myth—became one of the Intifada's most memorable symbols. The other central and perhaps even more significant symbol was the Palestinian woman, who for the first time in the history of her culture was involved in and indicted for acts of subversion and sabotage and jailed in Israeli prisons.

During this unprecedented offensive, women wrote and circulated leaflets, joined in demonstrations and protests, scrawled slogans on the walls of buildings, hoisted flags, donated blood, violated curfews and closures, and helped organize alternative means of educating their children. Women defied the Israeli army's policy of confiscating Palestinian agricultural produce. They physically tried to prevent Palestinian boys and men from being arrested. "Behold our women," one revolutionary leaflet proclaimed, "a fighting force comparable to that of our men. A giant step has been taken towards the equality of Palestinian women."

While the role of the Palestinian woman was unusual in this society, it was not unlike the role of all women when their men are off fighting or held as prisoners of war. They found themselves in charge of educating the children, of working in the fields, of running the family business. Even after the men were eventually released from jail but still required to observe the curfew imposed by the Israeli army that prevented them from resuming their normal activities, women continued to run the financial and emotional aspects of their lives.

Feeling their own power and independence, women throughout the West Bank and Gaza began to shorten their skirts, wear trousers, and leave their heads uncovered. Zahira Kamal, a feminist from Gaza who had been a member of the Democratic Front for the Liberation of Palestine (DFLP) until she broke off to join a splinter group, recalls those days. "By breaking the chains of the occupation, the women also broke the handcuffs of their own existence."

The more liberal and intellectual portion of Palestinian society believed that the participation of women in the first Intifada was a positive step forward for women. In fact, Palestinian women became a beacon of hope for equality for their sisters throughout the Arab world. By actively participating, women embodied its twin goals: nationalism and social liberation. Zahira Kamal claims that, finally, the Intifada "not only challenged the Israelis for the first time in a way

10

that did not provoke negative world reaction, but it changed the second-class status of women within the Palestinian community."

Feminists and peace activists on the Israeli side agree. Nomi Chazan, a member of the Knesset (Israeli Parliament) from the left-wing Meretz Party and a close friend and colleague with Zahira Kamal through their work in the Palestinian and Israeli Women for Peace movement, says, "Perhaps more than a step forward to end occupation back in 1987, the [involvement of women] was a step forward in creating a democratic society where women are equal and not under the control of religious extremists."

The road to equality for Palestinian women, expressed in the desire for a better life as well as the right to actively participate in the resistance, turned out not to be smooth. There were formidable setbacks and backlashes that put an end to their struggling equally with the men. A little over a year after the beginning of the first Intifada, the influence of radical Islamic groups, such as Hamas and the Islamic Jihad, were gaining power in the streets, and, as a result, took a position against women participating in violent demonstrations. Islamic clerics were adamant that the woman's place was in the home with her family and not roaming the streets unchaperoned. The women's proper function in life was to give birth as early and as often as possible. Women were ordered to resume their traditional roles of wives, mothers, and homemakers, a demand that was eventually obeyed. It was a blow to the progress Palestinian women had made during the first year of the uprising, although not surprising coming from organizations that were steeped in fundamentalist Islamic doctrine.

What was surprising was that even among the more moderate Palestinian leadership, there was a unanimous decision to curtail the participation of women in the first Intifada, mainly because they feared any divisiveness between the various political and religious groups throughout the West Bank and Gaza would hurt the outcome of their struggle. As a result, regardless of the religious, political, or psychological reasons that united the extremists with the more moderate segment of Palestinian society over this issue, the result was that even among women themselves, equality became secondary to the success of the national cause. The change was swift and visible.

Shalom Harrari is a former Israeli intelligence officer who was in charge of the Occupied Territories for twenty years until his retirement in 2000. "The Hamas leadership issued a formal edict stating that women were not allowed out in public without covering their head with the *hijab* and wearing the *jilbab* [long-sleeved blouses and long skirts]," Colonel Harrari explains. Fathers and brothers were urged to supervise and control the behavior of female family members with the utmost strictness. "Had we protested," Zahira Kamal adds, "Hamas would have taken action against us, and with the Palestinians at variance with each other, Israel would have found it much easier to crush the uprising."

When the role of women diminishes in any political struggle, it is a sign that the role of women in general throughout society diminishes. When a Palestinian man, especially a father, saw his daughter being arrested and searched by male soldiers, it was unbearable for him. Given the economic problems that

12

diminished Palestinian men as the viable head of the family and the influence of the extremists that called for women to remain in the background, it was only logical that men would eventually resent the occupation more in conjunction with the involvement and arrest of their women.

The humiliation and rage that Palestinian men felt when their women were "handled" by soldiers forced the Israelis to adopt different rules. Shalom Harrari recalls how the army's role was very limited. "Basically, if we touched a woman to search her," he explains, "we touched her honor, which in turn implicated her family, and eventually her entire village felt it was their responsibility to defend her honor. In the end, the soldiers found themselves confronting the civilian population over the honor of their women."

While the majority of Palestinian women obeyed the edict, there were a few who began committing violent acts against Israeli soldiers and civilians that some analysts believe were a harbinger of things to come. Shalom Harrari contends that several left-wing communist and Marxist factions of the PLO encouraged women to commit what are known as *Jihad Fardi*, which translates into English as "personal initiative attacks." "In these kinds of attacks," he explains, "there are no formal organizations behind them. They are simply individuals who make the decision to attack and risk their lives because of largely personal reasons." According to Harrari, in the 1970s there were numerous incidents where men crossed the Jordan River into Israel with the Koran in one hand and a pistol or a knife in the other. "Knowing that there was a good chance they would be overcome and killed in the end," he says, "they attacked soldiers guarding Israeli fortifications and usually managed to take with them one or two soldiers before they were shot."

In 1988, after women were forbidden to venture out into the streets during the Intifada, many of those personal initiative attacks, not only on the Jordanian border but also within Israel proper, were committed by women.

Dr. Abdul Aziz al-Rantisi is an attractive man in his late forties who was educated in Jordan and trained as a pediatrician in England. Although his activities with Hamas, as the second in command as well as the organization's spokesman, keep him busy, he still lectures in pediatric medicine at the local university in Gaza. During an interview with Dr. al-Rantisi, he explained that it was easier for women to hide a knife or a pistol under their *jilbab* and pass through security than it was for men. "Those Palestinian women who dared to risk their lives by committing acts of Jihad Fardi," Dr. al-Rantisi explains, "were determined to continue to struggle against the occupation on an equal basis with the men."

Mohammed Dahalan, the former head of Yasser Arafat's security force in the West Bank who resigned to become the head of Fatah in Gaza and who is now the head of security in the new government recently formed by Abu Mazen, the new Palestinian prime minister, suggests a shift in perspective on women after 1988. "Not only did Palestinian women believe that by doing these actions they were maintaining their equality," Dahalan explains, "but the leaders of the various factions also realized that as long as women were dressed in the proper attire, they could be used more effectively to penetrate security and transport weapons."

Still, Shalom Harrari cautions that the incidents of women committing these actions were very few and in no way changed the rules that had been set down by the more militant factions like Hamas and Islamic Jihad. "It is only significant in that the

14

leadership understood," he says, "that our soldiers did not view women as big a threat as men."

Despite the lack of lasting progress for women, out of the devastation of the first Intifada came the first real Middle East peace initiative. In 1991, four years after the uprising began, what some of the more cynical among us thought was a false sporadic calm actually culminated in a peace conference between the Israelis and the Palestinians. Further, in a move that was considered a harbinger of women's rights, Hanan Ashrawi, an American-educated Christian Palestinian who taught English literature at Bir Zeit University in Ramallah, won an official position on the world stage.

As the spokesperson for the Palestinian Liberation Organization during that initial peace conference in Madrid, Ashrawi helped inspire a sense that the PLO was a bona fide political entity rather than an international terrorist organization. The conference culminated with that now-famous handshake between the late Israeli prime minister Yitzak Rabin and PLO leader Yasser Arafat on the White House lawn, under the beaming gaze of then U.S. president Bill Clinton, on September 13, 1993. Subtly, Ashrawi herself had sent a message to the world: Not only could a woman in a male-dominated Arab society become the voice of reason in an area fraught with conflict, but a Christian woman in a predominantly Muslim society offered all Palestinian women evidence that they could finally participate in the creation of a Palestinian state on an equal basis to the men.

There seemed to be a new era dawning in that region of the world, not only of peace but of gender equality. Ashrawi even tried to organize a parliament of women to oppose a burgeoning movement toward radical Islam. For a while, Ashrawi's progressive rhetoric gained momentum, especially given her status as one of only a few women professors at Bir Zeit University. But once again it was not to be. After the failure of the Oslo Accord, not only did Hanan Ashrawi fade from the political arena in the years that followed, but the influence and control that the extreme Islamic groups regained changed the climate at home. Hamas activists increased their control of the streets throughout the West Bank and Gaza and even gained control of the Christian student council at Bir Zeit University. Ashrawi's voice was silenced.

With their dreams of equality and a better life ultimately dashed in the first uprising, the role of women in the current Intifada, which began in September 2000, was destined to change. So was the entire nature of the uprising. Suicide bombings in the West Bank and Gaza and throughout Israel proper signaled the unleashing of a new terror weapon. In the beginning, this new and deadly tactic was planned by extreme Islamic groups and im-plemented by men, all of whom were against any peace accord with Israel and in favor of the creation of an Islamic state in its place.

Suicide attacks became the ultimate "smart bomb" of the poor. They were efficient and spectacular, and there was no fear that the perpetrator could be caught and interrogated. But even more significant is that those who strapped on explosive belts or drove bomb-laden cars into civilian areas became instant superstars throughout the West Bank and Gaza. It was then that Yasser Arafat and his more secular Fatah organization, along with several militant factions under the auspices of his group, realized the success of these missions in crushing the morale, spirit, and hope within Israeli society. More significant, he saw how public opinion had shifted away from his secular organization to the radical Islamic movements.

In the summer of 2000, Arafat was seen as a negotiator who had been too willing to make concessions with both the Americans and the Israelis. His role as president of the Palestinian Authority was at risk. He had failed to keep promises to the Palestinians concerning the area of a potential state, he was incapable of forcing Israel to dismantle old settlements and stop building new ones, and he had proved himself ill-equipped to control the sentiment in the streets, which was increasingly in favor of the Islamic Jihad and Hamas.

It was for those reasons that Arafat made a decision that he believed would ultimately guarantee him a wider base of power to confront the opposition at home as well as in Israel. The beleaguered Palestinian leader judged that for the good of the people in the long term, to avoid a militant Islamic regime in the area, he would give his tacit approval to suicide attacks, not only to wreak havoc throughout Israel but also to control his detractors and elevate his standing within the community.

Curiously, it was not the first time that a secular Arab leader had followed the example of an ultra-religious opposition party. In 1985 in Syria, the late president Hafez al-Assad, an Aleuwite Christian, recruited people from the Syrian National Socialist Party in Lebanon in an attempt to "secularize" suicide bombings and to garner support in the street away from the religious portion of the population.

In September 2000, at the outbreak of the current Intifada, the al-Aqsa Martyr's Brigade began taking credit for suicide bombings and other attacks in the name of Allah. In hindsight, it was a logical development. The current uprising, called the al-Aqsa Intifada from its inception, was based on the notion that Israel had plans to destroy the al-Aqsa holy mosque in Jerusalem. In a very real sense, by unleashing the al-Aqsa Martyr's Brigade, Arafat responded to his people's demand to implement actions instead of words. But while Hamas and Islamic Jihad had no problem finding men who were willing to die in the name of Allah, Arafat had great difficulty mobilizing those loyal to his political faction to commit acts of martyrdom.

Ehud Ya'ari, an Israeli television journalist and terrorism expert, explains. "There were major problems with this Intifada from the beginning. It was never a real uprising because it is a top-down operation that started from the leadership on down and not with the people on the streets, on the ground level, the way the first Intifada did."

For the first few months, despite Arafat's willingness to unleash his forces to commit suicide attacks, he found that he was unable to get the masses involved in military operations. "There was an inner conflict," Sari Nusseibeh, a Palestinian intellectual, explains. "Generally speaking, the majority of Palestinians were against the Intifada but were desperate enough to commit violent acts in response to the brutality of the occupation."

What Arafat needed was a weapon that would impress his Islamic opponents and terrorize his Israeli enemy. To resolve his floundering political control over the Palestinian Authority, Arafat shifted the emphasis of his military operations onto a very special kind of suicide bomber.

18

CHAPTER TWO

ON THE MORNING OF JANUARY 27, 2002, more than one thousand Palestinian women came to hear Yasser Arafat speak in his compound in Ramallah. It was an address intended specifically for them. To thunderous applause and cheers, Arafat stressed the importance of the woman's role in the Intifada. Flanked by his ever-present loyal guards and advisers, he made it clear that women were not only welcome but expected to participate in armed resistance against Israeli occupation. "Women and men are equal," he proclaimed with his hands raised above his head and his fingers forked in a sign of victory. "You are my army of roses that will crush Israeli tanks."

Arafat's usual rhetoric and zeal notwithstanding, what made this particular speech different—and changed forever the nature of the Palestinian-Israeli conflict—was a phrase he used, words

19

that would become his mantra in the weeks and months ahead. "*Shahida* all the way to Jerusalem," he said, coining on the spot the feminized version of the Arab word for martyr, *shahide*, which previously existed only in the masculine form. He repeated it over and over again until the crowd, with raised fists, took the cue and chanted along with him: "*Shahida, Shahida . . .* until Jerusalem. We will give our blood and soul to you, Abu Amar [Arafat's nom de guerre], and to Palestine."

"You," he continued, his arm sweeping across the group of women and young girls, "are the hope of Palestine. You will liberate your husbands, fathers, and sons from oppression. You will sacrifice the way you, women, have always sacrificed for your family."

Tragically, the terrible success of the suicide bomber marked a new, dark phase for Palestinian women. That very day, Arafat found his first *shahida*.

On the afternoon of January 27, 2002, Wafa Idris, a twenty-six-year-old Palestinian woman, blew herself to pieces in a downtown Jerusalem shopping mall, killing one Israeli man and wounding 131 bystanders. Although Idris is the only female suicide bomber not to leave a videotaped confession of her impending martyrdom, within forty-eight hours of the attack the al-Aqsa Martyr's Brigade, the military arm of Arafat's Fatah movement, had claimed responsibility for the bombing.

As word spread, mourners gathered at the Idris house in the middle of the al-Amari refugee camp in Ramallah, where leaders of al-Aqsa arrived with candy and posters emblazoned with Wafa's image. There was an atmosphere of joy, "a wedding with eternity," one neighbor described it, as Mabrook Idris, Wafa's mother, distributed the sweets to the neighborhood children in celebration of her daughter's death.

Wafa Idris got up early that Sunday morning, dressed, brought one of her nieces a glass of fruit juice, and woke her mother to say good-bye. She told her that she was rushing because she was late for work at the Red Crescent. But Idris never showed up for work. The director at the Red Crescent office in Ramallah, Dr. Mohammed Awad, claims that she was not supposed to work that day, since she came in only on Fridays.

In reconstructing the events leading up to Wafa Idris's final journey from Ramallah to Jerusalem, what we know now is that she made her way without incident across the checkpoint at Kalandria. According to Mohammed Hababa, a Tanzim (military arm of Fatah) operative and ambulance driver for the Palestinian Red Crescent who is now in an Israeli prison, he was one of the people who planned the attack in which Wafa Idris was killed. He says his accomplice was a man named Munzar Noor, who also worked for the Red Crescent in Ramallah. Under questioning by Israeli authorities, Hababa claimed that Wafa Idris was able to pass the checkpoint from Ramallah to Jerusalem in an ambulance.

In Jerusalem, dressed in a smart Western-style coat with a muffler wrapped around her neck and chin, and with her doe-brown eyes and long curly hair, perfect makeup, warm smile, and beautifully manicured nails, Wafa Idris attracted only positive attention and admiring glances as she entered a shoe store on Jaffa

Road. No one around her could have known that in the knapsack she carried were ten kilograms of explosives strapped with nails to make the damage from the blast even more deadly.

According to a sales clerk in the store, Idris appeared preoccupied and nervous as she browsed. There is no doubt that Wafa Idris was a woman who would have enjoyed shopping in Jerusalem, trying on beautiful clothes and shoes, being able to buy the things that she admired in old magazines she read at the Red Crescent headquarters every Friday, between tending to injured or dying Palestinian victims, before she returned home to family. But fate had other plans for Idris. According to a customer who was severely injured in the blast, Idris suddenly turned and rushed toward the door, paused, and reached inside the knapsack to take out a lipstick and compact. But as she tried to hold open the door with one foot while holding the mirror so she could apply her makeup, the knapsack got stuck. Twisting it in an attempt to free it, it suddenly exploded, killing Idris instantly along with Pinhas Toukatli, an eighty-one-year-old Israeli man. Scores of people were injured in the blast.

At first the bomber was misidentified on the Hizbollah television station as Shahanaz al-Amouri from Al-Najah University in Nablus. The world press picked up on the name after Israeli security forces, the Shin Bet, confirmed that Al-Najah was a hotbed for suicide bombers. While policy at Al-Najah University student council is controlled by Hamas, Mahmoud al-Wahar, the Hamas leader in Gaza, refused to say whether his group was behind the bombing. That was not surprising, since Hamas and the Islamic Jihad had not yet issued a *fatwa*, or religious decree, giving women permission to participate in suicide bombings.

That would come later, after the political implications of Idris's act had reverberated throughout the West Bank and Gaza.

As the hours passed and Wafa did not return home, her mother became distraught. When news of the explosion on Jaffa Road reached her in the al-Amari camp, including the detail that the suicide bomber was a woman, Mabrook Idris says, "My heart began to pump faster. I feared it was her."

At the time of Wafa's death, Khalil Idris, her brother, was wanted by Israeli authorities. During my interview at the home of a senior Fatah commander, at first he claimed that it was he who had persuaded the al-Aqsa Martyr's Brigade to allow his sister to have the honor of being the first Palestinian woman suicide bomber. At the time, his version of the story was that his sister had begged him for months to put her in touch with the appropriate people to be trained for such an action. He said, "She was desperate from seeing all the children injured and killed by Israeli soldiers while she was working for the Palestinian Red Crescent."

According to Khalil, two weeks before his sister died he brought her to the house of another senior Fatah operative in Ramallah, where he claims she was told that she had been chosen out of all the women in the refugee camp and throughout the Occupied Territories to become the first *shahida*. "It was because she had demonstrated bravery and resistance to the brutality of the Israeli soldiers as she rode in the ambulance gathering up the broken bodies of the young fighters who were injured as they resisted the occupying forces, and because she had often expressed a desire to contribute to the Palestinian struggle, and because she was a child born after the second Naqba, or catastrophe, the humiliating defeat of the Arab armies during the Six-Day War in 1967," Khalil explained.

Hours later, the story of Wafa's recruitment and participation in the attack changed. The same senior Fatah leader who had arranged the meeting between myself and Khalil contacted me in Jerusalem and asked me to come back to Ramallah for another on-camera interview. "While it is true that Wafa Idris begged us to let her be a martyr, to die for Palestine, she was not chosen to be a martyr," he explained. "The truth is that she was chosen to help her brother Khalil pass through the checkpoint from Ramallah to Jerusalem. The plan was that Wafa, dressed in Western clothes and carrying the bomb in a knapsack, would not be stopped and searched."

The following day, Khalil Idris was arrested by Israeli authorities. During an interview with him several days later in the Russian Compound, the central Israeli police station in East Jerusalem, where he was being held temporarily before his arraignment, he changed his story as well. "I was destined to be the martyr," he said. "My sister, like all women, was there to help me and all the other *shahides* to die for Palestine and for Allah."

Long after the fact, in the fall of 2002, when the Israeli military raided Yasser Arafat's compound in Ramallah, documents were confiscated that added yet another twist to the story. Apparently hours after the attack, Colonel Toufiq Tirawi, the head of general intelligence on the West Bank, attempted to cover up the fact that Wafa Idris was a member of Fatah in Ramallah and to discourage the al-Aqsa Martyr's Brigade from claiming responsibility for the attack. Tirawi did not want the international community to make the connection between Fatah, Arafat's organization, and the al-Aqsa Martyr's Brigade, a known terrorist organization. To achieve the cover-up, Tirawi approached Khalil Idris, already wanted by Israeli authorities, and offered to arrange safe passage into Jordan for himself and his family if he would deny that Wafa had, indeed, carried out the suicide mission in the name of the al-Aqsa Martyr's Brigade. According to Tirawi's report, at first Khalil refused to "sell his sister's blood for his own gain." But after his wife put pressure on him, he agreed. Unluckily for Khalil, the Israelis arrested him before Tirawi could spirit him and his family across the border into Jordan.

Ehud Ya'ari, the Israeli television journalist and terrorism expert, supports that version when he explains that al-Aqsa and Yasser Arafat himself tried to convince Wafa Idris's family not to publicize the fact that she was a member of a woman's organization called the Fatah Mothers. "In the very beginning," Ya'ari says, "Fatah felt a bit uncomfortable about the use of women. When they saw the reaction in the street, however, they realized that the feeling was unanimously positive, which was when they advised the family not to express grief or sorrow but to rejoice in the fact that their daughter had died in the name of Palestine and in the process had set an example for other women."

The Fatah's claim, through al-Aqsa, that Wafa was one of theirs unleashed a burst of spontaneous praise throughout the Arab world. An editorial written by Halim Qandil, the acting editor of the Nasserites weekly magazine, *Al-Arabi*, announced, "She is Joan of Arc, Jesus Christ, and the Mona Lisa . . ." Yasser

Za'atrah wrote in the Jordanian daily *Al-Dustou*, ". . . her suitcase of explosives, which is the most beautiful prize any woman can have, her spirit was raging, her heart filled with anger and her mind unconvinced by the propaganda of coexistence." The Egyptian opposition weekly *Al-Usbu Nagwa Tatav* compared Wafa with the daughters of George W. Bush. "Bush, who leads an oppressive society, thinks he can educate the world and yet he cannot even educate his own daughters. Note the difference between our culture, based on beautiful and noble values and on the value of martyrdom, and the materialistic Western culture. This proves that whatever may be, victory will be ours because we have culture and values."

And, finally, Adel Sadew, a psychiatrist who heads the Department of Psychiatry at the University of Cairo, openly compared Wafa Idris to Jesus Christ when he wrote, "Perhaps you were born in the same city, the same neighborhood and in the same house. Perhaps you ate from the same plate or drank from the same cup, the water flowing through the veins of the holy city and who placed a child in Mary's womb. Perhaps the same holy spirit placed the martyr Wafa and enveloped her pure body with dynamite. From Mary's womb issued this martyr who eliminated oppression while the body of Wafa became shrapnel that eliminated despair and aroused hope."

The evening of Wafa's death, not only did leaflets begin circulating around the al-Amari camp, stating that the al-Aqsa Martyr's Brigade claimed responsibility for the attack, but by dawn, posters appeared as well throughout Ramallah that added a religious connotation to her death. Wafa Idris was portrayed in a touched-up photograph wearing a green headband with the words "Allah is the answer," carrying a Kalashnikov rifle, and back-dropped by the Islamic flag on which was written "Allah Akhbar."

Immediately after the bombing, Wafa's sister-in-law, Wissim, spoke up in a televised statement, saying that Wafa had often told her that it was better to die a martyr's death than to live in humiliation. Mabrook Idris's initial public response of pride and joy that her daughter had given her life for the Palestinian cause alluded to her daughter's personal suffering at the hands of the Israelis. "My daughter was shot in the head with rubber bullets," she claimed. Wafa's childhood friend Raf'ah Abu Hamid went further when she attributed religious and political motives to Wafa's action. "Her love for her homeland and her love for martyrdom was such that I don't think that if she had children it would have changed her mind," the young woman proclaimed. "She was strong-willed and active and always wanted to join demonstrations. She would always say that she wished she could sacrifice herself for the country."

Shalfic Masalqa is a psychologist and professor at Hebrew University who lives in the upscale Arab neighborhood of Beit Zafafa, near Jerusalem. Dr. Masalqa believes that the atmosphere that has "captured" the West Bank and Gaza allows "this plan of suicide to flourish." Still, he cautions, "it is a general idea that does not explain individual cases. For instance, in times of war there is less schizophrenia and less depression. When a nation is at war, the mental health of the population usually gets better. In our society, in this time of war, the general atmosphere is full of hopelessness and I think it is because of the occupation, which is different than a classic war, which brings people to have ideas of death rather than ideas of life. It is the atmosphere that is the main stimuli and not the religious, political, or nationalistic reasons."

And yet Masalqa believes that even as this "culture of death" has permeated Palestinian society, there are still differences between a *shahide* and a *shahida*. "There are two different dynamics," Dr. Masalqa explains. "When an adolescent boy is humiliated at an Israeli checkpoint, from that moment, a suicide bomber is created. At the same time, if a woman becomes a *shahida*, one has to look for deeper, more underlying reasons. There are obviously cases where mental illness plays a part, since not all marginalized women within the Palestinian society kill themselves. Pathology plays an important role in these cases. Not all people who try to kill themselves and kill others are desperate to such a degree that they simply cannot tolerate their pain. Often there are other, more personal reasons."

Disturbingly, no such differences may exist among children, the next generation. In May 2001, Dr. Masalqa conducted a study in which he collected data from three hundred eleven-year-old Palestinian boys and girls concerning their dreams. "Based on my research," he says, "there was no difference in their articulated belief that dying a martyr's death was the highest honor they could achieve. There was no difference between girls or boys in their willingness to sacrifice themselves. What makes this study particularly interesting is that the average child of that age has not yet been politicized or exposed to the same stimuli as adults. What these Palestinian children were exposed to, however, was the

28

Israeli occupation which resulted in their inclination or tendency to be a martyr, or *shahide* or *shahida*. Until then, there had been no female suicide bombers and suddenly my research showed that there was no difference between boys and girls. I remember thinking at the time that it was interesting that a woman had not yet done that kind of action. Of course, several months later, Wafa Idris did, and after that women began trying, and sometimes successfully, to blow themselves up."

Dr. Masalqa goes on to say that within the Palestinian population, boys and girls witness the same brutality and experience fear equally. "There is something in the atmosphere that touches everyone," he explains, "and that can explain a major part of the phenomena: hopelessness, helplessness, despair, thinking of death rather than of life, which is the opposite to human nature."

Dr. Iyad Sarraj, an eminent Palestinian psychiatrist, concurs, although he cautions that "the inhibitors in Palestinian society for suicide should be very strong . . . especially in this culture, it is a sin to take one's life." He continues, "However, there is a religious explanation for this, and also a psychological definition since anyone who dies because of the enemy in our culture is called a martyr—anyone, even someone who dies a natural death. For instance, if someone is stopped at a checkpoint and has a heart attack or soldiers won't let a sick baby pass to go to hospital, or even a prisoner who was released and years later, after enjoying a normal life, suddenly dies, he is a martyr. Martyrs are like prophets in our culture, they are holy people, not ordinary soldiers who fight to defend their country."

When it comes to the differences between a regular suicide and a *shahide* or a *shahida*, Dr. Sarraj is very precise when he explains that taking one's life according to the Muslim religion means taking a life that belongs to God, not to the person. "But if a person takes his or her life as a martyr, if they die for God, that is a different story. They are giving back to the owner, God, the life He lent her and that is highly glorified and brings the martyr to the status of prophet."

If Wafa Idris is a pioneer for women kamikazes, she is also a woman who broke the rules of her society. Days after Wafa's death, during an interview with Sheik Ahmad Yassin, the spiritual head of Hamas, from his home in the Sabra neighborhood of Gaza, he claimed that "a woman martyr is problematic for Muslim society." The sheik explained, "A man who recruits a woman is breaking Islamic law. He is taking the girl or woman without the permission of her father, brother, or husband, and therefore the family of the girl confronts an even greater problem since the man has the biggest power over her, choosing the day that she will give her life back to Allah."

Shortly after my interview with Sheik Yassin, Dr. al-Rantisi, the spokesman and second in command of Hamas, also spoke on the subject from his home in Gaza. While he chose not to address Sheik Yassin's comments, he maintained that not only Wafa Idris but hundreds of other women beg to be suicide bombers, whether they are active members of al-Aqsa, considered to be the more secular military organization, or whether they attempt to join Hamas.

"Every day, women, even married women, want to be

shahida," said Dr. al-Rantisi. "We try to tell them that they have things to give in other areas and not specifically in military areas. But it is difficult to dissuade them. In Bethlehem alone there are two hundred girls willing and ready to sacrifice themselves for Palestine, and obviously it is much easier for women to go through checkpoints. They arouse less suspicion, which is why, in my opinion, soon these women will be needed. In Ramallah and Nablus as well, as many women as men are ready, and some have already been trained in using weapons, and many of those women are also housewives, mothers, and students."

On February 18, 2002, only weeks after Wafa Idris's death, the al-Aqsa Martyr's Brigade officially opened a woman's suicide unit in her honor, the Shawaq al-Aqsa, or "those who miss the al-Aqsa mosque." The condition for membership in the group was that participating women had directly or indirectly been wounded by Israeli soldiers. At the same time, a tape began circulating throughout the Occupied Territories and Gaza. A woman, covered and veiled so it was impossible to see her face or discern her identity, talked about the role of women as *shahida* and discussed how a woman should be equipped and prepared to participate in suicide bombings. At the end of her discourse, she warned that this was only the beginning, as women were now a full and equal part of the struggle against occupation. "We are prepared to die in equal numbers to the men," she said.

Since the tape was made after her death, the woman on the tape was not Wafa Idris, but it was filmed in such a way as to create a doubt or give the impression that it was the final farewell video that Idris never made.

Yasser Arafat had called for a *shahida* on the day Wafa Idris died

31

without really being prepared that his demand would be answered before he had a chance to evaluate the emotional and political reaction among the Palestinian people. Then again, the most accurate method of conducting a popularity poll throughout Palestinian society has always been to observe the reaction "in the street" after an event occurs. "The [Palestinian] leadership sends up a balloon of sorts," explains Ehud Ya'ari, "and if the population carries it afloat rather than pops it, they realize they have hit upon a winning proposition. In the same way, the suicide bombers all make a video before their death and that has become a trend, just as the women who blow themselves up all wear the green headband with 'Allah Akhbar' written on it. That also has become a trend. It was then that the whole question of the religious legitimacy of martyrs in general prompted debate within the Muslim community and ended with a *fatwa* which encouraged and blessed women to do the same."

As it turned out, Arafat's words had an effect on the population far beyond his intentions and, as became evident in the following months, ultimately served to unite the secular Fatah movement with the religious Hamas and Islamic Jihad organizations. While Wafa Idris's death set a precedent for other women, it also served to save Arafat from a political defeat that would have cost him his pride and perhaps his life.

In July 2002, during another meeting with Sheik Ahmad Yassin in his home in Gaza, when I asked him to explain his position on *shahida*, he changed from what he had previously told me immediately after Wafa's death; obviously he was also influenced by the opinion in the street. "We are men of principle," the sheik proclaimed, "and according to our religion, a Muslim woman is

32

permitted to wage Jihad and struggle against the enemy who invades holy land. The Prophet would draw lots among the women who wanted to go out with him to make Jihad. The Prophet always emphasized the woman's right to wage Jihad."

There is no definite way to know the personal reasons that drove Wafa Idris to detonate a bomb in the doorway of a shoe store at 11 Jaffa Road in downtown Jerusalem. Those who knew her well, the few with whom she shared her feelings, have been able to offer only glimpses into her life. The truth is that she did not confide in her close girlfriends or in her mother that she had decided to die. All the other reasons that could validate her motives have become part of Palestinian history under Israeli occupation.

What is known, and about which there is no doubt, is that she set an example for numerous other women throughout the West Bank and Gaza who have tried to become *shahidas* in the name of an independent Palestinian state. The most mysterious aspect of the cult of death that has permeated Palestinian society, especially when it comes to *shahida*, is the transition that each woman makes from bearer of life to killing machine.

In January 2003, I visited Mabrook Idris. She told me that the Israeli military had received permission from the High Court in Jerusalem to destroy her home. Fortunately for her, the bulldozers were unable to maneuver through the narrow alley, as neighbors had created an obstacle path of wrecked cars to block them. "It is only a question of time," she says, "before they succeed."

Her son Khalil is still in prison, serving a sentence until 2020. His wife, Wissim, and their four children still live with her. Mabrook Idris's other son, Saban, spends his time playing cards and watching television. The constant closures in Ramallah have made it impossible for him to work.

Ahmed, Wafa's former husband, visited Mabrook Idris while I was there. He explained that he tries to stay in close touch with the family because he believes that had he not taken another wife and started a family, Wafa would still be alive. "I think about her all the time," he says through his tears. "I will always love her." As I was to later learn, Wafa's marital history was a key component in her story.

Mabrook Idris always believed that ending one's life was forbidden in the Muslim religion, except under one exceptional circumstance: to die in the name of defending Islam and Allah. Her daughter, the young woman who was destined to become the first female martyr, utilized that circumstance as a means to end her life.

Sometimes Mabrook Idris manages to convince herself that her daughter's death has meaning, since the battle cry of the Islamic fighting armies, as well as the cry of the suicide bombers as they attack, is 'Allah Akhbar.' She tries to justify her daughter's death as an action that defends the one true God and the only authentic religion, just as she tries to take comfort in the fact that her daughter is now revered and admired as the first woman to fight and kill the enemy on an equal basis to the men in their society. Most of the time, she cries. Martyrdom, she shrugs, not suicide. "What's the difference, my daughter is dead."

To the Palestinian population, Wafa Idris is a heroine. To Yasser Arafat, she is his first *shahida*. To her mother, she is the daughter who will never come home again. Wafa Idris reminds me of that woman I met in the Sabra refugee camp so long ago. I can still hear her words: "You can take a lesson from us Palestinian women. We die in equal numbers to the men."

34

CHAPTER THREE

THREE MONTHS AFTER Wafa Idris blew herself up to become the first Palestinian *shahida*, long after the mourners had gone and the excitement had worn off, I went to the al-Amari refugee camp near Ramallah to meet with Wafa's mother for the first time. The inside of the house had been made livable again by friends and neighbors with money supplied by the Fatah movement.

Dr. Abdul Aziz al-Rantisi, the charismatic spokesperson for Hamas, admitted during an on-camera interview that, depending on who takes responsibility for the attack, either Hamas, Islamic Jihad, or the Palestinian Authority distributes a lifetime stipend of four hundred dollars a month to the families of male suicide bombers; he points out that the families of *shahidas* like Wafa receive two hundred per month. It would seem that even in death women are not treated equally.

During the same interview, Dr. al-Rantisi confirmed the news reports that Iraqi president Saddam Hussein, since the beginning of this current Intifada and until his political demise, rewarded the family of every Palestinian suicide bomber with $25,000 and donated another $25,000 to rebuild those houses destroyed by the Israeli military. In February 2003, for instance, after the Israeli military had destroyed the homes of several suicide bombers in Jenine and Gaza, there was a ceremony where Salam Rkad, one of the leaders of the Arabic Front, an Iraqi-based organization, presented a check for more than $100,000 earmarked to rebuild the destroyed homes. Rkad was arrested shortly after that and is currently in an Israeli jail.

According to Steven Emerson in his book *American Jihad: The Terrorists Living among Us*, the money granted by Saddam Hussein rarely reached the families directly. By the time it was transferred through certain pro-Iraqi factions of the PLO and various shell companies, deposited in several different bank accounts, and after cuts were taken out by local leadership and commissions to middlemen were paid, there was not much left for the families—probably only one tenth of the original amount. Of course, that never stopped the "photo opportunity" when a check for the entire $25,000 is shown being presented on camera to the families. Once that happens, whether or not they ever actually get any money is debatable. What is certain is that their houses are rebuilt, although undoubtedly for much less than $25,000.

Even so, it is unwise to discount the allure and impact of the monetary rewards that the families receive. In a society where the per capita income is about $1,000 per year, it is not impossible to imagine that a family could spare one child, especially if they are convinced that he or she will end up in Paradise.

Saddam Hussein also promised to build a plaque honoring Wafa in one of the main squares of Baghdad. After the United States/British military action, it is unknown if that plaque, if it was ever built, is still standing.

Only fifty-six years old, Mabrook Idris looks far older, and feels years older as well, she says, given her weak heart. Greeting me in her shabby living room, she holds the tattered poster of her child, which she picks up automatically the moment I appear, seemingly by rote after so many months of practice when local dignitaries, neighbors, friends, and Western journalists have visited her to pay their respects. "Thank God," she says. "I am proud that my daughter died for Palestine, proud that she gave her life for us all. Thank God, thank God . . ."

But after an hour of sitting with her, talking with her, listening to her, Mabrook Idris is weeping. "If I had known what she was going to do, I would have stopped her," she says. "I grieve for my daughter." Finally, Mabrook Idris stops talking about death and begins to talk about her daughter's brief life.

Wafa was born in the al-Amari refugee camp in 1975, conditioned to Israeli occupation and experienced in street fighting. "We once had a home in Ramla," Mabrook adds wistfully, "but in 1948 we were forced to flee. Wafa never knew any other home but this." She makes a sweeping gesture with her hand.

37

She is silent for several minutes as two of her grandchildren, the children of Kahlil, scramble next to her on the sofa. She hands them each a poster of their heroine aunt and instructs them to kiss Wafa's image. Their mother, Wissim, Mabrook's daughter-in-law, sits nearby, cradling an infant. The whole family shares the three-room house with Mabrook, as did Wafa before she died. At one point during the interview, Wissim recalls Wafa once saying that she would like to be a martyr. "But only once," she insists. "When she saw pictures on television of a suicide attack committed by a man, she said that she wished she had done something like that."

As had been previously arranged, three childhood friends of Wafa's arrive. Ahlam Nasser, who worked with Wafa at the Red Crescent, Raf'ah Abu Hamid, and Itimad Abu Lidbeh are still visibly shocked by the death of their friend. But while Raf'ah claims that she had absolutely no inkling that Wafa harbored such violent intentions, Itimad remembers how in 1985 she and Wafa traveled once a month to the north of Israel to visit their respective brothers who were in an Israeli prison. "Our trips up north continued right into the Intifada in 1987," Itimad explains. "When Khalil, Wafa's beloved brother, was arrested for being a member of Fatah and sentenced to eight years in prison, Wafa told me that she didn't care if the Israelis killed her, she would always try to see him on visiting day." Mabrook Idris agrees that the hardships of the occupation hit Wafa hardest then. "My two sons worked as taxi drivers and they helped support us. When one son was arrested by the Israelis and the other lost his job because of the curfew, my daughter was desperate."

* * *

According to Dr. Boaz Ganor, the director of the International Policy Institute for Counter Terrorism in Israel, among Israeli political analysts and terrorism experts there are three schools of thought that explain suicide bombings. "My personal view," Dr. Ganor says, "is the main factor for suicide attacks is the nationalist and religious influence. There is a concrete belief that he [the bomber] will gain rewards in Paradise while contributing to the Palestinian people. He is giving his life to the nation."

Emanuel Savin and Ariel Merari, both experts in terrorism as well, add other variables to the equation. Dr. Savin believes it is the socioeconomic situation that motivates suicide bombers. "It is the horrible situation under occupation," Dr. Savin says. "Based on research I did in Algeria, I have to say that Israeli occupation is the main motivation for the Palestinians' readiness to commit suicide attacks."

Dr. Merari believes that the ultimate act is brought about by social pressure on individuals. "As soon as they make their final videotape, which forces them to state their intentions immediately before they set off on their mission, it puts the suicide bomber in a situation that he can't get out of. From the minute he makes that tape, he or she is doomed to carry out the attack. If not, the tape exists and he or she is branded a coward. Up until the Palestinian leadership forced terrorists to make that tape, it was easy for anyone to brag about their willingness to contribute to the Palestinian cause and not do anything about it."

Iyad Sarraj, the renowned Palestinian psychiatrist from Gaza who has studied the phenomenon of suicide, with a particular

39

focus on the cultural influences within Palestinian society that produce *shahides* and *shahidas*, further believes there is a crucial connection between the first Intifada and the current wave of martyrdom within the Palestinian society. "The children who threw stones and Molotov cocktails and confronted Israeli soldiers in 1987," Dr. Sarraj says, "and who watched their fathers and other male relatives being beaten and humiliated by Israeli forces, are the young men [and women] who are the martyrs of today."

Mabrook Idris supports this view. When the first Intifada erupted in 1987, Wafa was twelve years old, and her mother says she reacted in the same way that hundreds and thousands of other Palestinian children who were deeply affected by the first real display of rebellion and confrontation against Israeli occupation did. "A friend lost an eye," she explains, "and that affected Wafa very deeply."

Mabrook maintains that her daughter was motivated more by nationalist fervor than by religion, even if she attributes that fervor to God's destiny for her daughter. "She was a Muslim," the woman explains, "which made her fearless, but the injustice of the Jews made her act."

And yet Raf'ah Abu Hamid is convinced that her friend, regardless of her patriotic zeal and courage, could never have planned and implemented the suicide mission on her own. "She had to have someone behind her," Raf'ah says. "How could she get the bomb? How would she know how to explode it? We never learned anything like that on television or on the street."

How indeed?

Ahlam Nasser quickly explains that it is not difficult to make contact with an organization and to volunteer as a martyr. "Every group, Hamas, Islamic Jihad, and the al-Aqsa Martyr's Brigade," she explains, "has an office in every city in the West Bank and Gaza. People who want to become martyrs know exactly where to go." And then she offers another interesting observation about Wafa. "But I don't understand. She was so happy when she was working. She was always so encouraging and optimistic to everyone she cared for. I never heard her say anything about violent retaliation or hate. It was only while we were waiting at the office for a call that she seemed depressed. Once she was looking through an old magazine and told me how she wished she could buy all the pretty clothes she wanted." The young woman shrugged. "But which one of us didn't wish that?"

It is then, at that point in the discussion, that Wissim Idris suddenly changes her mind when she says that she never really took her sister-in-law seriously when she claimed she wanted to become a martyr. Instead, she maintains that Wafa was never quite the same since her husband divorced her several years before. The three friends agree, while Mabrook, tears welling in her eyes, sighs heavily. Apparently, while Wafa Idris was known for having an independent mind and a profound feeling of resentment against the occupation, she also had a reputation as a troubled young woman who was prone to bouts of melancholy and depression. Without prompting, Mabrook Idris offers another piece in the puzzle of her daughter's decision to die: Wafa had been a constant target for mocking after her husband divorced her.

"My daughter's husband divorced her because she couldn't have children," Mabrook says. "Wafa knew she could never marry again because a divorced woman is tainted . . . She was young, intelligent, and beautiful and had nothing to live for."

★ ★ ★

As is the custom in Palestinian society, along with other Arab cultures, a dowry is paid to the prospective wife's family by the father of the groom. Mabrook Idris explains that because of the hardships of Israeli occupation, because her husband had died of natural causes when Wafa was a little girl, and because her sons have children of their own to support, her daughter was not worth a handsome sum, which would have ensured that her daughter would have a husband who could offer her a relatively comfortable life.

"When Wafa was very young," she begins, "we decided to marry her because the only thing we had that made my daughter a prize was that she was young and would have more years to bear children."

In 1991, at the age of sixteen, Wafa married her first cousin, Ahmed, who also lived in the al-Amari camp and tended a small chicken farm along with his father and older brother. Fortunately for Wafa, according to her mother, it was a love story, since her daughter had had a crush on Ahmed, who was ten years older than she, since she was a small child. But the euphoria of the union and the hope that she would have a satisfactory life as a wife and mother was dashed when nine years later social pressure forced Ahmed to divorce her. After years of trying to get pregnant, in 1998 Wafa delivered prematurely a stillborn female infant. The family was devastated, and Ahmed, according to his description of events after the tragedy, was humiliated. During an interview with Ahmed later, he explained how he had been disgraced by the tragedy. "At first my family blamed Wafa, and

42

then they blamed me," he says. "They said that I was too weak to provide an infant that would survive in her womb."

After the trauma of the stillbirth, a local doctor told Wafa and her husband, in the presence of their families, that she would never be able to carry a child to full term. Ahmed is vague and obviously embarrassed when pressed about her medical problems. No, she didn't see a prenatal specialist or a fertility expert, and in fact she had been diagnosed by a general practitioner rather than a gynecologist. No, she had no particular tests such as an MRI or a sonogram, and it was only after her ordeal that the hospital staff determined she could never have another child.

Was Wafa's plight just another example of the hardship of living under Israeli occupation? Was she a victim of poverty and ignorance? There are more questions that Ahmed cannot answer and that the local doctor, when interviewed, also was unable to resolve. Would things have been different if she had had access to the best medical treatment? And what happened after she lost her baby? Did she suffer from postpartum depression? Was her judgment affected? Was medicine prescribed to alleviate her psychic pain?

It is as impossible to answer those questions as it is dangerous to diagnose so long after the fact. Ahmed claims that after she lost her baby, Wafa stopped eating and stopped talking. She stayed in bed all day and all night, and she refused to get up to clean the house or cook his meals. Ahmed admits that he was "crazy with worry" and unable to cope with the situation. "I called her brother Khalil," Ahmed explains, "to try and help, but she remained unresponsive."

Mira Tzoreff is a professor at Ben Gurion University whose research is in the field of women's history in the Middle East from a sociocultural point of view. Her doctorate is on Egyptian women in the period between the two world wars. Tzoreff explains that throughout the Occupied Territories and the Arab world, a woman is dependent legally and socially. When she shops or travels or is obliged to sign a legal document, it must be done under the scrutiny of her husband. In every aspect of her life, a man—either a father, brother, or husband—makes all her decisions and takes care of her. "It is called *bila-umri* or 'not without my dearest one,'" Tzoreff explains. "In Wafa Idris's case, because her father was dead, it was her oldest brother, Khalil, who was charged with the responsibility of his sister's life."

After Wafa's marriage, Ahmed took over from Khalil, but in the event of a problem that put the marriage at risk, custom dictated that the husband consult with his wife's father, or in this case with Khalil. According to Ahmed, he also consulted his spiritual leader, a local Imam, who quoted to him from the Koran a special passage that offered instructions about disobedient wives. "In the marriage institution," Ahmed says, "the husband is the driver of the car, he is at the wheel and it is he who sets the rules that guides the family to serenity and happiness. When it comes to handling problems, Allah has set down rules or guidelines that a man can follow when a wife is disobedient."

From his Imam, Ahmed learned that there were two different kinds of disobedience in the Koran. "Rebellion, ugly things she does," he explains, "or just simple disobedience."

The Imam suggested that before Ahmed could define his wife's particular case, he should watch a weekly television talk show broadcast from Egypt called *Life Is Sweet*, which featured a certain Dr. Mohammed al-Hajj, a professor of Islamic Faith at the University of

Amman. Once Ahmed understood what constituted the different degrees of wifely disobedience, he was able to assess the problem with Khalil. "She did not disgrace me in public or disgrace herself and the sanctity of her womanhood," he explains. "She merely disobeyed me when I ordered her to get out of bed and take care of the house, the meals, my family, my clothes."

(Ahmed offered to let me borrow a videocassette of the talk show during our interview, which I viewed on the VCR in my Jerusalem hotel room. One of the segments, both fascinating and terrible, showed a psychiatrist dressed in a Western business suit sitting with the host, both men surrounded by blocks of wood in varying sizes. As he explained which block should be used on the woman for which offense, he seemed completely relaxed and cheerful, as if what he was advising his audience was as normal or banal as offering a recipe. In another segment, the host, a serious young man who nodded encouragingly to all his guests, even those who phoned in to express their opinions, cautioned his audience about sadomasochistic couples who enjoyed the physical punishment set down in the Koran and, therefore, should be exempt from practicing them.)

Itimad Abu Lidbeh, Wafa's close friend, describes what she believes was Wafa's state of complete "inertia." "When she lost her baby, she lost the will to live. I never understood why she reacted like that, but she did. She was a woman in enormous pain, and although she never said the words, I sensed she had no desire to go on living."

Dr. Israel Orbach, a professor of psychology at Bar Ilan University in Tel Aviv whose specialty is studying suicide and suicidal behavior, maintains that suicide "is a very subjective experience . . .

45

A family member or friend might see the person's pain as something marginal or insignificant, but for the person who suffers, it is unbearable mental pain. As for Wafa Idris, it would appear that she carried an inner turmoil and pain for years, and the loss of a child was the culminating factor that made the process come closer to a final resolution."

Iyad Sarraj, the psychiatrist and writer from Gaza, is not convinced that Wafa Idris ended her life because of only one reason. "I believe the woman who does this is an exception to the rule, because basically women are the source of life," he says. "There is no doubt that there were other psychological reasons or symptoms which drove this woman to suicide. Perhaps she was depressed, and since sacrifice is the way for liberation and the way out and that affects people very strongly, especially with all the humiliation and violence on the Israeli side, because of this, it brings out the worst reaction in people. In other words, the cultural, religious, and nationalistic reasons, combined with her own personal depression, gave Wafa the reason and the courage to do it."

A fatal cocktail? Martyrdom that is rewarded in Islam by everlasting life at Allah's table in Paradise, combined with the political and economic oppression of an occupying force and exacerbated by personal problems caused by constraints from one's own society that make life unbearable. What if the idea that women who die as martyrs will finally achieve equality to men were added to that equation?

Dr. Tzoreff not only accepts Dr. Sarraj's analysis but adds her own reasoning about how Idris achieved the dubious honor of becoming the first Palestinian *shahida*. "If we take Wafa Idris," Dr. Tzoreff explains, "the ultimate *shahida*, who is she after all?

She is a talented young woman, married and divorced because she was sterile, desperate because she knew perfectly well there was no future for her in any aspect of the Palestinian society. She knew better than anyone else that the only way for her to come out against this miserable situation was to kill herself. Look at her funeral and what the Palestinian leadership said about her, calling her a national flower and the embodiment of Palestinian womanhood. She knew her own society and the limitations they put on her and on women like her and she understood better than anyone else that she had nothing left, no hope, no future."

One might wonder why Wafa Idris, an intelligent and attractive woman, didn't just leave, run away. Wasn't it possible for her to travel to Amman, for instance, where she could have found work in a hospital or even interim work in someone's home as a companion or menial work as a housekeeper until she could find something better?

"That is a very complicated question," Dr. Tzoreff says, " and more than that, there is a complicated answer. In this society, you can't run away, leave your family and friends, because if you do, you are a disgrace. The burden on you is even greater than if you stay. The disgrace on your family is even greater."

When Wafa Idris, a twenty-six-year-old divorcée, was sent back to her childhood home by her husband, she became a financial burden on her family, which was already overwhelmed with small children whose fathers were either unemployed or in prison. "Her intent at this point," Tzoreff says, "is not important, even if she was the pioneer of a wave of women martyrs. Wafa Idris was not chosen by mistake. She was from the lowest social economic strata of Palestinian society and she didn't have a father.

47

All her problems with her failed marriage and sterility made her an abnormal person. She could never remarry, and her chance to be self-sufficient was zero. There is no doubt that the people who chose her, if they did, did so because they knew she had no future. And I'm quite certain that the recruiters asked themselves how the family would react if they found out that she had been chosen as the first woman suicide bomber."

Iyad Sarraj acknowledges the fact that it is not inconceivable for large Palestinian families who live far below the poverty line to sacrifice one child so the others could have a better life. "Don't forget," Dr. Sarraj cautions, "there are monetary rewards for the families of every suicide bomber." He pauses. "And in our religion, martyrs don't die. They simply move to Paradise and live a better life with dignity."

Ahmed, Wafa's former husband, is a gentle man, quiet and profoundly shocked by what happened. After the stillbirth, he was relieved to learn from his local Imam that the first step in "rehabilitating" his wife was nothing more harsh than to banish her from his bed, and if that didn't work after several days and she did not stop bringing the "family into hell," he could proceed to the second step. Banishing Wafa from his bed was moot, since she was silent and as listless as a child. In fact, she had grown gaunt and thin because she refused to take any nourishment and, according to her mother, her hair had begun to fall out. And so a week later Ahmed proceeded to the second step, which was gentle admonition, accompanied by another video that he was given by the Imam to play for Wafa at home, which concerned the proper behavior of a woman toward her husband. Had he been rich, Ahmed says with regret, he might have enticed Wafa with money or gifts, but of course that was not an option.

After several weeks of this crash course in good wifely behavior, instead of getting better, Wafa grew worse. She cried inconsolably day and night. The presence of her mother, her sisters-in-law, and her friends did nothing to assuage her grief. The wisdom of Islam, the Imam told Ahmed, was vast, and since his wife was suffering from a physical ailment, she would be spared from the usual subsequent punishment as stated in the Koran: a beating with a thick block of wood, but never in the face or hard enough to cause fractures or wounds. Instead, Ahmed was instructed to give her a "gentle beating" with a handkerchief or a toothpick.

When she still did not improve, however, Ahmed broached the possibility that he take another wife, as was permitted in Islam, on the advice of his family and his spiritual guide. But when he brought up the subject to Wafa, she became hysterical. Beside herself with grief, she spoke for the first time in months to make it clear that she loved him and was not prepared, under any circumstances, to share him with another woman. More discussion ensued, and finally, in the spring of 1998, after several weeks and repeated efforts to convince her to change her mind, Ahmed divorced her. Two weeks later he married another woman.

With her heart and spirit broken and her physical health in decline, Wafa Idris watched Ahmed's marriage procession winding its way down the main road of the al-Amari refugee camp from her bedroom window. But what made the situation even more unbearable for her was that the entire camp knew the reason why she had been cast aside. *"Sterile,"* they whispered behind her back—an incomplete woman, unable to bear children, unable to provide soldiers to fight the Israeli occupation.

Less than a year later, Ahmed and his new wife had their first child, and a year after that, their second. After the children were born, Wafa still wanted to return to Ahmed, but he told her that his current wife was against it and had already threatened that she would leave him and take their children if he allowed that to happen.

During my time with Wafa's family and friends, I heard differing opinions of what had driven Wafa to the ultimate act of self-destruction. Most ascribed to her an inner zeal and anger that justified the "cult of Wafa" that permeated Palestinian society in the months following her suicide. Even her aunt, Mabrook's sister, claimed that she got divorced not because she couldn't have children but rather because she didn't want them. "She was too independent," the aunt explains. "She preferred to study. There is no truth about her being sterile. Wafa was a fighter with a strong sense of patriotism. She was destined to become a martyr."

There is no one who knew her, however, who doesn't agree that the young woman with the sensual smile, soft brown eyes, and curly dark hair derived enormous satisfaction from her work as a volunteer for the Palestinian Red Crescent. Everyone around the al-Amari camp agrees that Wafa's greatest pleasure in life, next to her adored nieces and nephews and her widowed mother, were those people whom she comforted and tended to every Friday when she rode in the Red Crescent ambulance. According to her mother, Wafa always told her that the only thing that gave her any purpose in life was her role as voluntary nurse. Wissim Idris agrees but adds that her husband, Khalil, Wafa's brother, was angry with his sister for working as a volunteer. "He wanted her to earn money," Wissim says. "But Wafa always said that she could never take money for saving lives. It was her contribution to the struggle."

When I visited the Red Crescent later that same trip, Dr. Mohammed Awad, the director of the Red Crescent office in Ramallah, admitted that he had still not "gotten over the shock." Talking about Wafa, he described her as a "hyper person." "She never walked," he says with a smile, "she always ran and shouted and laughed." He pauses. "We had a good friendship." Again, he pauses. "She made good coffee."

While Awad praised all his volunteers, he had especially kind words to say about Wafa's willingness to brave bullets to evacuate the wounded. "Friday, the day she worked," Dr. Awad explains, "was an especially violent day, since Palestinian men and boys emerged from the mosques, after hearing a fiery sermon by an Imam, burning to take action against their occupiers."

During several interviews with Shin Bet operatives—the Israeli internal secret service, comparable to the FBI—who routinely patrol Ramallah and the al-Amari camp undercover, they claimed that Red Crescent ambulances often carried bombers and their bombs toward the checkpoints on the way to their targets in Israel. When I shared this with Dr. Awad, he objected strongly to any connection between Idris's work with the Red Crescent and her suicide, dismissing the accusation as a "desperate attempt on the part of Israeli authorities to build a profile" that would explain a life that would culminate in the ultimate honor of becoming the first *shahida*.

"The Red Crescent helps all people," Dr. Awad claims, "regardless of religion, color, citizenship, or any other classification. Our staff is trained to save lives and relieve pain and suffering. This act contradicts our humane values and will not prevent us from helping soldiers and even settlers when necessary." He pauses. "Believe me, if I had any idea she intended to do this, I would have tried to stop her."

Days later, during an interview with Liat Pearl, the spokesperson for the Israeli border police, she revealed that prior to the attack by Wafa Idris, they had stopped and arrested several known Hamas operatives who used Red Crescent ambulances to transport militants on their way to commit actions within Israel, as well as confiscated weapons hidden under stretchers and in metal containers filled with medicine. "Last October," she said, "for instance, in Qalqilya, Nidal Nazal, a member of Hamas and the brother of Natzar Nazal, a leader of Hamas, worked as an ambulance driver for the Palestinian Red Crescent. When we arrested him, Nazal admitted that as a driver he served also as a messenger between Hamas headquarters in various West Bank towns, carrying money and weapons."

As in most issues concerning the Israeli–Palestinian conflict, there are always two sides to the story. The Palestinians accuse the Israeli military of preventing ambulances from passing checkpoints to evacuate the sick and wounded, while the Israelis claim that the ambulances are often a means to get by security and commit violent acts against civilians within Israel proper. In truth, it is likely that Wafa Idris's handlers would have found a way to get by security.

The last thing that Mabrook Idris said to me when I left her house that day was a request to help her retrieve her daughter's body. I promised to try, and did in fact talk to a contact in the military who was part of the contingent assigned to the West Bank. It was then that I learned the rules that applied to all Palestinians who commit terrorist actions.

The law in Israel states that when a Palestinian suicide bomber dies or is killed while committing an act of terrorism against civilians or soldiers within Israel proper, his or her body is never released to the family. Instead, it is buried in an unmarked grave in a large cemetery in the north of Israel.

The only way the body of a martyr or *shahida* is returned to the family is if he or she dies somewhere within the Occupied Territories or Gaza. Only then is the body released for a proper Muslim burial and the honor of a martyr's funeral, with the coffin paraded through the martyr's hometown or village while thousands follow behind, firing rifles and guns in the air.

A month after her daughter died, Mabrook Idris honored her daughter's memory with an empty pine box. At least two thousand Palestinian mourners marched in the streets of Ramallah behind the empty coffin, which was draped with Palestinian flags and pictures of Wafa, chanting and carrying posters of other Palestinian heroes in a display of pride and joy. A large photograph of Wafa was displayed prominently in the main square of Ramallah, and it remains there today. Ceremonies in her honor were held all over the West Bank and Gaza. Elementary school children as well as adolescents throughout the Arab world chanted Wafa's name every day before classes began, and there were ads in newspapers from various social and religious organizations that praised her for her bravery and lauded her as an example of the "new breed of Palestinian womanhood." "Wafa we love you," a group of fifteen-year-olds chanted on their way to school.

During the symbolic funeral for Wafa Idris held by the Fatah, one of the council members eulogized her in the following way: "Wafa's martyrdom restored honor to the national role of the Palestinian woman, sketched the most wonderful pictures of heroism in the long battle for national liberation." And from as far away as Cairo, an Egyptian film producer named Fatuh memorialized Wafa in a television program broadcast throughout the Arab world, and then later in an article entitled "An Oscar Winner," which appeared in the Egyptian government opposition daily newspaper *Al-Wafd*. She wrote, "This is not a typical film; the heroine is the beautiful and pure Palestinian woman Wafa Idris, full of life. I could find no better than she, and I could find no film more wonderful than the one that pierces Israel's heart. From Paradise where she is now, she shouts with all her strength the glorification of the dead, enough glorification of the victories of your forefathers, their part—and now it is your turn."

Between then and the end of 2003, five more women would take this final directive to heart.

CHAPTER FOUR

THERE WAS A BRIEF MOMENT IN THE HISTORY of the Israeli–Palestinian conflict when there was a realistic hope for a comprehensive peace that went beneath the surface of the agreement; when the determination was palpable when it came to guaranteeing a bright future for the next generation; when both sides wanted to enjoy economic prosperity; when doing business took precedent over making bombs.

During the period of the Oslo peace accord, between 1993 and 1996, the balance of power in the region tilted in favor of Yasser Arafat's more secular organization, Al-Fatah, over the Islamic fundamentalists who were determined to undermine any viable and concrete peace accord. The Palestinian people were hopeful, and the Israelis were determined. Boaz Ganor, the director of the International Policy Institute for Counter

Terrorism in Israel, says that the years of Oslo were "the best years. The economy tripled, and unemployment was for the first time in low double digits. The average Palestinian loyal to Arafat was against any kind of [violent] actions, since they saw that he had arrived as the president of the Palestinian Authority, which gave the people a degree of self-autonomy. There was hope."

Yasser Arafat, the newly installed president of the Palestinian Authority, was accepted by Israel and the international community as a partner who could lead the Palestinian people toward the implementation of a two-state solution. Even the radical elements within Palestinian society, such as Hamas, by ideology adhered strictly to what is called *fietna* in the Koran, which states that war between Muslims is forbidden. And, for the sake of peace in the Middle East, the world chose to forget Arafat's past transgressions, among the most spectacular the attack on the Israeli athletes during the Munich Olympics in 1972 by Black September, a terror group led by Abou Iyad and under Arafat's control, or a subsequent terror operation that resulted in an international arrest warrant issued in 1976 by the United States against Arafat for murder.

On that occasion he had ordered his Black September operatives to kill a Belgian chargé d'affaires, Guy Eid, and the American ambassador to Khartoum, Cleo Noel, at the Saudi Arabian embassy in Khartoum on March 1, 1973. Proof of Arafat's involvement was revealed on a tape that the Israelis had recorded when they intercepted a telephone call made by Arafat from his then-headquarters in Beirut to the terrorists who had penetrated the Saudi embassy. "Nahir al-Bard," Arafat said—in English, "cold river"—the signal that would begin the slaughter.

In January 1993, at the beginning of the Oslo peace process, that warrant was finally annulled. A year later, Arafat, along with Shimon Peres and Yitzak Rabin, won the Nobel Peace Prize.

That moment of hope between the Israelis and the Palestinians, however, was as brief as it was fragile. For reasons either steeped in recent historical events; or because of the Israeli policy of stalling when it came to affecting promises made within the context of the peace accord that resulted in Arafat losing control to the extremists; or based on the reinterpretation of certain passages of the Koran by the religious fundamentalist element within the society, that climate of optimism slowly diminished until it finally disappeared.

Imams preaching in the mosques who once advocated the notion of peace between Muslims began clouding that message with an ominous nuance when they qualified their words by saying, "In the end, with the help of Allah, there will be Islamic land throughout the entire region." According to Abdul Aziz al-Rantisi, spokesperson for Hamas, his organization has always believed that the timing for a Palestinian state was not important. "Our faith allows us to believe," Dr. al-Rantisi says, "that in the end, with the help of Allah who will ultimately decide, we will eventually win and have an Islamic state on all the land of what is now Israel, including all of the West Bank and Gaza." And Sheik Ahmad Yassin, spiritual leader of Hamas, predicts that Israel will disappear in twenty years. "Islam will overpower and win by sheer numbers," Sheik Yassin said during an interview at his home in Gaza in July 2002. "Israel can delay the moment of the last confrontation but it will come and we will win."

Eventually, whether voluntarily or because he had no choice, Arafat came to the conclusion that terror, or the concept of armed struggle to achieve national liberation, had always gotten him more than had negotiation.

Boaz Ganor maintains that Arafat was educated in "violence" by the Israelis rather than by politics. "Arafat wanted to break the Israeli society," he says, "and he believed that it was only a matter of time before Israel was broken. His biggest problem is that he couldn't make the transition from terrorist to politician, which is the reason why Arafat doesn't have control today, not because he can't but because he chooses not to take control. He has managed to convince the Palestinian people that if they just wait and suffer, in the end it will all pay off. As usual, he is playing a dangerous game, but that's because he's an expert at those kinds of games. His particular psychology is that he likes to walk on the edge. He did it in Lebanon and in Jordan and he's doing it here."

Mohammed Dahalan, formerly the head of security for the Palestinian Authority, and now leader of Al-Fatah in Gaza, explains the complicated relationship between Fatah and Hamas and, more specifically, Arafat's problem in controlling all the different factions within the Palestinian Authority. During an interview with Mr. Dahalan at his office in Gaza in January 2003, he made it clear that, as a member of the Fatah Revolutionary Council, he speaks for Fatah and not the Palestinian Authority. "Fatah is the protection for the Palestinian Authority," he says, "and the only protection for any peace process. But there are problems. In essence, while the PA is secular and democratic, there are factions within the organization that have a problem with democracy and are at risk of being swallowed up by the more religious factions."

In an interview at the American Colony Hotel in East Jerusalem in January 2003, Nihad Abu Ghosh, one of the leaders of the Democratic Front for the Liberation of Palestine (DFLP), states unequivocally that his organization is against killing Israeli civilians and gives credence to Mr. Dahalan's thesis. "There are already more than one hundred prisoners from the DFLP in Israeli prisons," Abu Ghosh says, "which means if I encourage suicide bombers, I will have even more wives and children to worry about than just the families of men who are alive and in jail. At least with them, I only have to worry for twenty years until they are released."

At the same time, Abu Ghosh admits that it is difficult to control the young people in his organization. "We are losing people to the religious parties because we discourage suicide bombers and the religious groups take them, especially in Nablus and Hebron. I try to tell them [our young people] that when we hit the settlements, we control public opinion to dismantle them and we influence immigration and even the settlers to rethink their policy for safety. If we commit suicide attacks in Tel Aviv, we make [Prime Minister] Sharon stronger in his position that settlements like Ariel or Netzarim are as much a part of Israel as Tel Aviv. But at the same time, it is very difficult for me to adhere to our Marxist philosophy that men and women should fight equally and then tell our women that they should go to the trade unions and struggle for equal wages instead of committing military actions. Our young people scoff at the idea of peaceful demonstrations, since the most attractive aspect of our struggle is the military actions."

Abu Ghosh went on to say that not only is the DFLP losing members to the more religious organizations, but Arafat, because he has been isolated and marginalized by the Israelis, has lost control over the people. "To be in control," Abu Ghosh explains, "Arafat needs money, communications, people to be able to come freely to his office. Now, nobody can get in or out. The world has a choice. Either they can think that Arafat is a prisoner of the religious groups in our

59

society or that he is a prisoner of the Israelis." He shrugs. "Either way, he is powerless."

As a result of what has become a conflict between political and religious ideologies within the Palestinian society, as well as within Israeli society, there are now too many variables obstructing what was once an automatic equation for peace, whose formula included a quid pro quo exchange: the dismantling of settlements, which would bring about an eventual cessation of violence and of course suicide attacks; or an Israeli withdrawal to the 1967 borders with the guarantee of safe borders and the automatic creation of an independent Palestinian state. If history has taught both sides anything, it is that the Palestinians will not give up the struggle and that the Israelis will not be pushed into the sea.

Despite the PLO's consistent inability to meet its avowed goals and the suffering the organization has brought upon its own people, to the majority of the Palestinian population, especially those who have lost a family member at the hands of the Israeli military or their homes and land after any one of the previous five wars—war of independence (1948), Suez War (1956), Six-Day War (1967), Yom Kippur War (1973), and Lebanon War (1982)—Yasser Arafat remains the preeminent symbol of the cause. The question is, can a mere symbol have credibility within the international community and in the end lead a nation into statehood? Or does it take a more pragmatic politician who understands that people everywhere want a sound economic program that guarantees them income, jobs, health care, and all the other benefits that contribute to a safe and dignified existence. In the world of terror, money may be the root of all evil, but in the world of diplomacy, money is the root of all goods.

Still, during that moment of hope for a comprehensive peace,

Arafat was nonetheless perceived as the only barrier between his people and the success of their enemy. And if some people judged that he had changed since 1952 when he founded the Union of Palestinian Students at Cairo University in Egypt, which later became Al-Fatah, it is only because memories are short. From the beginning, his organization was affiliated with the Muslim Brotherhood in Egypt. And that alignment was the reason why the Popular Front for the Liberation of Palestine (PFLP)—a communist-based group founded in December 1967 by Dr. George Habash, originally established in Beirut in 1949 as the Arab Nationalist Movement (ANM), also by Dr. Habash—was as an alternative to the Fatah organization. While both movements advocated Arab unity as a prerequisite for the liberation of Palestine, PFLP, under the influence of national liberation movements worldwide, adopted a Marxist-Leninist ideology to attract members. The nuance was that Fatah, given its association with the Muslim Brotherhood, was forced to make limited concessions to certain Islamic restrictions set down by the Muslim Brotherhood, while the PFLP was not.

Throughout the late 1970s and early 1980s, one of the ways that the Fatah differed from those Palestinian factions such as the PFLP that are steeped in Marxist and communist doctrine concerned its very selective use of women in more spectacular attacks. One woman in particular participated in these actions and remains a heroine throughout the Arab world.

On September 6, 1970, the PFLP hijacked four airplanes. Two of them, one American plane and one Swiss, were forced to land on an abandoned airfield near Zarka in Jordan, named Dawson's Field by the British Royal Air Force during the Second World War. There, the crew and passengers were held hostage inside the planes in the heat of the desert for four days and four nights. Meanwhile another hijacked American aircraft was flown to Cairo airport, where the crew and passengers were released before the plane was blown up. The fourth hijacked aircraft was Israeli, on its way from Tel Aviv to London. The hijacker responsible for that action was a woman named Leila Khaled. Assisting Khaled on that El Al flight was a man from San Francisco named Patrick Arguello.

Khaled, a stunning young woman in her twenties, boarded the plane wearing a blond wig and carrying two bombs in her bra. There is no doubt that as a woman, even under the watchful eye of Israeli security, she was able to penetrate the plane more easily than a man. The hijacking attempt failed. The Israeli guard on board killed Arguello and subdued Khaled. Before Arguello died, however, he managed to shoot and injure the Israeli guard. In an attempt to save the injured man, the pilot flew on to London, a shorter distance than had he tried to return to Israel. Despite his efforts, the injured man died en route and, upon arrival in London, Khaled was arrested by British police.

On September 9, a British plane on a flight home from Bahrain was hijacked and the pilot was forced to fly to Dawson's Field, where the other two aircraft were still held on the ground. The PFLP demanded the release of three of their members imprisoned in West Germany, three in Switzerland who had killed an Israeli pilot, and Leila Khaled; if not, all the planes at Dawson's Field would be blown up at three o'clock the following morning. The release of *fedayeen*, or Palestinian freedom fighters, from Israeli prisons was also demanded.

The Israelis refused to negotiate. The British, West German, and Swiss governments complied. Although Israel had refused the demands of the terrorists, most of the passengers were set free and the remaining forty were taken to a refugee camp and imprisoned. Then, as the Jordanian army watched helplessly, the aircraft were blown up. Leila Khaled, briefly detained in London, was subsequently released after several weeks of incarceration. She returned to Syria. On March 7, 1988, Khaled made a statement that "women must become an equal fighting force with men to liberate Palestine."

Leila Khaled voiced almost the same sentiments when I interviewed her at her office at PFLP headquarters in Amman, Jordan, in May 2002. She is fifty-six years old and still an active member of the Central Committee of the Popular Front for the Liberation of Palestine. "I still believe," she said, "that the only way to claim our land is through armed struggle, and men and women should struggle for our homeland equally because all of us suffer equally under occupation." But when I pressed her on the use of women as suicide bombers, she had a surprising response. "We in the PFLP have always considered men and women as equal. My comrades accepted me from the beginning and called on me to do the military actions years ago. There was no difference and I never felt as if I didn't have their respect. Today there is a big religious influence in our society, and that is the reason why there are so many suicide bombers. When the religious leaders say that women who make these actions are finally equal to men, I have a problem. Everyone is equal in death—rich, poor, Arab, Jew, Christian, we are all equal. I would rather see women equal to men in life."

★   ★   ★

The similar ambitions of Islamic Jihad ideology, which defines its first
and principal objective as an Islamic revolution throughout the
Middle East, and Arafat's Al-Fatah, whose goal is the creation of a
Palestinian state as well as the "right of return" of Palestinian
refugees to their original homes on what is now Israeli soil, has been
a convenient basis for tight collaboration between these two groups.
In the beginning of his tenure as president of the Palestinian
Authority, despite ideological differences, Arafat understood this.
Arafat reasoned that in order to dilute the increasing power of the
Jihad activists, who called for an escalation of the "armed struggle"
against Israel throughout the Occupied Territories, he would recruit
a reserve of their young religious fighting militants into his own
group. The Islamic Jihad and Hamas needed Al-Fatah's broad social,
economic, and political infrastructure in the Occupied Territories
and its connections into Jordan and other Arab countries that
provided the large sums of money necessary to support their military
and political enterprises.

Indeed, during Arafat's address to Palestinian women on January
27, 2002, when he called for their participation in the Intifada, he
made reference to the religious doctrine consistently stated by the
extremist religious groups when he said that "Israel will disappear in
the same kind of crusade as happened in 1211."

Mira Tzoreff, professor at Ben Gurion University, believes that
currently in Palestinian society, nationalism is a euphemism for
religion. "One cannot think of a dichotomy between a religious and
secular movement, although originally Fatah was established as
secular but now there is a process of Islamization of the Fatah and

secularization of the Hamas, which is the basis for their united power within the West Bank and Gaza. Fatah needs the Islamic discourse in order to strengthen itself and be able to go to the Islamists and tell them that you are part of us, we embrace you, and we can't afford to lose you and your support or we lose our nationalistic goal of creating a Palestinian state. Later on, Arafat can worry about how not to make Palestine an Islamic state, although he knows very well that by that time there will be someone else in charge and someone else with that problem. As it stands, all he cares about is that he is remembered for achieving Phase One of the Palestinian struggle for independence."

"Phase One" is a phrase that has sparked heated debate on both sides of the Green Line and emotional disagreement within political parties on the same side of the struggle. Dr. Boaz Ganor perceives the process of creating a Palestinian state as divided into a three-stage strategy. "First he [Arafat] wants the creation of a Palestinian state in the West Bank and Gaza, with the capital in East Jerusalem," Dr. Ganor explains. "Then he will take control of Jordan, which has about 80 percent Palestinians, and overthrow the Hashemite kingdom. The only thing that stops Arafat from doing that now is the absence of a Palestinian state in the West Bank and Gaza. The problem for him is not if he could win at this point but that a Palestinian state in Jordan would negate his claim to a Palestinian state throughout Judea and Samaria. The third stage would be to encourage the Israeli Arabs, who are Palestinians and who comprise about 23 percent of the population, to rebel. He will begin by encouraging them to go to the international community and accuse Israel of being an apartheid state. Why should the Israeli Arabs raise the flag of David or sing the national anthem that alludes to Jewish soil? Or, why is it that every Jew brings his cousins from anywhere in the world and they are given automatic citizenship and yet an Israeli Arab can't? And do you know what? The international community will buy it."

Dr. Ganor goes on to say that the "right of return" was one of the points of contention during the Oslo peace process and the subsequent Camp David accords, which ultimately caused their failure. "What broke discussions in Camp David and then in Taba," Dr. Ganor explains, "was that Arafat did not gain enough when it came to allowing the 'right of return' for the Palestinian refugees. The more Palestinians who lived in Israel meant that the demand for the last stage would provide a stronger argument. The bottom line is that since 1994, Arafat has been trying to prove to the world that he was the lesser of two evils, between the extremists and his own PLO. He was the good option and they were the bad. The truth is that I see no difference at this point between Arafat and Hamas."

Ismail Abu Shanab was the number three in the hierarchy of Hamas and the director of Sheik Yassin's office in Gaza. Married and the father of ten children, he died when an Israeli helicopter fired missiles at his car on August 21, 2003. It was approximately 11h20 in the morning and Abu Shanab was on his way to the University of Gaza where he was a professor of architecture. After the fact, he was a poor choice for a target of murder, since for Israeli journalists, moderates and foreign correspondents who always looked for a sane voice to explain the situation, Abu Shanab was a thoughtful, pragmatic and sensible human being. According to Roni Shaked, a journalist from *Yediot Aharanot*, one of the most widely read daily newspapers in Israel, the Israeli government targeted Abu Shanab to "send a message to all Hamas leaders that their days were numbered."

During an interview with him in June 2003, only two months before his death, he acknowledged that his organization (Hamas) had a three-point agenda. "We are in agreement with Fatah and Yasser Arafat," Abu Shanab states, "when it comes to continuing the Intifada, strengthening the unity between our organizations, and getting rid of the occupation. There is no state without resistance, but we nonetheless agreed to curtail military actions while Yasser Arafat was in negotiations with the United States and Israel. Ten years later and we are no better off. Now Fatah is participating in this resistance, and if there is any doubt, Fatah claimed responsibility for the double martyr operation in Tel Aviv [January 6, 2003, in which at least twenty-two people were killed, mostly foreign workers, and more than one hundred injured]. Nobody is talking about stopping the Intifada as long as there is occupation. Fatah said that Palestinians have the right to continue in the face of assassinations, collective punishment, and military raids by the Israelis."

Notwithstanding Abu Shanab's insistence of unity between Al-Fatah and Hamas, when I asked him if Arafat was still in control, he demurred. "There is no doubt there is tension and disunity within Fatah," he replied. "That is an interior situation within Fatah and we cannot interfere in that situation. Obviously, between us, there was once an ideological confrontation, since we are working towards a religious state and Fatah was looking for a secular one. But now there is no problem, since for the moment we are all concentrating on getting rid of the occupation. After that, we will see what kind of a state we build for the people."

In another example of the disunity that is endemic within the Palestinian Authority, Mohammed Dahalan insists that it was not Arafat directly but the al-Aqsa Martyr's Brigade, the military arm of Fatah, that took credit for the Tel Aviv bombing in January 2003, which occurred almost immediately after Arafat called for a complete cessation of violence. "There are some loose cannons in the field," Mr. Dahalan says, "who don't listen to orders; splinter groups, gangs who take revenge, uncontrollable factions. Fatah has an increasingly big problem to control their own people, so when Arafat condemned the attack, he was partially sincere. His problem is that he refused to listen to me when I was in charge of his security service to crack down on the splinter groups. He was afraid he would lose his popularity, and he is not ready to pay that price for a strict condemnation." Mr. Dahalan shrugs. "That is why I resigned."

On January 20, 2003, after meetings in Cairo between Hamas and Fatah, Nabil Shaath, a close adviser to Arafat, outlined provisions for a new constitution for an eventual Palestinian state. Among the points he made was that Islam would be its official religion. When I pointed this out to Abu Shanab, he added that during the meetings in Cairo not only did Fatah agree to creating an Islamic state, but Fatah never asked Hamas to stop suicide attacks. "Any statement he [Arafat] made," Abu Shanab says, "was for the Western audience. Behind the scenes there was a united and unanimous movement to continue suicide attacks."

Professor Mira Tzoreff explains that when Arafat, a secularist, talks about the Koran, he is simply pulling from his basic heritage. "Arafat has to do that to be legitimate for his people," Tzoreff explains, "to talk to them in the language and terminology they understand. In the end, he turns the Islamic *shahide* or *shahida* into a nationalistic one, or a martyr for the nation rather than a martyr for Allah."

Conversely, the Islamic Jihad and Hamas need Fatah to legitimize them and their nationalism so they are not left out or marginalized either. "The Palestinian society was historically, in its essence, not a religious one," Tzoreff says. "Any support the Islamists could get from the so-called secular part of the society made them stronger. Now things have changed, and it is the secular portion of society that needs the Islamists more."

While it is an accepted fact that those who are members of Hamas and Islamic Jihad are practicing Muslims, it is a misconception to view the Fatah movement as nonreligious or secular. According to Sheik 'Abd-Salam Abu Shukheudem, the chief mufti of the Palestinian Authority Police Force, "There is not one Muslim Palestinian who considers him- or herself secular. It is the West that considers al-Aqsa a secular organization, but we are all Muslims practicing Muslim beliefs. We believe in Paradise and the rewards that are offered there as much as those you call fundamentalists."

Shalom Harrari, the former Israeli intelligence officer, explains, "Every paper sent out by the Palestinian Authority under Yasser Arafat begins with 'In the Name of Allah.' Arafat united his forces with the religious forces so that now, religion and politics go together"

The strongest belief that the Islamic Jihad, Hamas, and Yasser Arafat's Fatah organization share is that armed struggle is the only way to liberate Palestine. For the latter, armed struggle is done under the banner of nationalistic and patriotic duty, while for the former, it is a religious duty for every Muslim to liberate Islamic land.

CHAPTER FIVE

UNTIL WAFA IDRIS BECAME THE FIRST *SHAHIDA*, suicide bombings had been the province of Hamas and the Islamic Jihad, the militant Islamic movements whose goal has always been to create an Islamic Palestinian state and, by consequence, to prevent Yasser Arafat and his Palestinian Liberation Organization from entering into a peace accord with Israel.

In keeping with Islamic tradition, suicide bombers had always been male, under the age of thirty, religious, unmarried, highly politicized, and unemployed. Even those suicide bombers who were educated for the most part also faced bleak futures, given the lack of opportunity under Israeli occupation. Many had spent time in Israeli prisons or had male relatives who had been wounded, killed, or imprisoned by Israeli forces.

Among Muslims in general and Islamic militants in particular, the influence and teachings of the Koran are paramount. For the past fourteen centuries the Koran has guided their religious fervor and dictated the principles and morals of secular life as well. Martyrs, according to the Koran, earn eternal glory by "dying for the sake of Allah" and are rewarded with eternal life next to their Lord. According to the Koranic verse that opens each installment of the newspaper biographies of those men— and now women—who died while committing an act of martyrdom, "Do not consider those who are slain in the service of Allah as dead. Indeed, they are living by their Lord."

While using women in suicide attacks is a major break with tradition, until the late 1970s "conventional" male suicide bombers were rarely used at all in the Middle East. Until then, religious leaders had not yet interpreted the passages in the Koran that "condemn the taking of one's life as a sin" to mean that "giving one's life in an act of martyrdom is a responsibility and duty that is honored by Allah and respected as the ultimate act of religious devotion by all His followers."

The unity between the Islamic Jihad, Hamas, and Arafat's organization has as its genesis a long history of cross alliances between religious and political Palestinian groups that date back to the 1970s. Only by tracing several key political events in Palestinian history can the use of women as *shahidas* be understood as an obvious outcome of those alliances.

In the early 1970s in Lebanon, three Islamic groups—al-Tahrir al-

Islami, al-Jihad, and the Muslim Brotherhood—formed a federation under the name of the Islamic Jihad. Not only did this federation operate openly in Lebanon, but it eventually gathered strength and an enormous presence in Jordan, the West Bank, and Gaza. For fundamentalists supporting all three groups, Islam was the solution to their woes. Despite their apparent unity, however, there were philosophical differences between them from the inception.

Both al-Tahrir al-Islami and the al-Jihad stressed that the Arab–Israeli conflict was not limited to land, but rather was a fundamentally religious conflict where Israel was seen as the spearhead of the West in the center of a Muslim world. They believed that the elimination of Israel was the first step toward the return of all Muslims to the faith and to the establishment of an Islamic state on all Arab land, including Palestine. Born out of the secular political parties' failure to give Muslims a dominant position in the twentieth century—Islamic guerrilla fighters, or mujahideen, were mostly young men who were highly educated but unable to find proper employment in the stagnant economies of the Middle East and North Africa—Islam became an appealing alternative. Israel was seen as the predominant symbol of that failure.

The Muslim Brotherhood, originally founded in the 1920s in Egypt by a schoolteacher named Hassan al-Banna to fight the occupying British army, was less concerned with the Palestinian problem than it was with spreading Islamic culture and social work throughout the West Bank and Gaza. Its members claimed that a solution to the Palestinian problem would come about only *after* an Islamic state was established in Palestine, which depended on their spreading the religious and cultural teachings of Islam throughout the area. Before launching upon an armed struggle throughout

72

occupied lands, the Muslim Brotherhood believed that the first step was to develop its infrastructure in the Gaza Strip and the West Bank by means of Islamic indoctrination. Any changeover into violence at that point risked the relative freedom of religious practices they were allowed by the Israeli security forces. But the al-Tahrir al-Islami and the al-Jihad argued that armed struggle was a divine obligation that should begin immediately.

Another serious difference between the three groups emerged as a result of changes within the Islamic community after the Iranian revolution and the rise of fundamentalism that spread from Iran into Lebanon and Syria in 1978. At that point, the al-Tahrir al-Islami and the al-Jihad, unlike the Muslim Brotherhood, adopted the revolution in Iran led by the Ayatollah Khomeini as their model. Under the influence of the mullahs in Iran, the bravery of the Iranian soldiers during the Iran–Iraq War became legendary and served as a symbol to every fighter opposing Israeli occupation within the West Bank and Gaza. Photographs appeared everywhere in which Iranian soldiers were seen going into battle with the "key to Paradise" on a chain around their necks, a symbol of their willingness to die for Allah while conquering the "infidel enemy."

It was during that period, in Syria, that Ali Akbar Mohtasehemi, the Iranian ambassador to Syria, created Hizbollah, or the Party of God, an extremist political and religious movement dedicated to the creation of an Iranian-style Islamic republic and the removal of any non-Islamic influences throughout the region. Under the spiritual leadership of Sheik Muhammed Hussein Fadlallah, a Shia cleric in Lebanon, the movement joined forces with smaller Shia political parties, such as the

Hussein Suicide Squad; Da'awa, the Lebanese branch of the Iraq-based al-Da'awa al-Islamiya; and dissatisfied members of the older Islamic Amal.

Iranian officials actively supported and assisted the movement of twelve hundred members of the Iranian Revolutionary Guards, the Pasdaran, to Baalback in the northern Bekaa Valley of Lebanon. The Pasdaran contingent not only fought against the Israelis and the Southern Lebanon Army (SLA), backed by Israel and based in southern Lebanon, but also provided Hizbollah's fighters with a combination of ideological indoctrination, vast financial support, and military training and equipment. The Iranian presence was a key factor in Hizbollah's transformation from a loose network into a well-organized and highly disciplined movement with a sophisticated guerrilla force.

By the end of 1982, Hizbollah in Lebanon had received the blessing of Iranian mullahs to use what they considered the ultimate weapon of destruction—suicide attacks, or the "poor man's atomic bomb"—a policy that was refined and improved throughout the rest of that decade.

Dr. Fathi Shekaki, a physician originally from Gaza and the author of *Khomeini: The Alternative and the Islamic Solution*, was the leader and founder of the Islamic Jihad movement in Gaza, along with Sheik Abed al-Aziz Ouda, who had been a teacher in Gaza. In 1984, Sheik Ouda was arrested and sentenced to eleven months in an Israeli prison. When he was released, he and Dr. Shekaki resumed their activities with the Islamic Jihad in Gaza until both were permanently expelled. Ouda settled in Syria, while Shekaki went to southern Lebanon, where he enjoyed good relations with Hizbollah and Iranian forces, as well as with the leadership in Syria. The Palestinian Islamic Jihad, the faction that Dr. Shekaki headed, became one of the largest Islamic Jihad groups in the Occupied Territories.

It was under the direction of Dr. Shekaki that the first of a series of suicide attacks in Lebanon occurred, beginning in 1983 with the explosion at the U.S. embassy in Beirut, which killed approximately sixty people. The most spectacular of those attacks was the truck bombing of the American Marine installation in Beirut on October 23, 1983, at six-thirty in the morning. More than 240 soldiers and civilians were killed. The attack was timed to coincide with the suicide bombing of a French paratrooper base a few kilometers away.

Despite the success of several spectacular attacks, it was difficult to find volunteers willing to get into trucks loaded with explosives and take their final journey to Paradise. According to a former member of the group, a close associate of Dr. Shekaki who has since defected and lives in Kuwait, the handlers would often "incorporate two switches in the cars and tell the drivers that they could detonate the bomb and run. . . . For this reason," the defector says, "those early attacks were called 'park and run' bombings, although in reality the handlers would blow up the driver along with his car by a long-distance detonator switch, turning an unwilling and unknowing victim into a martyr."

After his assassination in Malta by the Israelis in April 1995, Dr. Shekaki was succeeded by Dr. Abdullah Shala. He continues to direct the group's activities and their operatives from his base in southern Lebanon, where he recruits youth from the Palestinian refugee camps and trains them to carry out attacks in Israel with the help and assistance of Hizbollah.

★   ★   ★

At the same time that Hizbollah was building its powerful infra-structure and laying the groundwork for future suicide bombings, other events were occurring that ultimately affected the fate of Yasser Arafat and the PLO. Saddam Hussein, aware that he was losing support throughout the Arab world during the early years of the Iran-Iraq War, which began in 1980, strategically acknowledged the Jihad in his speeches at the time. He referred to Arafat as the "little Saladin," a leader who was struggling to conquer those who would "prevent an Islamic Palestine." In reality, Hussein's political agenda was not the plight of the Palestinians or to embrace the edicts of fundamental Islam, but rather to combat the zeal of the Iranian soldiers who con-sidered the battle against Iraq and Saddam Hussein's Baath regime one between Islam and the infidels.

While Saddam Hussein's comments may have served to elevate Arafat's stature and, as a consequence, garner support throughout the Islamic communities in the West Bank, Gaza, and Lebanon, a series of events was about to shake up politics in the region. On June 3, 1982, in London, the Israeli ambassador to the court of St. James, Shlomo Argov, was attacked on the pavement in front of the Dorchester Hotel in London. Although Ambassador Argov survived, he suffered a severe head wound and never fully recovered his mental faculties before his death in the autumn of 2002.

Three members of the Abu Nidal organization were arrested, tried, and found guilty of committing the attack. In retaliation, and because of constant Katuysha rocket attacks launched by Hizbollah across the border of southern Lebanon into Kiryat

Shimona in northern Israel, Israel began a series of bombing raids on PLO bases in Lebanon that culminated in a full-fledged offensive. On June 4, 1982, the Israeli army slammed across the northern border into Lebanon in a full-scale military operation called Operation Peace for Galilee, ostensibly to rid southern Lebanon of the PLO and Hizbollah guerrillas.

Because the PLO had no air force, they relied on direct Syrian assistance to defend them. In the beginning, Syrian ground and air forces did engage the Israelis, but after losing twenty-two planes in the first three days of the fighting and subsequently more than fifty more, as well as the destruction of their surface-to-air missiles in the Bekaa, Hafez al-Assad, the Syrian leader, withdrew. On the fifth day of the fighting, Assad agreed, under pressure from the United States, to a cease-fire with Israel. Previously protected by the Syrians, the PLO leaders suddenly found themselves facing the Israelis alone; Syria had no intention of fighting a "hopeless" war with Israel merely to save Arafat's organization. Nor would any other Arab nation come to the aid of the Palestinians, and in fact several announced that there would be no regrets if the PLO were destroyed entirely.

The silence from the Arab world and the lack of active or even tacit support came as a shock to the PLO leadership and remains today a source of contention between the Palestinian population and their Arab neighbors. In the end, Philip Habib, an American diplomatic envoy, negotiated an agreement with the Israelis, the Lebanese government, and with the ex-premier of Lebanon, Sa'ib Salam, for the PLO to be permanently expelled from Lebanon.

On August 21, 1982, PLO forces began their withdrawal from

their base of operations in Lebanon. Approximately six thousand soldiers from the Palestinian Liberation Army (PLA) set off along the Beirut–Damascus highway, along with some six hundred women and children. Another eight thousand PLA members left by sea for the Syrian port of Tartous. Other PLA fighters went by sea from the port of Beirut to more distant destinations. It took twelve days for all the contingents to leave, although their departure was, on the surface at least, not dishonorable. They paraded through West Beirut as if celebrating a victory, bearing their personal arms and shooting wildly in the air. From his base in Beirut, Arafat first went to Athens, where he was received warmly, before he set up his new headquarters in Sidi Bou Said in Tunisia, where then-President Bourghuiba welcomed him.

On September 14, 1982, Bashir Gemayel, the Christian Phalange president of Lebanon, was assassinated. His murderer, Habib Chatouni, who had planted a Japanese-made, electronically triggered bomb behind a wall panel in Gemayel's conference room, was a member of the Syrian Socialist National Party (SSNP). Chatouni's affiliation directly implicated the Syrians in Gemayel's death and subsequently accounted for their choice of Amin, Bashir Gemayel's brother, to succeed him. While Bashir enjoyed good relations with the Israelis, Amin had always been favored by the Syrians. After Bashir's death, and with continued sporadic attacks by remaining PLO and PLA fighters, the Israelis focused their attention on several thousand Palestinians who remained in refugee camps in West Beirut.

The Sabra and Shatilla refugee camps, according to the Israelis, sheltered between two and three thousand terrorists among the civilian populations. On several occasions, even before Bashir

Gemayel's murder, the Israelis had asked the Lebanese army to go in and "clear them out." The Lebanese consistently refused. On September 16, 1982, Kataeb militia men (part of the Christian Phalange army) entered the two camps and, with the help of Israeli forces stationed on the rooftops illuminating the area below with spotlights, massacred what they claimed were approximately three hundred "terrorists." On Saturday morning, September 18, it became apparent to the press, Red Cross, and other international observers who were finally allowed access to the camps that there had been a wholesale massacre of more than seven or eight hundred Palestinian civilians and militants by the Christian militia, aided by Israeli military forces. While the international community heaped opprobrium on Israel and the Lebanese Christian forces, the more extreme Arab groups were determined to exact revenge.

Living conditions under the occupation continued to be abysmal throughout the West Bank and Gaza, and in June 1987, Hamas—in Arabic, an acronym for *Harakat al-Muqawama al-Islamia*, meaning "courage and bravery"—was created as an outgrowth of the Palestinian branch of the Muslim Brotherhood. In the very beginning, Hamas was primarily engaged in political activity, such as running candidates in West Bank Chamber of Commerce elections. Basing their philosophy on the tenets of the Muslim Brotherhood, Hamas, like the Muslim Brotherhood, was against armed struggle, which threatened to diminish the freedom they enjoyed from the Israelis throughout the West Bank and Gaza when it came to indoctrinating members into an ultra-religious concept of Islam.

When the Intifada broke out on December 11, 1987,

however, Hamas activists realized that *not* participating in an armed struggle, when the entire population had risen up against occupation, would damage their image and cost them support. Any past differences between the Islamic Jihad and the Muslim Brotherhood were eliminated when Hamas joined the uprising and therefore adopted, by tacit accord, the policies of the Islamic Jihad to wage war against the "infidel occupiers of holy Islamic land." The consequences of the uprising not only had political repercussions throughout the various competitive militant groups, but it also ultimately changed the balance of power throughout the Middle East.

With the bitter memories of the events in Lebanon in 1982 and the growing strength of Hizbollah across the border, Palestinians were determined to actively resist Israeli occupation rather than remain passive, which would have cast them in the eyes of the world once again as victims. The revolt began in the streets and slowly filtered up to the top echelon of the Palestinian leadership. One of the founders of the PLO, along with Yasser Arafat, was Khalil al-Wazir, or Abu Jihad (his nom de guerre). Abu Jihad became the link between the PLO in Sidi Bou Said in Tunisia and the local leadership of the uprising throughout the West Bank and Gaza. His wife, Um Jihad, a symbol of resistance to the occupation, was an inspiration to the burgeoning feminist movement as a liberated woman, helpmate to her husband, and fighter in her own right. Her husband put her in charge of the

Martyr's Fund, which looked after the families of those men killed or jailed during the Intifada.

On April 15, 1988, mere months after the beginning of the Intifada, Israeli commandos led by future prime minister Ehud Barak embarked on an elaborate sea mission that ended in the assassination of Abu Jihad in his home in Sidi Bou Said in front of his wife and infant son. It is significant that when he was alive and directing the Intifada, the success of his operations depended largely on the participation of the Islamic Jihad and eventually Hamas, which frowned upon women's participation in the violence. After his death, his widow was careful to follow all of her late husband's directives to make the Intifada a continued success.

As a woman who was seen as a national treasure, Um Jihad, the widow of a Palestinian hero and martyr, nonetheless came out against the participation of women in the Intifada in an effort to maintain a united Palestinian front to combat the Israel military. "It is difficult for women to participate," she said at the time, "because they are forbidden to go out at night alone to demonstrate and confront the soldiers." Further, she explained that because women were obliged to wear their traditional long dresses that made it difficult for them to move around, and since they were forbidden to wear pants or clinging outfits, they were at a disadvantage. "The danger is if they [women] understand that disadvantage and begin dressing inappropriately. If soldiers see them, they will bring dishonor to their families."

After the murder of Abu Jihad, Sheik Assad al-Tamimi, the scion of a distinguished family in Hebron, with the blessing of the Iranian government and in cooperation with Yasser Arafat's Al-Fatah, began to recruit young Palestinians, including active Fatah members, for a new Islamic Jihad faction called Belt al-Muqades, based in Jordan. Sheik al-Tamimi's credentials were impressive enough to garner respect from both the secular and the religious factions of Palestinian society. He had once served as imam of the al-Aqsa mosque in Jerusalem in the 1960s, and when his term of office expired before the Six-Day War in 1967, al-Tamimi went to the West Bank and joined the Muslim Brotherhood, where he remained until after the Iranian revolution. In addition to creating the Belt al-Muqades, al-Tamimi, no longer an active member of the Muslim Brotherhood, also organized additional Islamic Jihad cells in the Occupied Territories and courted various Jihad groups that had already coalesced there. For a while, most of the Jihad factions in the Occupied Territories were either associated with al-Tamimi or subordinate to him.

In view of his close ties with the Iranians, as well as with Fatah—especially with the organization's strike force at the time, which was known as the Western Sector—al-Tamimi was the natural replacement for Abu Jihad, serving as the liaison between Fatah and Islamic Jihad activists. In this way, al-Tamimi was able to forward funds he received from Iran, Fatah, Saudi Arabia, and other Arab countries to Jihad factions on the West Bank and throughout Gaza.

Despite Saddam Hussein's attempt to "Islamize" Arafat and his Al-Fatah movement during the Iran–Iraq war, cooperation between Fatah and the Islamic Jihad group deteriorated sharply after the assassination by the Israelis of Abu Jihad. During a 1989 interview with Salah Khalaf, or Abu Iyad (*nom de guerre*), the eventual head of Black September and a founder of Fatah along with Yasser Arafat and Abu Jihad, he indicated that the death of

82

their old friend had a profound effect on Arafat's vision of a protracted military struggle with the Israelis.

"Abu Jihad," Abu Iyad told me, "was a man who had on-the-ground experience. The Palestinian people loved him and trusted him because he was one of them. When he died, they were less apt to take orders from a stranger or someone they considered an outsider." My relationship with Abu Iyad continued until his assassination in Sidi Bou Said by what is now thought to be militants attached to the late Abu Nidal, the leader of a more militant faction of the PLO that was against Yasser Arafat. A jovial man and an astute politician, Abu Iyad realized, even during the hopeless days of the first Intifada, that an eventual peace accord with Israel was an inevitability. During an interview that I did with him and with then Israeli defense minister, Yitzak Rabin, which was published in the *Journal de Dimanche*, a French weekly newspaper in early December 1988, both men stated their belief and hope that a dialogue and eventual peace accord was in the future.

On December 7, 1988, Arafat formally accepted U.N. Security Council Resolutions 242 and 338. Standing before the U.N. General Assembly in Geneva days later, Arafat called on Israel to join in peace talks aimed at resolving outstanding differences. Arafat told the assembled U.N. delegates, "The PLO will seek a comprehensive settlement among the parties concerned in the Arab-Israeli conflict, including the state of Palestine, Israel, and other neighbors, within the framework of the international conference for peace in the Middle East on the basis of Resolutions 242 and 338 and so as to guarantee equality and the balance of interests, especially our people's rights in freedom, national independence, and respect the right to exist in peace and security for all."

Resolution 242 was made after the 1967 Six-Day War and stated that Israel should retreat from Occupied Territories in exchange for safe and secure borders. Curiously, there is a discrepancy between the French and the English texts. The French text states that "Israel should withdraw from *all* territories," while the English text, which is considered to be the binding one, states that "Israel should withdraw from *the* territories." United Nations Resolution 338 was made after the 1973 Yom Kippur War and is considered a parallel resolution that essentially reiterates the principles of 242.

By accepting the resolutions, however, Arafat was accused by the Islamic Jihad of recognizing the existence of the "Jewish entity," which caused a rupture between Fatah and the Islamic Jihad. A dire consequence of that rupture was that Fatah terminated its assistance and financial support to Jihad groups in the Occupied Territories. As a result, Sheik al-Tamimi became closer to pro-Syrian and other rival organizations of Arafat's, such as the PFLP-General Command under the leadership of Ahmed Jibril. Eventually, the Jibril front allowed Sheik al-Tamimi access to its radio station in southern Syria, which enabled him to broadcast announcements of Islamic Jihad activities throughout the West Bank and Gaza. Once again, there was dissension within the ranks, as not everyone within al-Tamimi's organization was pleased with the break with Arafat or his new alliance with Syria and the PFLP-General Command.

In September 1990, Sheik al-Tamimi's assistant Ibrahim Sarbal defected and, along with several other activists, established a rival faction called the al-Aqsa Martyr's Brigade, which functioned under the auspices and with the cooperation and support of Al-

Fatah. It was then that Saddam Hussein once again tried to mobilize Yasser Arafat and his followers throughout the Occupied Territories to support his invasion of Kuwait.

In aligning himself with Saddam Hussein against the United States and its coalition force of Arab nations, Yasser Arafat once again made the wrong political decision for the Palestinian people. Until his defeat, however, Saddam Hussein claimed, along with Arafat, that they were together in the name of Allah, against the United States and their coalition of "infidels," and were united in eradicating Israel from the map. He even changed the Iraqi flag by writing on it "Allah Akhbar." Gathering momentum from Saddam Hussein and determined to break out from under the defeat of their Arab brothers, Palestinians continued to choose violence as an alternative to humiliation under Israeli occupation.

By the time the Gulf War ended and Saddam Hussein had been defeated and marginalized by the rest of the Arab world, not only did Yasser Arafat pay an enormous financial price, given the loss of millions of dollars that once poured into the West Bank and Gaza from oil-rich Gulf states, but the radical factions within the Occupied Territories and Gaza had been sufficiently incited and mobilized to create daily violence, which took many lives on both sides of the struggle. In response, Israel's Prime Minister Yitzak Rabin took a step that would ultimately lead to the emergence of a new and even more efficient terror weapon within his own borders.

CHAPTER SIX

ON DECEMBER 13, 1992, Nissim Toledano, an Israeli border policeman from Lod, was kidnapped and assassinated by Hamas. Ehud Barak, the chief of staff under Prime Minister Rabin, suggested that the Israeli government should deport approximately one thousand Hamas members across the border into Lebanon. The idea was to send them away for one year to avoid creating negative international opinion that the Israelis were embarking upon a "transfer" policy, whereby Palestinians were systematically expelled. Sholomit Aloni, the minister of education and a member of the left-wing Meretz Party, opposed Barak's idea, and the Knesset was compelled to quickly strike a compromise.

On December 16, the Israeli security service and police rounded up approximately sixteen hundred members and supporters of Hamas and Islamic Jihad and deported 415 people:

250 from the West Bank and 165 from Gaza. The Act of Deportation was signed by the High Court in Jerusalem on the morning of December 18; that afternoon, Prime Minister Rabin formally expelled them to Marj al-Zahour in southern Lebanon, an area that became known as No Man's Land because of its barren and bleak lunar-like surface. The international press focused on their plight.

As it turned out, by deporting the Hamas members, Rabin played right into the hands of extremists. As the deportees languished throughout the harsh winter of 1992–93 in No Man's Land, they were the captive audience of fundamentalist mullahs who nourished not only their bodies with food but their minds with radical Islamic ideas. The result was the beginning of an unholy alliance between Hamas, who are Sunni Muslims, and the Shiite Hizbollah, during which Hizbollah shamed Hamas for their reluctance to participate in suicide bombings. Hani, a bearded twenty-two-year-old Hamas disciple who currently lives in Gaza, was a small child when he was deported with his father. Now his neighbors say that he is "destined for martyrdom." "We were taught then," Hani recalls, "and we understand now that this [the liberation of Palestine] is a religious war. It has nothing to do with land."

By late 1993, when public opinion forced Prime Minister Rabin to allow those deported members of Hamas back into the Occupied Territories, they had been completely indoctrinated into the practice of suicide bombings by their Hizbollah spiritual guides. By then, Islamic Jihad members throughout the West Bank and Gaza were organized into small secret cells and maintained contact with the higher Jihad leadership in Jordan. This leadership, generally composed of senior Islamic Jihad operatives who had been expelled from Israel, directed the activities of its people in the Occupied Territories by giving them instructions through various channels such as newspapers, radio, and television, as well as covering their expenses and meeting their daily needs. One indicator of the relative strength of the Islamic Jihad, even before the Hamas members were allowed back, was the success of a general strike called by the organization on December 6, 1992, to commemorate the fifth anniversary of the first Intifada (the traditional date honored by the PLO and its supporters is December 11). As Dr. al-Rantisi, one of those who was expelled in 1992, explains, "[The Israelis] have tried that tactic [expulsion] many times before. They thought the situation would be quiet because all the military members and even political leaders were expelled, injured, dead, or in jail. Believe me, we were then and we are now an organization in which the people are the source of all the military and political actions. Palestinian people can do military operations without the leaders."

During the final two years of the first Intifada, which officially ended in 1993, Yasser Arafat came to the conclusion that it was in his interests to try a path other than violence in order to achieve an independent Palestinian state. His reasoning was not without logic. Arafat believed that based on the positive reaction of the international community to the Intifada, which had turned in favor of the Palestinians, he had a moral victory to justify his participation in a peace initiative. In addition, he knew that his people were weary of street fighting and feeling hopeless about their economic situation. For Arafat, it was the moment when he believed that peace through negotiation and conciliation would not imply that he was in a weakened position that had forced him to compromise with his enemy.

When Arafat shook hands with Prime Minister Rabin in September 1993 under the beaming eyes of U.S. President Bill Clinton in an historic ceremony on the White House lawn, it was the culmination of months of negotiation that promised to be the beginning of a new era of peace. But if the Intifada that began in 1987 can be credited for that historic handshake, it was the reluctance of the Israeli government to implement promised withdrawals from the Occupied Territories that produced renewed hostilities and violence on the part of the Palestinians.

Almost immediately after that White House ceremony, Hamas and the Islamic resistance movement, along with the Palestinian Islamic Jihad (PIJ), carried out more than thirty suicide attacks in the West Bank and Gaza, killing more than a hundred people and injuring hundreds more. In the beginning, Hamas and the PIJ focused their attacks on military targets in the Occupied Territories and on Israeli settlements, but quite rapidly the focus shifted to civilians in central cities and crowded areas within Israel proper.

On February 16, 1994, Dr. Baruch Goldstein, an American physician specializing in emergency care who had immigrated to Israel as a member of Meir Kahan's extremist Kach party, massacred twenty-one Palestinians and injured dozens more as they prayed at the Cave of the Patriarch in Hebron. The response was immediate; Hamas and the other Islamic Jihad groups carried out another spate of suicide attacks, once again within Israel proper. What ensued was not only a series of violent reprisals by both sides, but a schism within both the Palestinian and Israeli societies, where the extremists took over in the streets. The assassination of Yitzak Rabin by Yigal Amir, a Jewish fundamentalist and member of the Kach movement, on November 2,

1995, was one of the final acts that irrevocably ended the peace process. The other was the assassination on January 3, 1996, of Yaiah Ayash, the Hamas member known as the Engineer, who designed the first suicide belt. According to Shimon Peres, the acting prime minister, the Israeli-sponsored assassination was a move designed to cripple the morale and the efficiency of the Hamas terror network. Instead, it served only to inspire Hamas and Islamic Jihad members to commit even more acts of terror throughout Israel and the Occupied Territories.

The climate became increasingly violent. The influence of the Islamic Jihad became even more prevalent when they took control of all the universities in the West Bank and Gaza, including the Christian ones like Bir Zeit in Ramallah. As Shalom Harrari, the former Israeli intelligence officer, describes it, "The Islamic religion was hijacked by about forty or fifty thousand sheiks of the Muslim Brotherhood, who preached the liberation of Palestine and the destruction of the Jewish state as the religious, nationalistic, and moral obligation of all Muslims."

As suicide bombings became more prevalent in the late 1990s, not only did they create terror throughout the civilian population in Israel, but they also hit the business community hard, as investment money began to pull out. Eventually Yasser Arafat realized that if terrorist attacks and suicide bombings affected the economy of Israel, the Palestinians would be the first casualties. More out of pragmatism than a sense of commitment to the peace accord,

Arafat did not participate in any attacks within Israel until it became clear that the Israeli government had no intention of putting a moratorium on the construction of new settlements, as outlined within the Oslo peace accords. In fact, after Benjamin Netanyahu was elected prime minister in 1998, the promised 10 percent Israeli withdrawal under the Oslo Accords dwindled to 2.5 percent.

Under pressure from his people, who blamed him for Israeli intransigence when it came to the settlements, Arafat gave his consent that Al-Fatah, under the auspices of the al-Aqsa Martyr's Brigade, would begin to commit terrorist attacks within the Occupied Territories. The beleaguered Palestinian leader had already realized that the new heroes of the Palestinian quest for independence were those men who died in suicide attacks under the banners of the Islamic Jihad and Hamas, a trend destructive to any hope of resuscitating the peace accord, but a fact that was diminishing his own popularity.

After the talks at Camp David in July 2000 between Arafat, Prime Minister Barak, and President Bill Clinton failed, Arafat declared that the Oslo Peace Process was dead. Despite the Israeli perception that Barak had offered Arafat "more than any other Israeli leader," the Palestinians balked that the 21 percent of the Occupied Territories offered was not a contiguous chunk of land but rather made up of small parcels, so that they would still have to pass through Israeli checkpoints to travel from Ramallah, for example, to get to Jericho or Bethlehem.

According to Mohammed Dahalan, the leader of Fatah in Gaza and at the time the chief of security for the Palestinian Authority, Barak believed that regardless of what the Israelis offered, it would be acceptable to the Palestinians. "Arafat asked me to meet with

Barak and explain how we cannot conclude the agreement the way it is," Dahalan explained. "I sat with him twice, each time for two hours, and tried to explain that he was wrong to assume that the Palestinians would accept his terms, and I am a peaceful man. The three main differences had to do with territorial guaranteed security, which included settlements, land and security, and Jerusalem; those were the three main issues. The Israelis offered 91 percent from the West Bank without the area of Jenin, Jerusalem, Latrun, and the Dead Sea area, which meant they were only offering us 85 percent. And if we had accepted, it would have been with eight conditions. Under the issue of security, there would have been five everlasting locations for Israeli troops forever in Palestinian territories, which meant that we had no real autonomy. There would be blocks of settlements that would have divided the West Bank into three parts from Jerusalem to Jericho; and Jerusalem would have been divided into three parts: the Old City, Haran, and the neighborhoods outside the wall; and there would have been early-warning stations that would be controlled and managed by the Israelis."

Dahalan claims that he reported his discussions with Barak to Arafat, who instructed him to make several counteroffers. "The criticism at the time and even now throughout the international community and especially in Israel and the United States was that Arafat never made any counteroffer. It was reported that he just refused everything Barak offered and walked away. That isn't true. I made counteroffers and in fact I even told Barak that the phrase from the beginning, about 'giving' us back our land, was incendiary. One of the concessions we made was to swap land, in other words to offer the Israelis the right to have settlements in

Jerusalem, in return for not dividing the city into three parts. Another big concession we made was to accept only 22 percent of Gaza and the West Bank. But then Barak came back with the counteroffer of controlling our 22 percent. The biggest problem was Barak's ego. He was a one-man show and he functioned on his own. He initiated Camp David and he wanted to be the one who decided how much to give. He was not a partner."

The general response throughout the Occupied Territories to the breakdown of the peace accord was to resume violent opposition to occupation. Under pressure from the United States to put an end to the violence, Arafat was forced to challenge his two strongest political opponents, Hamas and Islamic Jihad. Arafat's stature as "statesman," coupled with his desire not to alienate the European community, provided the incentive for him to adhere to the American demand. And, for a while, he actually succeeded in breaking the base of those two militant factions, which accounted for the gang fights between Islamic Jihad and Hamas militants and Arafat's Fatah members.

The result of this internecine conflict, however, was that Arafat suddenly found himself confronting two different enemies: Islamic Jihad and Hamas, who wanted to overthrow him as the leader of his people, and Israel, who wanted to undermine him in the eyes of his people. Not only were the lives of Fatah members threatened by both Israeli intelligence and the militant arm of the extremists, but the situation deteriorated to the point where Arafat's security forces were prevented by the militants from arresting members of the Izz al-Din al-Qassam Brigades, the military wing of Hamas, in turn causing further repercussions from the Israeli military.

★ ★ ★

Boaz Ganor claims that Arafat refrained from using his full ability to deal with Hamas and the Islamic Jihad. "He never started to fight them," Dr. Ganor says. "He never collected their illegal weapons. Arafat wanted to position himself as the underdog, as incapable of fighting Hamas." During that period of internal tension, when Arafat was unsuccessful in satisfying either Israeli demands or Palestinian expectations, his oft-repeated statement was, "I am making 100 percent effort to control the violence, but I can't guarantee 100 percent success."

Ironically, up to this point Arafat and his Fatah militias were still considered moderate by both Israelis and the Palestinians, and they ideologically supported his stated goal of establishing a Palestinian state next to Israel. Even the Tanzim, the armed wing of Fatah that had been set up in 1995 by the Palestinian Authority and the Fatah leadership as a quasi-military force to offset the growing power of the Palestinian Islamist groups, was not viewed as an extreme organization. Nor was the al-Aqsa Martyr's Brigade.

In the summer of 2000, though, realizing that his role as president of the Palestinian Authority was at risk, Arafat made a decision that would ultimately guarantee him a wider base of power to confront the opposition at home as well as in Israel. According to Mohammed Dahalan, who resigned as head of the Palestinian Authority security force because, in his words, "Arafat was unwilling to reorganize the force so it would be effective in dealing with the violent factions," Arafat found himself in a position where he was fighting for his life. "He refused to cut down on the number of security officers so that one person, me, could give orders," Dahalan said. "By allowing the security force to be too big so there were too many different directors, he diluted its power. But had he listened to me, he would have made even more enemies within the militant population."

As Dr. Ganor points out, "When the al-Aqsa Brigade saw that Hamas was taking a lead in the Intifada and threatening their status in the street by a spate of suicide bombings, they adopted the suicide strategy in an even more sensational way by utilizing the one weapon that the Islamists could not, according to the Koran, which was women and young girls."

When Arafat's al-Aqsa Martyr's Brigade claimed Wafa Idris as their own, the timing was perfect. Al-Aqsa did not want to be left out of the martyr race, again taking a back seat to Hamas and Islamic Jihad, which used religious fundamental edicts to train and implement young men as suicide bombers. The use of female bombers marked a tactical shift by those loyal to his faction to elevate their prestige and popularity on the street. During the first two years of this second Intifada, by unleashing this new army of women, Arafat's al-Aqsa Martyr's Brigade, for a while, achieved equal footing on the street with more radical religious elements that were moving toward deposing him as president of the Palestinian Authority. Finally, Arafat's Tanzim and the al-Aqsa Martyr's Brigade were able to steal the banner of martyrdom that was growing so popular throughout the West Bank and Gaza.

At the same time, Arafat still managed to say one thing in Arabic and another in English to satisfy both his position at home and his stature abroad. While the leadership of Hamas and Islamic Jihad never condemn suicide attacks, Arafat systematically does so in front of the international media. According to Dr. Iyad

Sarraj, the Palestinian psychiatrist, however, when Arafat does condemn them, everyone in the streets, including the leadership, understands the nuance of politics. "He is forced to pander to the United States president by condemning the attacks," Dr. Sarraj says. "Arafat has a serious problem. He told me, and you can quote this, that 'those people who commit these acts in Tel Aviv may be obstructing my road to Jerusalem, but they are guaranteeing my lease in Ramallah.'"

Not to be outdone by Arafat's "army of roses" that would "crush Israeli tanks," less than a month after Wafa Idris's death, the mufti of Saudi Arabia, Abd al-Aziz Bin Abdallah Aal al-Sheik, made the following statement, which influenced the course of thinking of other religious leaders: "I am not aware of anything in the religious law regarding killing oneself in the heart of the enemy's ranks, or what is called 'suicide' . . . although the Koran permits and even demands the killing of the enemy; this must be done in ways that do not contradict the Shari'a [Islamic religious law]. There is nothing that differentiates between men and women *shahides*."

On February 25, 2002, Dr. al-Rantisi stated in an article in the *Al-Ayat* newspaper, published in London and Beirut, "Suicide depends on volition. If the martyr, whether a man or a woman, intends to kill him or herself because he or she is tired of life, it is suicide. However, if he or she wants to sacrifice his or her soul in order to strike the enemy and to be rewarded by Allah, they are equally considered martyrs. We have no doubt that those carrying out these operations are martyrs."

Days later, in another interview, the mufti of Saudi Arabia stated in the *al-Hayat al-Jadida* newspaper, published by the

Palestinian Authority, "The great difference is between martyrdom, which is allowed and even desirable in Islam, and suicide, which leads to torments in Hell on Judgment Day. In the Koran, the Prophet Mohammed instructed both men and women to die for the sake of Jihad."

Finally, on February 26, 2002, the "Scholars of Al-Azhar" at the Al-Azhar Center for Islamic Research published their own religious ruling in support of suicide attacks. "When Muslims are attacked in their own homes and their land is robbed, the Jihad for Allah turns into an individual duty, for men and for women equally. In those cases, operations of martyrdom become a primary obligation and Islam's highest form of Jihad."

On February 27, 2002, Darine Abu Aisha, a brilliant student from Al-Najah University in Nablus, blew herself up at the Maccabim checkpoint near Jerusalem. Unlike Wafa Idris, Darine has the dubious distinction of being the first female suicide bomber to leave a videotape. She is also the first and only one so far to have killed herself under the auspices of Hamas.

CHAPTER SEVEN

BY WEST BANK STANDARDS, the Aisha family could be considered privileged. Beit Wazan, the area in Nablus where Darine Abu Aisha lived with her parents and eleven sisters and brothers, is a village on the outskirts of the bustling city, far from pollution and congestion and a world away from the grim warren of alleys and tightly packed dwellings that are synonymous with Palestinian refugee camps. The stone house in which Darine grew up is large and well furnished, with an attractive covered veranda that overlooks a lush expanse of olive groves and orchards of apples, pears, and plums. Inside, there are no signs of the typical wall decorations that honor the martyrs of this and the previous Intifada.

Mohammed, Darine's father, always earned a good living for his wife and children in construction and, when times were

98

quiet, by exporting his olives and fruit into Israel and across the Allenby Bridge into Jordan. He was one of the fortunate ones who never had to endure the indignation of crossing into Israel to work at the menial jobs available to most Palestinian men. Unlike the majority of Palestinian families who were displaced after 1948 and again in 1967, Mohammed and his wife, Nabila, both came from Nablus, as did their parents and grandparents. In fact they are first cousins and were married in 1968 in a concerted decision to keep the large land holdings of the two families united, given the changing political situation after the Six-Day War.

Nabila Aisha is an attractive woman of fifty-eight who wears a pristine white *hijab* (the scarf that covers her head, neck, and throat) and a long pale brown *jilbab*. Her hands are smooth, a sign that she has led a relatively comfortable life. Her fingers are adorned with gold rings, and gold bracelets cover both wrists. Mohammed, who is six years older than she, now suffers from an advanced case of diabetes and is nearly blind. The black glasses that cover his eyes and most of his face are designed to keep out the light. On the day of our interview he talked about the medicine for his condition that he was unable to get because of the curfew imposed on Nablus by the Israeli military. With seeming resignation, he indicated that he was hopeful that the Israelis would lift the curfew by the next day so that someone could go to the pharmacy and fill his prescription. It was always difficult to calculate, he explained, how many pills he would need, when the military government imprisoned people in their own homes without notice and kept them there without any inkling as to when they could resume normal life.

By the time that I was able to travel to Beit Wazan and visit the family, Darine had been dead for five months, having killed herself and injured several Israeli soldiers at the Maccabim checkpoint. Both her parents were resigned to the hopelessness of the situation. I had the impression that after the loss of their child there was nothing else that could happen that they would be unable to withstand, including the daily hardships of living under curfew.

There is a quiet dignity that prevails in the Aisha home, despite the palpable grief that is seen in the faces of Darine's siblings and parents. Curiously, Mohammed Aisha was mostly silent during the interview, sitting on the opposite end of the long sofa from his wife. He came to life only when she began to cry uncontrollably. Only then did he remove his dark glasses to wipe the tears from his own eyes. Shrugging helplessly, he gestured to his wife and asked rhetorically, "What can I do? She weeps all the time and there is nothing I can do to comfort her." He sighed. "This is our fate now, to mourn our child. My wife will never get better. This is it now. Our lives are filled only with the grief of having lost our daughter."

Darine Abu Aisha, Mohammed and Nabila's youngest daughter and seventh child, was twenty years old when she died. She was a brilliant student of English literature at Al-Najah University in Nablus. She had dark hair and eyes and a mischievous smile that her sisters describe as "captivating." Samira, a cousin who lives in the next house, which is also spacious and well appointed, claims that there were many suitors who came to ask for Darine's hand in marriage. "She refused them all," Samira explains. "She was only interested in studying." She pauses. "Sometimes people teased her and called her names because she refused to marry and have children. Her parents suffered because of this. Now they are better because they realize she had other, more important plans. She knew that her destiny was to become the bride of Allah in Paradise."

During the course of my conversation with Samira, her father, husband, and three little children joined her at Darine's house. It was then that she revealed that her own brother had died a martyr's death when he blew himself up in a spectacular terror attack at the central bus station in Netanya on March 4, 2001, killing three people and injuring sixty more. She reaches into her purse and pulls out a plastic key chain with the image of her martyred brother on one side and a picture of Darine on the other. "Another brother tried and failed to become a martyr," Samira says. "He is in an Israeli prison. It is difficult for us to visit him because of the constant closures."

According to Samira, Rashid, the brother who survived, also went to Al-Najah University and was close to Darine. "They were both very smart," she says, "and they both shared a deep belief in Allah." Samira's father and Darine's uncle, Atta, explains that before he was arrested, Rashid introduced Darine to several Hamas leaders at Al-Najah University. "When my oldest son became a martyr," he explains, "my second son only wanted to follow his example. While he waited for the right opportunity, he decided to help Darine reach martyrdom as well. He is very smart and studies the Koran day and night. He knew even before the others that Darine intended to become a martyr. It was because of him that she succeeded. Even if he failed in his own quest for martyrdom, he is respected because of the help he gave to Darine."

Before Samira and her family left to return to their own house, she encouraged her two sons, ages four and ten, to explain how they too hoped to become martyrs one day. The younger boy managed to articulate the words that his mother prodded him to say. "I want to be a martyr like my uncle." The older boy was reluctant, however, and instead stated that he wanted to go to university and become an "animal doctor." Samira apologized for him. "He is too young now. Later on he will understand that he should follow his uncle and his cousin, Darine. He doesn't understand. He thinks he knows what he wants." With tears in her eyes, Samira added, "It is the duty of every Palestinian mother to encourage her sons and daughters to become martyrs. I adore my children, but if I help them achieve martyrdom, it only means that Allah has chosen them because he loves them more than I do."

Darine's three sisters, while adamant that they would never commit an act of martyrdom, are fiercely proud of their sister. All three young women are dressed in identical white *hijab* and black *jilbab*. "Her [Darine's] action has made my parents sick," Muna, the older girl, says. "They are old now and we have to take care of them. If they had not been so sad, we would have done the same thing." And yet, there is no doubt in Muna's mind that Darine's decision to become a martyr was made not because she was influenced by her cousin Rashid, or by anyone else at Al-

102

Najah University, but rather because she "believed in her heart" the teachings of the Koran. "She knew she would go to Paradise and she understood that by becoming a *shahida*," Muna explains, "she would help liberate our land."

Darine's best friend, Nano Abdul, disagrees. According to her, Darine was brilliant, quick to grasp new mathematical equations, deeply interested in English literature, and prepared to debate the meaning of Chaucer or *Beowulf* as readily as she could discuss how anti-Semitism had influenced Jean-Paul Sartre's work. In fact, Darine had no doubt her major in English literature was not only something that inspired her but what she intended to teach on a university level after she graduated. "This has shocked me," Nano says. "And I am sure that everyone who knew Darine is shocked because this is not what she planned to do with her life. She was a leader and a feminist, someone who was not easily influenced by others and who stood up for what she believed in regardless of what her peers thought."

When asked what had been the motivating factor that pushed Darine over the edge of despair, Nano ponders the question for several moments before she begins talking again, this time barely above a whisper. "There was enormous pressure on her to marry," she begins. "Her family was pleased with her academic achievements but they still felt that she was at university only until she married and had children. They were very upset when she announced that she had no intention of ever marrying because she had no intention of becoming a slave."

One of the most interesting insights that Nano reveals is how Darine even managed to take a passage from Ernest Hemingway's *The Old Man and the Sea* and adapt it to her eventual decision to become a martyr. "She talked about the part in the book when the old fisherman who, upon reaching shore empty-handed and worn out after losing a struggle with a giant marlin, looks back at the sea and spits at it with scorn. Although he had not brought home his prize, he has struggled valiantly and was not defeated. For Darine, the struggle for Palestine, on a personal and national level, was the true meaning of her life."

According to Nano, Darine told her that there was no shame in losing the battle. The main thing was not to give up. "Within the limits of my ability," Darine told Nano, "and in the conditions in which I was raised, I will try to do everything possible to contribute to the liberation of Palestine, and in turn that will liberate me."

Nano claims that while Darine was brilliant, she was also frustrated because Al-Najah University couldn't offer her everything that she wanted to learn. "Theoretically, Darine was a bright, energetic young woman with everything to live for. Her family was comfortable financially, they were respected members of the community, and they were relatively untouched by the hardships of the occupation. But what I sensed in Darine was a frustration that went deeper than everyday inconveniences. And, as time went on, and she knew absolutely that regardless of her achievements at university, her fate as a Palestinian woman was sealed—an arranged marriage, six or seven children, a husband who probably wouldn't have the same hopes or curiosity about life as she did. Eventually she became nihilistic. Nothing mattered. Nothing excited her. Nothing pushed her to achieve more. She had gone as far as she could in this environment."

Curiously, it was only at the very end of her life that Darine actually discussed the struggles that she had waged personally as a daughter in a traditional Palestinian family and those she would encounter later on, as an adult woman seeking freedom in a society bound by numerous cultural restraints. "And yet," Nano says, "she never once considered abandoning religion because of the constraints it put on her. Instead, she was determined to do everything possible within the parameters of religion to make her mark and become independent and an exception to the rule."

Muna claims that not only was her sister brilliant, but she was "more interested in intellectual subjects than she was in politics. Darine considered herself a feminist in the global sense of the word," Muna explains. "She always said that in our society, human relationships were like a steel form into which we are poured by our family and which don't allow us to liberate ourselves from it and from the rules, dictated by tradition, which are so strict." According to Muna, Darine complained bitterly during those last months that her "life was meaningless and insignificant."

Often Darine would take long walks alone through the steep hills and deep valleys that are so typical of the topography around Nablus. She would wander even in those areas rife with danger from Israeli tanks or bullets that targeted randomly when a curfew was being enforced. Nano says that Darine would come to her house after those walks and talk about her anger and frustration. "Of course it was because of the occupation, but it was also because her parents were putting a lot of pressure on her to be an obedient, full-time childbearing and child-rearing spouse in a family where the husband was all-powerful and had absolute authority. Darine resisted that. She told me she would rather die."

And yet during my long conversations with Darine's mother and sisters, they acknowledged that she reacted extremely emotionally—more than any other family member—to an Israeli incursion into their village. "Once she fainted," her mother said, "and other times, she would scream and cry. It was difficult to calm her."

There were two defining incidents in Darine's brief life that sealed her fate. One of them happened only two months before she died. In December 2001, she had entered a literary competition with other women students majoring in English literature from all over the Arab world: Jordan, Egypt, Algeria, Morocco, Syria. Each student—and there were more than two thousand who participated—was required to write an essay on the subject of what being a woman in a Muslim society meant to them. Darine was aware that not all the women who entered the contest were observant Muslims, and yet she felt, according to Nano, that her concept of feminism was more "pure and true" than anyone could imagine, especially "for a woman who covered her head and body." Quoting from the Koran, Darine wrote that the holy book teaches that "all men and women are equal, that individuals should not be judged according to gender, beauty, wealth or privilege."

"The only thing that makes one person better than another is his or her character," she wrote. "I am a Muslim woman who believes her body belongs to her alone, which means that how I look should not play a role in who I am or what response I evoke from people who meet me. Wearing the hijab gives me freedom, because my physical appearance is not an issue. True equality means women don't have to display themselves to get attention."

While Darine did not win the contest, her paper was reprinted in a leaflet that was passed out in schools and universities throughout the West Bank and Gaza. A week later, after she had appeared on television and had become something of a celebrity as an example of a "liberated Muslim woman," the second and final incident occurred at an Israeli checkpoint near Nablus that sealed her destiny.

Darine's mother recounts the circumstances calmly, although through her tears she declares her belief that it was the culminating event that drove her daughter to die.

At the checkpoint near Nablus, there was the usual line of Palestinians waiting to pass, and Darine was near the front of the line, standing next to her good friend and cousin Rashid. Next to them was a woman who held an infant who was burning up with fever. The soldiers were refusing to allow the woman to pass through so she could walk ten meters to a waiting ambulance that would take her and her baby to the closest hospital. "Darine told me that the child was turning blue from lack of air. The baby was near death," Nabila says. Despite the pleas of the others who were witness to this tragedy in the making, the soldiers adamantly refused to make any exceptions until all the necessary papers were checked. "They refused to let the woman go in front of Darine and her cousin, even though they begged the soldiers."

At some point, after Darine made it clear that she spoke and understood English, she became the self-appointed spokesperson for the desperate woman. She pleaded her case. In response, several of the soldiers started whispering and laughing among themselves. Finally, one of them approached Darine and announced that they would let the woman through so she could put her dying baby in the ambulance if Darine's companion, Rashid, kissed her on the mouth. "My daughter was horrified," Nabila explains. "You understand, that is impossible in our religion, and yet my daughter understood that the life of this child was in her hands."

Darine tried to reason with the soldiers, explaining that she was a Muslim woman whose head was covered and in her modest attire and deep faith it was a sin to allow a man to kiss her unless he was her husband, and even then never in public. Without warning, one of the soldiers ripped the *hijab* off Darine's head. "She was humiliated," Nabila continues, "but by then the baby had stopped breathing and the mother was screaming." She covers her face with her hands and takes a deep breath. "What could my daughter do?"

What Darine did was quickly tell her cousin to kiss her, on the lips, so the baby could be saved. The young man complied, to the horror of the others who were witnessing the scene. As promised, the soldiers ushered the woman and her infant into the waiting ambulance. "The next day," Nabila says, "Darine gathered us together and told us what had happened. That evening Rashid came to our house and asked for Darine's hand in marriage."

It was a noble and sincere gesture, since the two families, after hearing the story, considered the incident to be serious enough to jeopardize Darine's chances of ever finding a decent man willing to marry her. But the trauma she had suffered and the humiliation at the hands of the soldiers was only intensified when she learned that her parents were insisting that she and Rashid marry. Darine refused. Not only was she outraged at the idea that she would be forced to stop her studies and marry a man who, even if he was her close friend, had no part in her plans for the future, but she was unwilling to change the course of her life on account of the immoral actions of a group of Israeli soldiers. According to Nano, Darine was completely honest with Rashid, which was when he promised to help her find another solution to the probklem so that her family would not be disgraced.

Deeply religious and intellectually curious, Darine was aware of the debate that raged throughout the West Bank concerning the *fatwa* by religious leaders that allowed women to participate in suicide bombings. "She was a feminist in the true sense of the word, she always explained to us," Nano says, "and she took the Koran very literally. The debate about the *fatwa* was a sign to her that she would make the right decision."

For the close circle of young women who took classes with Darine at Al-Najah University, the decision to become a *shahida* came, naturally, "from Allah." Nayfeh, another friend of Darine's and a student at Al-Najah, explained that "because she [Darine] took the Koran very literally, she accepted the new ruling for women . . . She claimed that it was too easy to change the rules for reasons that went beyond religion," Nayfeh said. "And she trusted the religious leaders to interpret the Koran correctly."

With this kind of thinking, Darine became Hamas's perfect new weapon.

Singled out because of her unwavering faith; sought after because she was intelligent enough to understand the political implications of a religious edict that summarily changed the rules; depressed and desperate because she was being forced into a marriage; aware that her refusal would bring disgrace to her family, since dozens of other Palestinians from Nablus and the surrounding villages had witnessed the traumatic scene orchestrated by the Israeli soldiers—for these reasons, Darine Abu Aisha, with the help of her cousin Rashid, decided to become the second female suicide bomber in the history of the Palestinian struggle.

Back in the Aisha living room, Darine's mother weeps inconsolably as she describes how she learned of her daughter's intentions. Minutes before she detonated her explosive belt at the Maccabim checkpoint near Jerusalem, Darine had called her mother to apologize for sneaking out of the house without permission, and to say her good-byes. When asked if she said anything to try and stop her, Nabila nodded through her tears. "I tried everything," she wept. "I told her I loved her, that she was killing me, that she was the daughter of my heart, my best child." She stops to catch her breath. "But it was too late."

That simple gesture—calling to apologize for sneaking out of the house without permission—is a telling one. Dr. Iyad Sarraj is visibly moved when he says, "For her, it was worse that she had left the house without permission than it was to announce to her mother that she was about to embark on a journey to Paradise. But in order to understand this, one has to accept the notion that in our religion and in this society, dying as a martyr is the highest honor anyone can achieve."

Several months after her death, Darine's distraught mother traveled to Al-Najah University to collect all her daughter's diplomas. They are displayed prominently on the walls of the family home.

CHAPTER EIGHT

ON THE SAME DAY that Darine Abu Aisha died, and only one month after Wafa Idris became a heroine throughout the West Bank and Gaza, Sheik Yassin, the spiritual guide of Hamas, suddenly announced that there was nothing in the Koran or any Muslim tradition that says women cannot fight equally to men. In fact, when Sheik Yassin realized that the al-Aqsa Martyr's Brigade, after claiming Wafa Idris as its own, was gaining popularity throughout the Occupied Territories, he issued a *fatwa* that not only gave permission to women to participate in suicide attacks but enumerated the rewards in Paradise that these female martyrs would receive.

Sheik Ahmad Yassin is barely sixty years old and is paralyzed from the neck down after suffering a spinal injury in a soccer accident when he was a teenager. After spending ten years in an Israeli prison during the period when hundreds of Hamas militants were deported to Marj al-Zahour, the sheik has been in increasingly fragile health. After I was given a *jilbab* and *hijab* to wear in his presence, Sheik Yassin received me in a large, brightly lit room with a beige linoleum floor containing a hospital bed and several chairs and tables at one end; the other end of the room was set up as an office. On one wall were books and numerous pictures of martyrs who had given their lives in the course of suicide attacks.

Wrapped in a pink gown and head-covering and with a pink Pashmina shawl draped over his lap, the sheik was attended to by a coterie of young Palestinian men who were there night and day to lift him from his wheelchair to his bed and to perform other nursing duties. His kind expression and gentle smile contradicted his words, translated from the Arabic by a Palestinian journalist, Reham Abdul Karim, who lives in Gaza. One of the first questions I asked him was, "How do you feel, Sheik Yassin, a man of God, when you hear that a young woman has strapped on an explosive belt and blown herself up in a market, killing dozens of Israeli men, women, and children?" His answer: "It is a good sign. Once women were squeamish about seeing blood or committing acts of martyrdom. Now they are willing to die for the sake of our cause. For me, it is a good sign that women are beginning to take up the fight alongside our men."

During an interview with me in January 2003, Sheik 'Abd-Salam Abu Shukheudem, the chief mufti of the Palestinian Authority Police Force—equivalent to the chaplain of an American police force—explained the seven rewards that male martyrs earn, according to Islamic tradition. "From the moment the first drop of blood is spilled, the martyr does not feel the pains of his injury, and is absolved of all his bad deeds; he sees his seat in

Paradise; he is saved from the torture of the grave; he is saved from the fear of the Day of Judgment; he marries seventy-two beautiful black-eyed women; he is an advocate for seventy of his relatives to reach Paradise; he earns the Crown of Glory, whose precious stone is better than all this world and everything in it."

When I ask Sheik Yassin what women martyrs receive in Paradise, he replies that they become "even more beautiful than the seventy-two virgins . . . If they are not married," he continues, "they are guaranteed a pure husband in Paradise, and of course they are entitled to bring seventy of their relatives to join them there without suffering the anguish of the grave." But when I ask him to show me where in the Koran these rewards for women are written, he smiles slightly and speaks in Arabic to the man seated next to him, who is taking copious notes. "It is my job and the job of other sheiks and Imams to interpret the Koran," he finally says. "The people have our trust. Women along with all Muslims have the right and the duty to participate in suicide bombings to destroy the enemy and bring an Islamic state to all of Palestine."

At the end of my interview with the sheik, I ask him and the man seated next to him if either of them have children, and, if so, have any of them died in an act of martyrdom. Sheik Yassin smiles and shakes his head as if my question were a sign of my complete misunderstanding of the Koran. "We do not choose martyrs to die," he says quietly. "Allah chooses them. So far, he has not seen fit to choose any of my children." The man seated next to him also smiles and says something in Arabic to the sheik before he answers my question. "Yes, I have children," he says. "But every Palestinian man or woman who becomes a martyr is a child of all the people. We do not differentiate."

113

The late Ismail Abu Shanab, who had been number three in the hierarchy of Hamas and the director of Sheik Yassin's office in Gaza, also explained during one interview how children are chosen as martyrs. "I have thirteen children," Abu Shanab begins, "eight boys and five girls. The Jihad spirit is knocking on all our doors, but if one of my children intends to do that he wouldn't talk about it with his father or mother. Allah chooses him. God knows that many want to become martyrs but of course not all succeed." But when I asked him how he would feel if one of his children became a *shahide* or a *shahida*, he avoided a direct reply and instead said, "The Israelis are responsible for all our suffering and loss. It is normal during occupation to think of becoming a *shahide*."

Before I leave Sheik Yassin's house that day, I ask if my cameraman can take a still photograph of me and the sheik together. There is more banter in Arabic before my translator tells me in English, "He agrees, but only if you promise not to tell his wife, since it is against Islamic law." Sheik Yassin and the other men laugh some more at what is obviously a private joke.

After the special *fatwa* was issued by Muslim leaders, Hamas spokesman Abdul Aziz al-Rantisi also agreed to address the Palestinian woman's place in the struggle as well as the rewards that she would receive in Paradise.

Dr. al-Rantisi was educated in Jordan and trained as a pediatrician in England. Although his activities with Hamas keep him busy, he still lectures in pediatric medicine at the local university in Gaza. On one of the occasions when I visited him at his home in Gaza, two of his sons were in the room, along with a bodyguard. In the middle of the interview, his oldest and favorite granddaughter, Amal, skipped into the room and crawled on his lap. Dr. al-Rantisi explained that Amal had recently had eye surgery to correct what he called a "lazy" right eye, which accounted for the patch she wore. As we spoke, he cuddled and kissed her and explained that she was the child of one of his three daughters. When the subject finally turned to women suicide bombers, Dr. al-Rantisi made it very clear that in the Koran, women are not only expected to share in the struggle but are even allowed to do so without the "permission" of their "male relatives." As for the rewards, he was very precise. "Satisfaction," he said. "In Paradise, women are satisfied, which is the most important thing, because there is no competition between men and women. Everyone gets what they want and are their own master. They achieve total satisfaction after death."

When I ask Dr. al-Rantisi the same question I had asked Sheik Yassin—if he were willing to sacrifice his beloved little grand-daughter—he does not hesitate to reply. "It is destiny. If Allah chooses her, she will go. It is not up to me." Al-Rantisi's ready response notwithstanding, his three daughters and their children all live comfortably far from the Mecca of the revolution. In August 2002, a tape recording was unearthed in Jenin of a conversation between Dr. al-Rantisi and his wife. On the tape, he suggests that he is now willing to sacrifice one of his own sons as a *shahide*. His wife, however, reacts violently and tells him that "over my dead body" will she ever "let one of her sons blow himself up."

Her reaction is not unusual. Indeed, up till now the children of leaders have not been involved in suicide missions but are usually sent off to Amman, Europe, or the United States to study, far from the trauma and danger of the Intifada.

Sheik Yassin and Dr. al-Rantisi are not the only visible leaders who protect their own children. Suha, Yasser Arafat's wife, and his daughter live in Paris, while Hanan Ashrawi's two daughters were schooled in a prestigious all-girls private Quaker school in Ramallah before they went off to study abroad. And, according to witnesses in jail, the first words that Marwan Barghouti, the military leader of the Tanzim, the fighting arm of Arafat's Fatah movement, uttered to his lawyer when arrested by Israeli authorities in March 2002 were, "Tell my wife to watch our sons and daughters so they don't go on a suicide operation."

Saeb Erakat, Arafat's chief negotiator and perhaps the most visible of all the leaders of the Palestinian Authority, has twenty-year-old twin daughters who are both studying in Amman, one in her third year of law school and the other in her third year of medical school. Erakat's eleven-year-old son is not yet affected by the cult of death that has permeated Palestinian society, although his fifteen-year-old son, according to what Erakat told me during an interview in his office in Jericho, is "suffocating under occupation . . . I'm very worried about him because he doesn't understand why he can't travel from Jericho to Ramallah to play soccer or ride horses."

The nonparticipation of the children of the leadership in suicide bombings is telling when it comes to identifying the conditions that characterize most people who are willing to blow themselves up. What I call the fatal cocktail is comprised of religious doctrine that promises the suicide bomber eternal life, economic and social deprivation that offer people no hope, nationalistic fervor that runs throughout society, and the hardships of living under an occupying force. In theory, all Palestinians live in the same environment, and the children of those men and women who are visible and vocal as the voices calling for the end of occupation and the establishment of an autonomous Palestinian state should be even more aware of the plight of their people. In theory, perhaps—but in reality this is clearly not true. As Nomi Chazan, member of the Knesset from the left-wing Meretz Party, says, "I have trouble with people who send other people to commit acts of martyrdom. If they believe in that practice so deeply, they should go themselves."

Concerning Yasser Arafat's condemnation of suicide attacks for the Western media, Dr. al-Rantisi is clear about his distaste for the chairman's tactics. "I would never put myself in Arafat's position," Dr. al-Rantisi says. "Arafat lost a lot of support in Gaza." He shrugs. "But the Palestinian Authority never had any sovereignty here in the Gaza Strip. Mr. Arafat doesn't have power here and he is losing his power in the West Bank when he condemns martyr attacks for the benefit of the American president or the United Nations or the European community."

As for the participation of women and the recent justification that religious leaders have found in the Koran that encourages them to fight and die alongside the men, Dr. al-Rantisi went a step further in his justification. "We are not only talking about equality when it comes to men and women," he explains. "We are also talking about the goal of turning Palestine into an Islamic state, which is not something to be feared or reviled by the Western world. First of all, is it [the creation of an Islamic Palestinian state] something so bad? The Israelis believe that a Jewish state is good, so why not a state only

117

for Muslims? If Jews should have a state, why not the same for us?

"And by the way, when we succeed," Dr. al-Rantisi continues, "which I am convinced we will, the creation of such a place would be for the sake of the United States as well, because an Islamic regime is much better than a democratic regime. For example, if you read a translated version of the Koran, you will see that we have to be just with our enemies, that we must not deprive them of their dignity. We have ethics that guide us in the treatment of our enemies, as we consider them as human beings. Given our ethics and values, Islam is a benefit to the whole world and especially for women, who are protected, sheltered, and revered by all society."

Ismail Abu Shanab not only agreed but offered several historical examples to prove Dr. al-Rantisi's point. "The Jews lived best under Islamic regimes in Europe," Abu Shanab said. "Remember that in Spain when the Muslims left, the Jews left with them. That's why we are not fighting Jews because they are Jewish but because they occupied our land. If they leave, everyone would be quiet. The Jews could live well under an Islamic regime here in Palestine."

When I ask Dr. al-Rantisi about the theory that there are two Islams, one that teaches the basic moral standards of humanity and another that adheres to violence in the name of Allah, Dr. al-Rantisi disagrees. "The West says there are two different Islams," he says. "One that is good and the other that sends bombers into the World Trade Center. The truth is there is just one Islam, and Hamas, for example, fights our occupiers but never kills any Jews outside of our occupied lands. We will not fight outside Palestine and we will not target Americans or anyone else throughout the world."

At the same time, Iyad Sarraj believes it is crucial to have a re-definition of Islam that will give all Palestinians living under Israeli occupation hope for the future. "We are not against Islam, but we want a redefinition of Islam that will give our people a dose of hope instead of despair for the future. We want Islam redefined in the context of humanity. One of the signs of failure in this part of the world, for Muslims and Jews, is that they are both victims of their extremist leaders. But it is far more tragic for us because our children are being taught in the mosques, on television, and in schools to die. I was brought up here in Gaza and went to all the schools and was never taught to hate. But if you are a little Palestinian child growing up next door to a settlement and you see Israeli children enjoying swimming pools when you have no drinking water, you don't learn how to love Jews. You learn how to be envious of them. When you have bombs falling on your house, you learn how to hate and not make peace. You don't need a teacher to teach you how to hate because the best teacher is Ariel Sharon. Fear and paranoia are intertwined, and the Zionist project has failed. It was supposed to give Jews a safe haven and instead it has given them constant bloodshed."

Manar television is Hizbollah's privately owned satellite station that broadcasts directly to Palestinians throughout the Occupied Territories and Gaza. Manar, which means "lighthouse" in Arabic, specializes in five-second spots that show Palestinian children confronting Israeli soldiers. The voice-over is in Arabic, and the Hebrew subtitles say, "One rock hurled by a child is stronger than the most sophisticated weapons."

After each suicide bombing in Israel, Manar broadcasts the

images as well as describes the details of the suicide bomber's life; it also airs images taken from Israeli television of the agony of the victims and their families. In all of Manar's broadcasts, the word "Israel" is never mentioned; instead it is referred to as "the Zionist entity." (When I was in Tripoli in 1986 after the American raid there to interview Moammar Ghadaffi for *U.S. News and World Report*, it was not only against the law to refer to Israel as anything except the "Zionist entity," but the Libyans prominently displayed a map of the Middle East in Green Square in which Israel was simply blacked out.)

Hassan Fadlallah, the news director of Manar television, is clean-shaven and relatively young to hold such a responsible position. His youthful appearance, though, belies his zealous militant beliefs. He explains that all Arab countries view Israel as an enemy. "We are only giving the region the television programming that they want," he explains. "Our ratings are very good, and people call us and write to us praising our efforts."

During Ramadan 2002, Manar broadcast a series titled *Knight Without a Horse* that was based on the late-nineteenth-century czarist book *The Protocols of the Elders of Zion*, which detailed a plan by the Jews to control the world. Although the book is banned worldwide, it still enjoys consistent sales and is used by Holocaust revisionists, Islamic extremists, and other groups that embrace anti-Semitism as proof of Israel's evil intentions and as justification of any military action taken by Arab nations. According to Mr. Fadlallah, not only Muslims but all people are beginning to see the threat that Israel poses to world peace. "When our martyrs choose to die in order to liberate Islamic land," he says, "that is proof of how desperate they are in the face of Israeli injustice."

* ★ ★

In 1985, Hizbollah published a manifesto stating that all Western influence, particularly from Israel and the United States, is detrimental to following the true path of Islam. Since then, nothing in their political or spiritual policy has changed. In fact, if anything it has become more extreme.

On the occasion of Jerusalem Day 2003, an annual military spectacle with a blatant "I Hate Israel" theme, members of Hizbollah dressed in black fatigues and green-and-purple berets and marched through the streets of Nabatiye in Lebanon, just across the border of northern Israel. Sheik Hassan Nasrallah, the party's secretary-general, urged followers to combat "the plan by the United States and the Zionists to control" that region of the world.

Sheik Nasrallah's headquarters is in a bland apartment building in a suburb of Beirut. Driving out of Beirut through towns and villages on the way to his office, one notes that the surroundings are almost identical to those in the West Bank and Gaza: lampposts and buildings are covered with photographs of revered *shahides*. The border between southern Lebanon and northern Israel is heavily guarded with land mines and an electrified barbed-wire fence, but the ideology of the fundamental Islamic groups on both sides of the frontier are the same, despite those man-built separations, when it comes to recruiting and training children and young adults for suicide attacks.

Inside Sheik Nasrallah's office, there are more photographs of martyrs and some of the most influential leaders of the Iranian revolution. Most prominently displayed is a large picture of the Ayatollah Khomeini.

121

The interview is brief. The sheik agrees to answer only two questions before I will be taken back to my hotel in Beirut.

"Is Yasser Arafat in control and able to effectuate a lasting peace accord with Israel?"

The sheik's response is clear and concise. "Even if Arafat wanted to enter into a peace accord, as he did at the time of Oslo, he is unable to do anything. He has little or no support or power among the Palestinians. I respect Abu Ammar, but he is nothing more than a memory, a symbol of a revolution that he led when he was relevant."

"With the collapse of the Soviet Union, who are the main sponsors of Hizbollah today?"

This time Sheik Nasrallah is not so direct. He prefers to discuss Hizbollah's role in arming Palestinian militants throughout the Occupied Territories. "We consider the Israeli–Palestinian conflict as our first priority," he says.

(According to Ariel Merari, the Israeli professor and terrorism expert, Hizbollah's two main sponsors are Iran and Syria. "We know that there is always the risk," Dr. Merari says, "that Syria and Iran will arm Hizbollah with missiles and other weapons to attack Israel across our border with Lebanon.")

The sheik continues. "When we send Katyusha rockets across the border into Israel"—primarily to the Shabaa Farms area, which is, according to Hizbollah, disputed territory—"we maintain our claim on the land. And, of course, we give our Palestinian brothers arms and suicide training so they can liberate Palestine from Israeli occupation. This is our strongest weapon and the only path to protect Palestinians and to regain Jerusalem and its holy sites. This is the only military strategy that the most powerful forces [Israel and the United States] have failed to prevent."

And with that, the interview was over.

CHAPTER NINE

THE FIRST TIME I MET Arnold and Fremet Roth was a month after their daughter had been killed in a suicide bombing attack in Jerusalem. Fremet is originally from New York, the daughter of religious parents who brought her up with a profound feeling for Zionism and a deep belief in Judaism. Her father was a rabbi who dedicated his life to teaching young children; Fremet, from the time she was a child, always knew that one day she would live in Israel.

Arnold Roth is Australian, an intelligent and articulate man who explains that until he met his wife when they were both law students in New York, he was not a religious Jew. They fell in love, and when he returned to Australia they corresponded for a year. "In fact," Arnold says, "I proposed to my wife in a letter." Fremet accepted Arnold's proposal, on the condition that they would eventually live in Israel and raise a family.

The arrangement was that they would marry in the United States and return to Australia for a year before Arnold settled his affairs, and then they would move permanently to Jerusalem. "One year became ten years," Arnold says, "and four of our seven children were born in Australia."

Arnold and Fremet Roth no longer have seven children. They now have six. Malki, fifteen years old, was their middle child and oldest daughter. Of the four girls, Malki resembled her mother the most. Tall and slim and a gifted musician who played classical flute and who had taught herself piano and guitar, Malki learned to handle most of her school and personal problems on her own. In a tribute that Fremet wrote after her daughter's death, she admitted that the opportunities to help Malki were usually limited. Caring for her youngest child, who was born profoundly retarded, blind, and physically handicapped, did not leave her a great deal of time for her other children. According to Fremet, not only did Malki shop for her own clothes and run her active social life at the Horev Girls School in Jerusalem, but she also helped her mother care for her youngest sister. Malki spent hours at little Haya's side, relieving her mother so that she could tend to other chores. And, when Haya was hospitalized, it was always Malki who spent the night in her room.

Despite the challenges and responsibilities that faced Malki, she was a well-balanced, wholesome teenager who loved her family and friends and derived enormous pleasure and satisfaction from her music. Often she would drag her guitar with her and strike up sing-alongs at every opportunity, even on the school bus. According to one friend, they were always "songs of the soul."

Nearly a year before she was killed, Malki and her friends wrote personal letters to God, in which they expressed their prayers and

125

requests for the upcoming Jewish New Year. Her youth leader agreed that all the letters would be opened and read aloud the following year. During the period of mourning, the youth leader brought Malki's sealed letter to her family. When they opened it, they read that Malki had prayed for success in school and in her youth movement, and she added the hope that the family would remain close and supportive of one another. Her request for her little sister Haya touched her parents the most. Rather than asking for a miracle or a cure or even an improvement, she simply requested that Haya learn to somehow convey to the rest of the family her displeasure or pleasure that their words and actions brought her. And, at the very bottom of the last page, Malki had written, ". . . and that I'll be alive and that the Messiah should come."

The person closest to Malki was not one of her six siblings or even her parents but rather a girl her own age named Michal Raziel. When the Roth family arrived in Israel in 1988 from Australia, they met the Raziel family, who were just about to leave Israel for a year abroad in England. In a series of happy coincidences, not only did the Roth family sublet the Raziel's flat in Ramot, a neighborhood in the north of Jerusalem, but they eventually became the best of friends.

When Malki was two years old, the Raziels returned from overseas. Within days, the Roths bought an apartment in the same complex, only two buildings away. From then on, the two little girls were constantly together. As they grew up, they remained the closest of friends. Aviva Raziel, Michal's mother, describes her family's relationship with the Roths. "We were the same kind of people, outgoing and always ready to help others."

Two weeks before Malki's death, for the first time in many years the whole family was together. Her oldest brother, twenty-three years old at the time, had just moved back home after finishing his time in the army; her middle brother, twenty years old, was preparing to leave for the army, while the youngest boy, seventeen, had just finished high school and was still at home before leaving on vacation after graduation. Along with Haya, Malki's two younger sisters—Rifka, eleven at the time, and Pesi, who was eight—were still living with the family. Arnold Roth remembers that there was a sense of gratitude that they were all together, healthy and alive. It was an especially exciting moment for Malki since she, along with Michal, were planning to leave on a two-week working vacation together in the Galilee, where they would be counselors at a summer camp. During those two weeks before she left, Malki kept up with her activities, spent time with Haya, visited friends, and made plans for the upcoming school year. Most of the time she played the flute and guitar, practicing so she would be proficient enough to join other musicians in the evenings around the campfire.

On August 9, Malki, along with Michal, left her parents' apartment in Jerusalem and headed to the home of another friend, who was due back from vacation the following day. As a surprise, the two best friends decided to decorate the girl's room as a welcome-home gesture. Afterward, they were planning to attend a meeting of the other counselors who would be together at the summer camp in the Galilee.

Given the spate of suicide bombings that occurred with regular frequency around Israel, Malki always informed her mother by cell phone of her exact plans. But on that day the decision to stop for a pizza at Sbarro's, a popular meeting place for teenagers in the center of Jerusalem, was made on the spur of the moment. Malki didn't call.

* * *

Zina (a pseudonym, used at the request of her family) is an attractive young woman, gregarious, intelligent, and, as friends describe her, "someone with an independent character." One of twelve children from a middle-class family who left Palestine for Jordan shortly after the 1967 war, Zina has a history of problems both at home and at school. In any other time and place, her life might have turned out differently. But even living in Amman, a city that is certainly more sophisticated and international than any number of towns or villages in the West Bank or Gaza, a young girl from a good Muslim home was expected to follow the rules set down by her father and her religion.

Beginning when she was an adolescent, Zina rebelled. She refused to wear the *jilbab* and the *hijab*, and as she grew up she told her friends and family that she intended to become an international journalist and live far from home. When she arrived at the university in Amman, she studied English until she became proficient, and eventually she got a summer job at an American television network, where she trained as an intern.

During an interview with Zina at the women's prison in Ramla, in Israel, where she will remain for at least twenty-five years, she claims that the relationship with her father became irreparable when she refused to marry a man her parents had chosen for her. "It wasn't that I had something against the boy," she explains. "It was the idea of an arranged marriage." She pauses. "Anyway, I was in love with someone else, a boy I met at university who came from Egypt. We had a secret relationship for several months, until one of my brothers followed me after classes and caught me with him in a café."

128

A family discussion followed, during which it was decided that Zina could no longer be trusted to go anywhere on her own. Her father refused to allow her to continue her studies and instructed his wife to keep their daughter locked in her room until he consulted with the Imam about her future. Within a month, Zina realized that she was pregnant. Terrified that her father and brothers would kill her if they found out, she decided to keep her condition a secret for as long as possible before she planned her escape to Egypt with the father of her baby. "I managed to get word to my boyfriend," Zina continues, "through a girlfriend of mine who had classes with him at the university." She begins to cry. "But when he found out, he was scared that my family would come after him. He left Amman suddenly. No one knew where he went, although I imagine he returned to Cairo."

Zina managed to keep her secret for another five months before her mother and sisters noticed that she had missed several periods and was putting on weight. They confronted her, and after several harrowing days of screaming scenes and beatings at the hands of her oldest brother, Zina finally admitted she was pregnant. It took several more days before she was beaten into revealing who the father was. According to Zina, the decision was made immediately. "I would have the baby," she relates, "and remain with the child in my father's house. My father told me I was lucky that the punishment was so light. Other girls in my condition would have been killed, since there was no possible way to find my boyfriend or his family and make him marry me." She shrugs. "My life was over."

Four months later, at the end of April 2001, Zina gave birth to a boy in her father's house. Despite the shame associated with the birth, her sisters and mother showered the infant with affection and eventually gave him to the oldest son to be cared for by his wife. "There was nothing left for me," Zina says. "I wasn't even allowed to keep my baby with me. He was to be raised as my brother's son."

The al-Masri family has its roots in Nablus and is considered one of the leading Palestinian families in the West Bank. Not only are they successful merchants, importing produce from Amman, but the most illustrious member of the family, Zafri al-Masri, was the mayor of Nablus during the early 1980s. In February 1986, before the Intifada erupted, Zafri al-Masri was murdered by Palestinian militants while walking to his office in the main square of Nablus. Because of his cordial relationship with the Israeli administration and his philosophy of cohabitation with the Israelis—which, he believed, would result in a better economic life for Palestinians— al-Masri was accused of "collaborating with the enemy."

Coincidentally, at the time of al-Masri's murder I was at the Noga Hilton Hotel in Geneva, Switzerland, with then defense minister Yitzak Rabin and his close adviser Eitan Haber, working on an interview for the French newspaper *Le Journal de Dimanche*, which would also include my interview with Abu Iyad. It was a Saturday evening when Haber rushed to my room on the sixth floor of the hotel to inform me that he and Minister Rabin were being called urgently back to Israel. Minutes before he left for Bern by helicopter to catch a flight, Haber explained that Zafir al-Masri had been assassinated and they feared more violence would ensue throughout the Occupied Territories. Until they were safely back in Israel, they asked me to remain at the hotel and not reveal what I knew. Obviously, they didn't want the news leaked before Minister Rabin could meet with his advisers and prepare for any violent clashes.

The murder was a shock to the Israeli civil administration, since al-Masri was one of several West Bank mayors who were potential partners for conciliation. But that fact alone, as well as the hatred he evoked from the militant factions within Palestinian society, caused the family to lose a great deal of respect and prestige throughout the community, which they never really regained until Malki Roth's death at Sbarro's in Jerusalem.

Shuhail Masri, a cousin of the slain mayor, remembers that time with sadness and regret. "He was a good man. . . . Zafri was not someone who would compromise his people. He wanted them to have a better life, and it was only when the militant forces in the area decided that he was in some way cooperating with the Israeli authorities that his death warrant was signed."

Shuhail goes on to explain that the family had never been religious and in fact had been considered one of the more Westernized among the Palestinian population. "When the Islamic influence became visible throughout the area, naturally it was just one more reason for Zafir to be targeted." He pauses. "I think it was more a question of his having a successful business, enjoying popularity among the people, and resisting any change that would cause our society to go backwards. All he wanted was that all the people in Nablus should live well and earn a living. He understood that if there were no problems, the Israelis would continue to allow the exports to go in and out between the West Bank and Jordan and would continue to let the Palestinian people cross into Israel to work."

In 1979, Shuhail Masri's youngest son, Izzedine, was born. A frail child with no particular interest in school, he was only eight years old when the first Intifada broke out in the West Bank. According to several of Izzedine's brothers, that was the moment when he changed and suddenly seemed to find a purpose to life. Shuhail Masri has a different opinion. "Izzedine didn't understand the meaning of the uprising because his life hadn't been touched by the occupation the way other boys' had been. For my son, going out into the street and throwing stones and taunting the soldiers was a game that he played with the other boys. It was a dangerous game, but something that was exciting and fun at the same time."

When Izzedine turned seventeen, he decided that he wanted to become a "real Muslim," as one of his friends explains. "He grew a beard and began praying regularly at home and at the mosque. He began talking more and more about driving the Israelis off our land."

In an effort to change his son's ideas and extricate him from an environment that he felt was detrimental to his future, Shuhail sent Izzedine to Detroit, Michigan, for the summer to study English, a city that has the largest Arab population in the United States.

In Detroit, Izzedine met a Palestinian student with whom he became close friends. Before long, the two young men were attending meetings at the Islamic Association for Palestine, which has close ties to Hamas. According to other friends, during that period in America Izzedine watched Hamas recruitment videos and read only pro-Hamas newspapers. By the time he returned to Nablus, instead of having become more Westernized and modern, he had become even more militant and religious. He began speaking about Jihad and the desperation of the Palestinian people. He began talking about dying a martyr's death.

CHAPTER TEN

THE SITUATION WAS UNBEARABLE for Zina after her parents took her baby away from her. She refused to eat. She refused to pray with the other women in her family. She refused to speak. She refused to help her mother and sisters. There were constant arguments in the house until finally, after her father suffered a massive stroke, it was decided to offer her an alternative to her confinement in her father's house. According to one of her sisters, it was "more because no one could stand the problems . . . We understood that she would never change, and my father was ill and my mother was getting old and just couldn't handle things."

One of Zina's brothers had contact with a cousin in the West Bank who was an operative in the Tanzim. Word had already spread from Amman to Ramallah that the family was having trouble with their oldest daughter. In late May 2001, Zina was told that the only way to redeem herself and her family was to leave Amman for Ramallah. On the condition that she prepare herself for an eventual military mission or even death in the name of liberating Palestine, she would be allowed to go to university there. Only after she successfully completed the mission would she be exonerated of her shame and be able, if she were still alive, to live a life free of constraints or punishment. It was an offer that immediately appealed to Zina. To her, it meant freedom and a chance to do something exciting and meaningful. It was a second chance at life.

Within days, she was sent to Nabi Salah, a village near Ramallah in the West Bank, where she moved in with her cousin and his family. Bright, aggressive, and bilingual, Zina immediately enrolled at Bir Zeit University to study journalism and telecommunications. To earn money, she became a "fixer" for Western journalists who came to Ramallah. A fixer arranges interviews for the foreign press with Palestinian leaders, acts as a translator, and usually arranges for a special car and driver to pick the journalist up at the Israeli checkpoint when he or she enters into Palestinian territory. Also, fixers know when it is relatively safe for reporters to make the trip into Palestinian towns, villages, and cities, especially when the area is under curfew. In other words, the journalist puts her or his life into the fixer's hands.

Because she had a Jordanian passport, Zina was able to pass easily across checkpoints, enabling her to travel unhampered to Jerusalem and other places within Israel. Not surprisingly, one of the first assignments she received from her cousin was to gather intelligence information for the Tanzim. According to Zina, she would provide the times when certain areas in Israel, including checkpoints, were the most crowded and would report as well on the most popular meeting places within the Occupied Territories for off-duty soldiers.

Eventually one of her contacts at the Tanzim told her that they judged her ready to help several women implement actual attacks within Israel. The first woman who was put in contact with Zina was Iman Aisha from Nablus. Under Zina's guidance, the woman tried to plant a package containing a bomb in the crowded Tel Aviv bus station, an attack that ultimately failed when the package was discovered before it exploded. Another woman who found herself under Zina's wing was Abir Hamdan, who, with a bomb in a shopping bag, attempted to board a bus between Tulkarim and Nablus. The bomb exploded prematurely and no one was injured except Hamdan. Ironically, when she woke up in the hospital and saw everyone wearing white, Hamdan was convinced that her mission had been a success and she had reached Paradise. In an effort to convince her that she was, in fact, in an Israeli hospital, the doctor told her he was a Jew. "Are there Jews in heaven?" he asked her. "No," Hamdan replied, finally prepared to believe that she had failed in her mission.

In the first of several interviews with Zina from prison, I asked her to describe her life back then, living near Ramallah, attending Bir Zeit University, and acting as an important asset for the all-male military arm of Chairman Arafat's Fatah. Her whole demeanor changed. Her face lit up. She was exuberant. "For the first time in my life," she said, "I was free and doing something meaningful for myself and for a political cause. I could study and not have to worry what people thought. But I also realized how difficult life was under occupation. A lot of people I knew were injured, and several had even been killed." According to Zina, when she first arrived in

Ramallah she had been grateful for a chance to begin her life again and to redeem herself. Within a month she was anxious to sacrifice herself for the sake of the Palestinian people. The problem was that until then, Zina had not proven herself since the missions that the Tanzim gave her had all failed.

Toward the middle of June, Zina made friends with another student at Bir Zeit named Mahmoud Douglas, who was not only an active member of Hamas but also an activist in Force 17, another military arm of the Fatah movement. Because of the sensitivity of his work, Douglas explained that he used the pseudonym "Hassan." As the friendship between the pair flourished, Hassan also told Zina that he was responsible for mounting suicide bombings within Israel and the Occupied Territories and in fact worked with one of the most successful bomb makers within the organization, a man named Belal Barghouti. According to Zina, it was Hassan who first broached the possibility that she could help him commit those actions within Israel, as she had the proper papers to pass the checkpoints. "I was also a woman," Zina explains, "which made it easier for me to pass through and walk around unnoticed in Jerusalem or Tel Aviv."

Eventually Hassan told Zina that he would recommend her as an active member in Hamas, which according to him was a great honor since the organization rarely accepted women. Zina was ecstatic. "It was an honor and I understood that from the beginning. There was no doubt in my mind that I wanted to join and kill my occupiers and even, some day, if circumstances called for it, to blow myself up in an attack as well." She smiles sadly. "What did I have to lose? I already lost my baby."

During the days that followed, Zina never stopped asking

136

Hassan if his superiors had approved her membership into Hamas. "This was my big chance," she explains, "and naturally I was anxious to get started and prove myself."

Within a week, Zina was told that she had been accepted. "Hassan was my sponsor," she explains. "He told me that I was only to take direct orders from him, except if he was arrested or killed. Then my new contact in the organization would be a man named Riyad Kasewani."

After her acceptance into the group, Hassan introduced Zina to Belal's brother, Abdullah Barghouti, who actually secured the explosives and designed the bombs that his brother built. "He also told me that in the event that Abdullah was killed or arrested, another man would be replacing him. He assured me that the strength of the organization was that if someone was arrested or killed they had people in place who would step in and take over."

From then on, Zina's days were filled with classes at Bir Zeit and regular meetings with Hassan at the university and eventually higher-level meetings at a secret apartment he rented in Ramallah that housed suicide bombers on their way to committing their attacks. According to Zina, she later learned that Hassan was also the mastermind for transporting the bombers to the designated areas, hiding them there, often for days, until he led them to the actual target. According to Israeli security forces, long after the apartment was searched and dismantled, the kitchen was filled with bomb-making materials.

During the interview with Zina, she admitted that eventually she and Hassan fell in love. "He inspired me," she said. "I wasn't afraid of anything, and soon I came to believe in everything he believed in and everything he did. He opened my eyes to life and to the possibilities that a woman could take advantage of, even within a religious environment. It was something my father never gave me. Suddenly, I had choices."

If love was an underlying reason for Zina's commitment to Hassan, he saw in her a perfect accomplice to deflect attention from any suicide bomber that passed through Israeli checkpoints. When I suggested this to Zina, even after all that subsequently happened, she refused to believe it. "He told me he loved me," she said tearfully. "He told me that he was organizing a bombing operation that would include me. How much more proof did I need?"

On July 20, 2002, Belal and Abdullah Barghouti were arrested by the Palestinian Authority, at a time when Yasser Arafat was forced to prove to the Israelis and to the Americans that he was in control of the violence within the Occupied Territories and was prepared to arrest known militants to prevent suicide bombings. Two days later, however, the pair were released for "lack of evidence," although when Zina asked Hassan why they had not returned to classes at Bir Zeit, he told her that the brothers were "in hiding" as they were still "wanted" by the Shin Bet, the Israeli internal security force.

During a meeting that evening in Hassan's apartment in Ramallah, in the presence of the Barghouti brothers, Zina says that she was informed of several daring plans, one of which was to kill an adviser to Prime Minister Sharon. "I understood that evening that my job was to kill civilians because I could pass by security. I also understood that killing civilians affected Israelis more than anything else. And I was prepared to do anything Hassan asked me to because I loved him." She cries. "He knew this was my last chance and he expected me to prove that I was worthy of his love."

138

On July 25, Zina was given her first real mission. She was to carry a bomb, concealed in a beer can, across the checkpoint from Ramallah into Jerusalem. While the bomb was being made, Zina was instructed to scout out the best location to place the bomb so that "it would do the most damage." "They told me they wanted a place with a lot of people. I knew Jaffa Road was usually the most crowded, which is why I decided to go there."

On July 27, in the company of her nephew she set off for Jerusalem. As predicted, the pair had no trouble getting through the checkpoint, and when they reached Jerusalem they walked together on Jaffa Road. "I still wasn't satisfied," Zina explained, "because I wanted to find the most populated area. From Jaffa Road I went to King George Street and looked around the Mahane Yehuda market area. Finally I decided on a supermarket called the Coop, on Jaffa Road. We went inside and I bought a bottle of water and wandered around the store until I found where the beer was kept. I knew that a bomb hidden in a beer can would almost certainly be successful."

Zina waited until she got back to Ramallah to report to Hassan in person, since he had warned her about using her cell phone, which was easily traceable by the Israeli security forces. Three days later, on July 30, at ten-thirty in the morning, Hassan met Zina at Bir Zeit University. According to her, he said that they would be taking a back road in Ramallah that would lead into Jerusalem. Belal Barghouti would meet them there and give her the bomb.

An hour later, on that dusty deserted road, Belal Barghouti met the pair and showed Zina the bomb as he carefully inserted nails into it to do, as he explained, "more damage." Before he placed the device into a plastic bag to put inside the beer can, he also explained how to

139

detonate it. "All I had to do," Zina says, "was to push a button which would trigger the time mechanism so it would explode approximately one hour later. I had enough time to get away."

Zina put everything into her bag and went by collective taxi from Ramallah to Damascus Gate in East Jerusalem. When she arrived there at twelve-fifteen, she changed into a skimpy halter top and tight pants to look, as she put it, "like any young Israeli girl." With the bomb in the beer can concealed in her purse, Zina headed toward the Coop supermarket. As she was about to enter the store, however, she noticed a security guard approach her to search her bag. Thinking quickly, Zina took out her cell phone and began speaking in English, pretending to be preoccupied and pretending as well to be an American tourist. The security man got distracted by other people and never checked her.

Once inside, Zina took a cart and walked unhurriedly up and down the aisles until she arrived at the beer display. Satisfied that she had found the same brand as the one she carried, Zina placed the bomb at the front of the shelf. It was exactly one-thirty when she detonated the timer. Leaving the empty cart at the door, she walked out of the market and continued on foot until she reached Jaffa Gate in East Jerusalem. There, she changed out of her Western outfit and waited. At exactly ten minutes past two the bomb exploded, and within three minutes Zina heard the sirens as ambulances and police sped toward the Coop. "I knew it was all because of me," she says, "and I was really happy because finally I had done something that worked. I knew that the bomb had exploded. It was only a question of counting the casualties."

As agreed, when Zina returned to Ramallah she went directly to the Internet center at Bir Zeit to meet Hassan so they could follow the events as they happened. But when he saw Zina was still carrying a plastic shopping bag from the Coop, he was furious. Pushing her out of the Internet center, he told her to "destroy the bag, to tear it up in a million pieces and throw them all around the campus."

When Zina returned home that night, she heard on the television news that nobody had been killed in the attack. "I was desperate," she says. "Another failure. Then I got angry. I called Hassan and told him that before I take another bomb, I wanted it checked out for defects so the next mission would be a success. If I tried again and nobody was killed, I would refuse all other missions and just stop. It was a waste of my time and there was too much risk involved for nothing."

Later that night, Hassan called her back to apologize. "He told me it wasn't my fault," Zina says. "The bomb was not as powerful as it should have been. The next time he promised he would check it out personally so there would be no problem."

According to Zina, she barely saw Hassan during the days that followed and feared not only that had he abandoned her as a coconspirator but that he had grown tired of her as a girlfriend as well. It was then that she discovered he had a wife and three children in Nablus. A tearful scene ensued, during which Hassan not only affirmed his love for Zina, but assured her that he was prepared to take her as his second wife when he was certain that she was completely committed to his beliefs and had proved herself for what he described as the biggest mission he had ever undertaken since joining Hamas. According to Zina, she wanted to believe him, but she also knew she wasn't in a position to make demands. "Everyone knew about me and my baby and they understood why I had been sent to live with my cousins. I just wanted to be able to prove to him that I was better than his wife or any other woman he ever met."

Two days later, on August 7, 2001, Hassan told Zina that he and Belal Barghouti had finally finished making another bomb, and to be patient. Her time had come.

Within twenty-four hours, Zina was rewarded for her faith and patience. Hassan explained that a suicide bomber, with Zina's help, would arrive in Ramallah for his last journey on earth. Once again, she was told to go to Jerusalem to find the most densely populated area. "He told me that if the attack was a success, which meant that more than twenty people were killed, he would finally consider me a valuable part of the organization." She pauses. "He told me that only then I could have the honor of dying in my own martyr operation."

When I asked Zina if dying for Allah was a sign of equality, she replied that it was "definitely a step forward for equality for women throughout the Arab world." Was it more important than living to share her life with Hassan, whom she claimed she loved? "Hassan told me we would be together forever since he planned on following me to Paradise," Zina answered. "He told me he loved me and we would be together forever in the next life."

On August 8, Hassan informed Zina that the potential suicide bomber was arriving in Ramallah from Nablus to prepare for his mission.

142

CHAPTER ELEVEN

Two weeks before he was chosen to die a martyr's death, Izzedine Masri had already proven himself worthy. According to Mohammed Abu Haji, a Hamas leader from Jenin who was subsequently assassinated by the Israelis in September 2002, all potential suicides undergo a sort of "crystallization," during which they are intentionally placed in situations where their lives are in danger. The "instructors" analyze and examine their reactions and their manner of behavior, including their facial expressions and body language. The purpose of this test is to make sure that the potential suicide bomber never betrays his intentions, or his fear. "If they fail the test," Abu Haji explained, "they are sent back home without any recriminations. If they pass, they proceed to the next step."

Masri passed the examination conducted by Hamas activists in

Nablus without any problem and was transported to a hiding place in Gaza that also served as his training camp and base of departure. According to Mohammed Abu Haji, from the moment he is chosen, the recruit is forbidden to tell his friends and family what he is about to do. Instead he is simply to disappear. Shuhail Masri was ready for the worst when his son walked out of the house, allegedly on his way for evening prayers at the mosque, and didn't return until two weeks later, as if nothing had happened.

In the hiding camp in Gaza, Izzedine was put through rigorous training. He was taught how to activate an explosive device and how to behave in crowds or in the presence of police or other security officials on his way to the target. When he was finally discharged, he was instructed to return home and carry on a normal life until he was contacted to report for active duty. Shuhail Masri describes his son's behavior when he returned home: "He was very quiet. He seemed at peace with everything. He prayed a great deal and told me on several occasions that I should never regret what God has in store for us in life."

Izzedine, like other suicide bombers, was not told where the attack would take place or the day that he would be summoned. According to Dr. al-Rantisi, spokesperson for Hamas, "Everything is done to prevent troubling thoughts or second thoughts in the mind of the martyr. We don't want our martyr visiting the target area in advance because he might imagine the reality after the bomb explodes," he explains. "And of course, we keep it a secret for security reasons." He smiles. "Although I must admit that men tend to keep secrets better than women."

After Izzedine returned home, he underwent a process of indoctrination and purification. "Our martyr looks at many,

many films, which show the atrocities the Israelis have done to our women and children," Dr. al-Rantisi explained. "He is shown films on Sabra and Shatilla and television images of young men being tortured. He sees films of Palestine and our olive trees and homes before the Jews invaded. He reads many, many books; of course the holy book, but also stories of how Jews have mutilated children, even Christian children. He is asked to read *The Protocols of the Elders of Zion* and there are lectures by learned men and prayers, many, many prayers."

On the day the indoctrination and purification ends, the potential *shahide* is instructed to write a will under the guidance of one of his Hamas handlers and to record a video, which is not only a farewell to his friends and family but an explanation that details his reasons for undertaking the mission. The text has been written for him in advance.

The video is made in one of several studios throughout the West Bank and in Gaza, depending on where the *shahide* happens to be. After the incursion by Israeli troops into Jenin in April 2002 and the fierce battle that ensued, I was there to film for my documentary. While interviewing several Hamas leaders who showed me the destruction of the houses and recounted how hundreds of innocent Palestinians had been slaughtered by Israeli troops, referring to the battle as the "massacre"—allegations that were eventually rejected by a committee from the Human Rights Watch and from the United Nations—the owner of the studio offered to show me the actual place where martyrs made their final videos. Although the shop was in ruins, he managed to salvage several interesting items: a papier-mâché model of the al-Aqsa mosque, plus numerous backdrops—one of photographs of other martyrs, another of an assortment of guns and rifles, yet another with pertinent writings from the Koran. The owner of the studio explained that each *shahide* had the right to choose his own setting, props, and backdrop for his final video. Almost all, he added, wanted to pose with the al-Aqsa mosque somewhere within camera view, as that was the "most holy symbol of this Intifada." The final tape is broadcast by Palestinian television after the martyr's death and circulated throughout the Arab world.

Two days before the attack, Izzedine Masri embraced his father and left the house, this time never to return. "I knew," Shuhail Masri says now, "deep in my heart I knew that I was supposed to feel joy that my son would be a martyr." He pauses. "But I was sick. This has destroyed me and my family."

Within hours of making the videotape, Izzedine was brought to Ramallah by a group of Hamas members who came from a city far from Nablus and who did not know him or his real name. According to Dr. al-Rantisi, this is how it should be. "Until the last day, everyone who has a role in the attack knows only his own precise duty and is not in contact with any of the other operatives."

Zina says she never knew or met the suicide bomber until the day of the attack. The only thing she had been told by Hassan was that she would be accompanying the young man from Ramallah to Jerusalem. But when Hassan told her of the plan to conceal the bomb in an oud, an Arab instrument that resembles a guitar, she refused. "It was just too obvious," she says, "to carry an oud through the streets of Jerusalem. I told Hassan we should put it in a regular guitar that wouldn't attract attention."

Hassan agreed and bought a guitar complete with a case, which he brought to Belal Barghouti to fit with the bomb. He also bought Zina a SIM card so she could contact him from Jerusalem using the Israeli phone service, a detail that made it more difficult for the Israeli Shin Bet to trace the call than on an Arab cellular phone exchange. Later that day, Hassan informed her that the martyr had arrived and would be spending the night in his apartment in Ramallah.

That evening, Hassan and Zina met Belal Barghouti in a café, where he explained the technicalities of the operation. During that same meeting, Hassan also told Zina that both she and the *shahide* would be wearing Western clothes. "The guitar, our clothes, the bomb material, my SIM card, and money for the taxi fare," Zina explains, "were all part of the budget that Hamas gave Hassan for the attack. Hassan also had to decide if security was particularly tight that day, and if it was, the mission would have been postponed."

On Wednesday, August 8, 2001, the evening before the attack, Izzedine Masri, as is the ritual, bathed and shaved off his beard. Instead of shaving his head, however, as is also the usual ritual, Hassan instructed him to dye his hair platinum blond, another detail that would make him look more like an Israeli "rocker," especially since he would be carrying a guitar.

Early Thursday morning, August 9, just after dawn, Zina finally met Izzedine. There is a faraway look in her eyes as she describes him. "He was calm and very polite," she recalls. "Very sweet, young, and not curious at all about knowing anything about me."

Did she wonder how he felt, knowing he was about to die? Was she tempted to ask him?

Zina smiles, and I interpret that smile to mean that the answer to my question is obvious. "He didn't believe he would die," Zina replies. "He believed he would be going to Paradise."

Dr. Mohammed al-Hajj, professor of Islamic Faith at the University of Amman and the chairman of the Association of Psychoanalysts, stated recently on the television talk show *Life Is Sweet*, broadcast out of Egypt, that "Contrary to the opinion of the West, the martyr loves life more than anyone else. This may seem strange to people who do not see the human soul as most Muslims see it, but the goal of our life is loyalty, sacrifice, and honor. When a martyr dies, he attains the height of bliss. And, as a psychiatrist, I can say that the height of bliss comes with the end of the countdown: seven, six, five, four, three, two, one, and then you press the button to blow yourself up, and then the boom, and then he senses himself floating to another life and he knows for certain he is not dead."

At eight-thirty in the morning, August 9, Zina traveled to Jerusalem alone to check out potential targets. When she returned to Ramallah several hours later, she informed Hassan that, dressed in a halter top and tight pants, nobody had paid any attention to her other than to make complimentary comments. "I was convinced there would be no problem for me or for the *shahide* to be in Jerusalem."

Accompanied by Hassan, Zina went to the market in Ramallah where Izzedine was waiting with his handlers from Hamas. He was wearing jeans, a T-shirt, and sunglasses. He carried a guitar in a case that contained the bomb. According to Zina, Hassan told her to

148

pray to Allah that the mission would be a success, and then he instructed both of them not to talk until they crossed the checkpoint and had arrived in Jerusalem. "He told us to pretend we didn't know each other so that if one of us was arrested," Zina explains, "the other one could get away." Handing Zina one hundred shekels for the cab fares, he left the pair at a taxi stand where they would get into a collective cab that would take them to Damascus Gate in East Jerusalem. Zina sat in the front next to the driver, while Izzedine, with the guitar on his lap, sat in the back.

When they reached the Qalandrya checkpoint, the driver announced that he didn't have the proper papers to cross with his taxi into Israel. Everybody had to get out and walk from that point on. Zina and Izzedine, along with the six other passengers, took the back roads until they reached Aram, the next checkpoint, where they found another taxi with the proper credentials. This time, the driver announced that any passenger who didn't have permission to enter Israel had to get out and make his way on foot across the checkpoint, where he would be glad to pick him up and take him the rest of the way into East Jerusalem. Izzedine handed Zina the guitar since she had a proper Jordanian passport and could remain in the cab with the other passengers. Holding the guitar case containing the bomb on her lap, Zina, along with the other passengers, passed the Aram checkpoint before stopping several kilometers down the road, already within Israel proper, until Izzedine appeared and got back into the car. "By that time we were talking and laughing together," Zina says. "We forgot to pretend we didn't know each other. I guess we were both nervous and relieved he didn't get caught."

When they arrived at Damascus Gate, Izzedine took the guitar from Zina and strapped it around his shoulders so it hung over his chest. "It was ridiculous," Zina said, laughing. "It was all wrong, so I told him to strap it over his back. Then I took off this little jacket I was wearing and showed off my halter top. We walked without attracting any suspicion until we reached Jaffa Road."

Zina suddenly admits, "It hit me then. Why did he seem so happy even though he knew he was about to die?" Was she scared at that point? "No," she replies. "I knew if we got caught, he had the bomb. I could say that I didn't know anything. He would be arrested. I had a chance of getting away."

Zina showed Izzedine Jaffa Road and told him that it was the main street for Jews to shop. "I pointed out the intersection of Jaffa and King George Streets, where there are four crossing lights. People cross in all directions and it is always very crowded."

On one of the four corners was Sbarro's Pizza.

Zina first suggested that Izzedine stand in the middle of the intersection and wait until the light changed so that people would be crossing in all directions, and if he was very lucky, perhaps a bus would be stopped there as well among all the cars. "I told him he could blow himself up there and cause a lot of casualties," Zina says. "I also told him if he didn't like that spot he could suggest another but it had to be here in the area, somewhere on King George Street because that was the busiest." According to Zina, it was then that Izzedine decided to walk into Sbarro's and blow himself up. "I didn't argue. After all, it was his decision," she says matter-of-factly.

Together, the pair walked slowly across the street and into the pizza restaurant. It was crowded, filled mostly with children and their parents.

CHAPTER TWELVE

ACCORDING TO SEVERAL WITNESSES who survived the Sbarro attack, Malki Roth and Michal Raziel stood together in line waiting to order their slices of pizza, chatting happily about their summer plans. One of those witnesses says that Malki noticed Izzedine and Zina immediately. In an atmosphere of fear and terror where every package, purse, or suitcase is seen as a potential bomb, Malki saw only a fellow musician.

"Malki had no suspicion that anything was wrong," Arnold Roth says. "People told me afterwards that she engaged the young Palestinian man and the girl with him in conversation as they waited for their pizza. She felt they were human beings. Little did she know that no, they weren't human beings, they were monsters in the service of a monstrous and barbaric society."

At 1:53, only two minutes before Izzedine detonated the explosives, Zina walked out of the restaurant. At precisely 1:55, the bomb exploded. Malki Roth and Michal Raziel died instantly. They are buried side by side at Har Tamir Cemetery in Jerusalem: two best friends who shared everything, from clothes to secrets—an unfailing friendship that continues after life.

Even before Zina reached Damascus Gate to make the trip by collective cab back to Ramallah, she heard the bomb and saw all the ambulances and police cars racing to the scene. She learned later that fifteen people had died, including seven children, and that more than 130 were injured. The bomb, it was reported, weighed ten kilograms and had been packed with nails, screws, and bolts. The restaurant was completely gutted, and every car in the area was destroyed. Within an hour, Hamas and Islamic Jihad claimed joint responsibility for the attack.

On her way back to Ramallah, Zina called Hassan on her cell phone and told him that the attack was a success. He already knew. They laughed. He praised her in the name of Allah. By the time she arrived in Ramallah and went to the secret apartment near the market, however, he was gone. The apartment was empty except for some bomb-making material left behind in the kitchen. Zina never saw him again.

During the interview in her prison cell, Zina was at first defiant. She had no regrets that so many teenagers and children had been killed that day. Her most frequent response was that they, the victims, had no business being there in the first place. "They should go back to Poland or Russia or America where their parents came from," she said. "If they hadn't come here to take our land, they would be alive today."

* * *

When the bomb exploded, Fremet Roth was watching CNN. It never occurred to her that her daughter was anywhere near Sbarro's Pizza. "I started screaming and crying because I had two other children out of the house and they didn't have a cell phone and I was afraid they were near there," she says. "I just didn't think about Malki because she never mentioned she was going there, and she always told me exactly where she would be. But I started calling her anyway, and I couldn't reach her. Eventually my other two children came home and I hugged them and was relieved and still I couldn't reach Malki on her cell phone, and then I couldn't reach her friend either. But I still wasn't worried because she had told me very precisely where she was going and everybody knows whenever there's a bombing, the cell phone lines are often disturbed."

Malki always kept in touch, especially after a bombing, and it is impossible not to be aware of a bombing, even if you are kilometers away. Whenever there is an explosion in Jerusalem, as has happened several times while I've been there, it feels like an earthquake. The walls shake, the ground below trembles, and there is no doubt that a bomb has gone off somewhere in the city.

"When I didn't hear from her for a couple of hours, and when Michal's family hadn't heard from her either, I started to worry. When my oldest son got home, we began calling the hospitals to see if she was among the injured, but she wasn't on any list."

It was too much to bear. Fremet Roth decided, along with Michal's mother, Aviva Raziel, to go to the hospitals and see for themselves if their daughters were among the injured. When they were only a few meters from Hadassah Hospital, Aviva

153

Raziel's cell phone rang. "One of her older children called to say that Malki and Michal had asked him to meet them at Sbarro's," Fremet says, weeping.

When they arrived at Hadassah, they were told that Michal Raziel's body had been brought in and identified. "Then I knew there wasn't any hope," Fremet Roth says, "but I still fought the reality and prayed."

Arnold Roth continues, "One of our neighbors is a doctor and he used his connections to look for any possible child matching Malki's description who might have been unidentified and unconscious. He ran into our apartment at eleven that night and said there was a girl on the operating table who matched Malki's description. So we drove over to the hospital, but it wasn't our daughter." He stops to collect himself. "But one of the doctors who was there came running over and said, 'Oh, you're looking for a fifteen-year-old girl, we just had one die on the table a few minutes ago. Why don't you go to the other room and check in out.'" He pauses again. "It wasn't Malki, but you have to know that this was a heart-breaking situation," he continues. "There were dozens and dozens of people who were injured and killed, and it was like the world was coming to an end, so when the doctor said he had another child, he was just trying to cope."

At one o'clock in the morning, when there was still no definite news of Malki, the Roths' two oldest sons volunteered to drive down to Tel Aviv to the morgue. Apparently it had taken so long to remove all the bodies because there had been so much debris and so many body parts that it wasn't until almost midnight when everything finally arrived at the morgue.

At two o'clock in the morning, the call finally came. It was

154

Malki's brothers. They were at the pathology lab. "We found our sister," they announced. "She's here."

There are always horrifying stories after each and every suicide attack in Israel, stories that circulate for weeks and months and that eventually become part of the tragic history of loss and pain. There are also stories that give people a modicum of hope that there are exceptions to the rules of hatred and vengeance that permeate the region.

One of the victims of the Sbarro's bombing was a man who had lingered for weeks after the attack in a profound coma. According to his wife, she had made the decision that when he died, which was inevitable given the extent of his head injuries, she would donate his organs so others could live. A week later, the woman called me. Her husband had died two days earlier and, as arranged with the hospital, his heart, liver, kidneys, and corneas had been donated to the hospital's organ bank. In an extraordinary set of circumstances, her doctor called her after she had signed all the legal forms to ask her a very specific question. "A Palestinian man in the hospital was next on the list for my husband's heart," she told me, "and the doctor wanted to know, given the circumstances of my husband's death, if I had any objections."

She had no objections and even agreed to meet the recipient after he had successfully undergone transplant surgery. The scene in his hospital room was one of those moments when blood feuds, biblical prophecies, and political grievances disintegrate under the weight of pure human emotion. The Palestinian man, his wife, and the Israeli widow embraced, the three of them, their arms intertwined as the two women leaned over the patient's hospital bed. There was nothing any of them, or any of us who witnessed the moment, could do except cry.

Two weeks after Malki's death, I meet with Arnold and Fremet Roth at their apartment in Jerusalem. One of the first questions I ask is how they feel about the so-called political strategy of suicide bombers. Arnold Roth responds. "What does this have to do with political strategy? This is barbarism without historic precedent. This isn't even kamikaze pilots. What did they think they were blowing up? A child buying a pizza?" He was quiet for several moments. "It's the randomness of the attacks that makes you go mad," he finally said. "And yet, I can't just hate. I guess because we are not hate-filled people where we hate all Arabs or all Palestinians."

After several moments, he continues in a passionate voice. "Here was one child, full of cultural values, sympathy for others, with her whole life in front of her, and here was another child, who knows what her background was, but some ugly man in some office, maybe in Ramallah, maybe in Gaza, manipulated and programmed and did everything he could to turn that child into a bomb."

Weeks later Zina was sentenced to twenty-five years in prison for her part in the Sbarro's bombing, convicted as an accomplice in the deaths and injuries of all the victims. She learned from the Israeli authorities that her lover Hassan had denounced her when he was arrested. He also implicated her in the attack when she placed a beer can in a supermarket in Jerusalem, as well as for her role in directing the two unsuccessful bombings involving other women. Several weeks after that, Zina's parents and two older brothers were interviewed from their home in Amman. They were asked the same question, about the political strategy or gains of suicide bombers. Her oldest brother spoke for the family. "It is the highest honor that any true Muslim can have. It is an honor for us that our sister helped a martyr achieve Paradise."

Zina's father was unable to speak. Upon learning of his daughter's fate, he suffered a second stroke. Zina's mother held her daughter's baby in her arms, and wept.

On September 23, 2002, exactly one month and fourteen days after the Sbarro's bombing, students at Al-Najah University in Nablus opened an exhibition of the bombing. It included a grisly reenactment of the aftermath of the attack, complete with papier-mâché body parts and pizza slices strewn across the room, as well as photographs of the actual scene of the disaster. Before entering the exhibit, students wiped their feet on the Israeli and American flags.

During my visit there, shortly before Israeli authorities demanded that the director of the university dismantle the exhibit, one of the students told me that the exhibit was dedicated to Izzedine Masri and to Darine Abu Aisha, the second female suicide bomber, who had attended Al-Najah University. He also told me that Al-Najah is considered the most radical of all the institutions of higher education in the West Bank and Gaza. Controlled by the student council, which is led by members of Islamic Jihad and Hamas, it has the distinction of having had at least 135 suicide bombers enrolled at the university since the beginning of the present Intifada.

CHAPTER THIRTEEN

THERE IS A SAYING IN ISRAEL that every time one Israeli dies, whether a civilian or a soldier, his or her death "pierces the heart of the nation." In such a small country, there are less than six degrees of separation among a population of nearly six million people. Everyone always knows someone who knows someone who is related to a casualty of war or a victim of terror. Since the beginning of the Intifada, the lives and deaths of Palestinians have become part of this equation.

Further, the physical proximity and the economic repercussions that every political decision and military action has for both Palestinians and Israelis mean that their fates are also closely linked, whether they chose them to be or not. A mother who loses a son who dies a martyr's death in Gaza, for instance, is forever connected to the victims of her son's attack. Death links the families inextricably for eternity, regardless of the religious or idealistic rationales that separate the two societies. Mothers grieve for their children, husbands for their wives, wives for their husbands, brothers for their sisters, and on and on, tragically linking more and more people in grief as the conflict continues and worsens.

Curiously, though the same piece of land has been fought over for centuries, there is a kind of contradiction that can be seen among both Palestinians and Israelis, even in harrowing times of war and certainly in moments when the occupied portion of the population rebels against its occupiers. One of the most poignant examples of that contradiction or ambiguity is evident in one special hospital, Hadassah, in Jerusalem, a city that is the symbolic and geographic focal point of the dispute. Not only do Palestinian and Israeli doctors and nurses work side by side as trusted colleagues, and in some cases even friends, but in this particular hospital they administer care to all elements of Israeli and Palestinian society. It is especially true during the current Intifada, when the kinds of injuries inflicted are so devastating, such as when Israeli soldiers wound Palestinian children or when Israeli citizens are maimed and killed in suicide bombings.

In the intensive care unit of Hadassah Hospital in Jerusalem, an Israeli doctor confers with a Palestinian nurse over the bed of a young Palestinian man who was critically wounded when his explosive device detonated prematurely on the ground of a nearby Jewish settlement. In the next bed is an Israeli man who was one of the casualties of that attack. A Palestinian doctor discusses with her Israeli colleague a new medicine that might be administered to ease the victim's pain.

When questioned about what they feel when obliged to treat

159

patients who are on opposite sides of the conflict, the Palestinian nurse and the Israeli doctor smile and offer the same logical response. Gimella, a nurse from a small Palestinian village near Jerusalem, says, "I leave my politics at the door when I come to work. All I see are people in terrible need of my expertise and care, and I administer it without any hesitation. My goal is to save lives. My patients have no nationality or religion." The Israeli doctor nods. "I have a Palestinian man in this bed who has a fierce infection from his injuries, and I have an Israeli man in the bed next to him who lost a leg and risks losing the other leg from a suicide bombing. I don't care how each of them got here. All I care about is that they will leave here alive."

To hear firsthand of the heartfelt compassion that transcends religious, political, and nationalistic boundaries and that prevails over an atmosphere of such gratuitous violence is an incredibly powerful experience. I spoke with one Palestinian nurse who was on duty during one of the many suicide bombings in Jerusalem.

"I was called down to the emergency ward by a series of alarms that went off throughout the hospital. I knew immediately that there had been another bombing. When I got there, I saw several women, obviously mothers, screaming and running after the gurneys that carried their injured children. One of my colleagues asked me to deal with a man who was hysterical, although not physically injured. The whole family had been on their way to a bar mitzvah when the bomb exploded, and he was not yet aware that two of his daughters were dead. It was up to me to tell him."

The nurse went on to explain that her name, which is obviously Palestinian, is written on a plastic-encased tag pinned to her blouse. "I didn't even think about that," she continues.

160

"All I thought about was how to tell this poor man that two of his children were dead." At that moment, the man's wife entered the emergency room and she, like him, was not yet aware of her children's fate. "It was just tragic," the nurse explains. "Every event is so personal because families are destroyed. These are not soldiers but people who were accidentally in the area. This wasn't a military confrontation. It was random carnage."

The nurse escorted the distraught parents into a small room, sat them down, and proceeded to explain gently that their daughters had succumbed to their injuries. "It was just unbearable to see these two people so broken, so grief stricken. One moment they were all on their way, as a family, to a joyous event, and the next minute they are in mourning."

The nurse spent several hours with the couple, eventually placing them in adjoining beds under sedation. "But right before I did that," she explains, "the man noticed my name and asked me if I was an Arab. I answered that I was a Palestinian. They both began to hit me and pull my hair until several guards came. I was frightened." She pauses. "But I don't blame them. How would I feel in their position if an Israeli nurse was tending to me after telling me that an Israeli had just killed my children? Working here like this, under these conditions, it's hard to say if this has changed my politics, because I try to separate politics and work, whether my patients are Palestinian, Arab, or Jewish. You just can't involve politics in medicine because if you do, it will influence you in a negative way to care for your patients. I grieve for all the parents who lose children and for all the children who lose parents. There is no easy answer."

In another example of this kind of schizophrenia that the

161

people here experience, all of them constantly so close in life and death, the Palestinian nurse's best friend in the hospital is her Israeli counterpart. They both work in the pediatric unit. Together, they tell this harrowing story.

Several weeks before the incident with the Israeli parents who lost two daughters, the sister and brother-in-law of the Israeli nurse were on their way home from work one evening when they were shot and killed by a Palestinian terrorist on the road leading to their settlement near Nablus. When she learned of her sister's death, the first person the Israeli nurse called was her Palestinian friend. As the two women stood together, their arms linked, talking to my camera, they each gave their own version of the tragedy and how it affected them.

"I was devastated," the Palestinian began. "In a way, I felt ashamed and responsible, which was irrational on my part since I felt the loss as acutely as my friend. I wanted to come to her house immediately and comfort her." She glances at her friend. "But I understood that it would have been delicate for the rest of the family. After the funeral, I called to ask if I could come to pay my respects while the family sat shiva [the required eight-day mourning period in the Jewish religion], but it was just too emotional for the family to accept me, a Palestinian, in their home under those circumstances."

The sister of the murdered woman is visibly uncomfortable. "Of course I wanted her with me," she begins in a soft voice. "When my sister was killed, I needed her there and I told her that." She shrugs. "At the same time, the rest of the family was so filled with grief and hatred that I knew it was impossible. I felt terrible. I felt as if I had not only lost my sister, but that I would lose a friend who was as close as a sister. I didn't know what to do. All I can say is that I was grateful that she understood."

Perhaps the situation might have been different had the victims not come from a settlement like Itamar, whose followers hold some extreme views, including not serving in the Israeli army because they do not recognize the state of Israel. "They are very religious," the Israeli nurse explains, "and are waiting for the Messiah to come, which is why they don't serve in the army to defend the country. These are not my views, but they were my sister's and of course her husband's."

These two close friends, one Palestinian, one Israeli, are good examples of another type of victimization in this ongoing war. Each suffers under the extremist views that have taken over her respective society and which determine, on each side, the political and military actions and the emotional reactions throughout the region. And yet, almost unbelievably, when they are at Hadassah Hospital, a sense of peace and cohabitation prevails, at least in the emergency room and the intensive care unit, where both women, along with other Palestinians and Israelis, work together as they all fight to save lives imperiled by this conflict.

At the end of the interview I ask each woman what it's like immediately following a suicide bombing, when the hospital staff is preparing to receive the broken bodies of the victims. The Israeli nurse answers first. "After a bombing," she says, "obviously the first thing that crosses my mind, of course, is my own family. I can separate myself from the nationality of my patients, but I cannot separate myself from my family. Within ten or fifteen minutes from the beginning of the event, a list starts coming over our fax machine with the names of all the victims, the wounded and the dead. So naturally I look to see if I know anyone on the list. It doesn't change anything, but at least I'm assured that I am not personally implicated." She pauses. "At least not this time."

The Palestinian nurse nods. "For me, it's the same thing, except I pray that no one in my family was the suicide bomber." She glances at her friend. "At least not this time."

Eli Picard is a pediatric surgeon at the Shaare Zedek Medical Center in Jerusalem. A small man with a ready smile and sincere demeanor, he and his family immigrated to Israel from France more than twenty years ago. While he is a modest man who is not prone to self-aggrandizing statements, he tells a story about a Palestinian boy of six whose life he saved.

"The child was critically ill, and for several weeks after I operated on him he lingered between life and death. Finally, when he pulled through the crisis and I knew he would recover, I told his father that his boy would live." Dr. Picard smiles sadly. "The man broke down and cried." Picard pauses. "Then, he opened up his shirt to expose his bare chest and said, 'Kill me, you can kill me, Doctor, if it makes your pain less.'" Again, Dr. Picard smiles sadly. "I told him to stop the nonsense. Killing him would not change my life. And, anyway, he wasn't responsible for what happened to my son. Killing him or any other Palestinian won't bring my beloved son back to me."

On the day of the Sbarro's bombing, Eli Picard's nineteen-year-old son, Eyram, was on his way to the restaurant to meet friends. Seconds after the bomb exploded, he called his father to inform him of the attack and to assure him that although he had planned to eat lunch there, the bomb had exploded before he could enter the restaurant, and so he was safe. Dr. Picard received the call from his son only five minutes before he was paged by the hospital to come immediately to the emergency room because there had been a terrorist attack and dozens of wounded were expected momentarily.

He hardly had time to think. When survivors of the blast were carried in, Eli Picard forgot about everything else except tending to the wounded. "It was a carnage the likes of which I had never seen before," he recalls. A religious man, he remembers doing triage in the ward, stanching the flow of blood and praying that this kind of atrocity would never happen again. He admits that he kept thanking God for having saved his own family from this kind of catastrophe. Three months later, however, tragedy struck the Picard family.

It was a Thursday night when Dr. Picard's oldest son, a parachutist in the Israeli army, called him at home. The doctor was spending a quiet evening with his wife on one of the few evenings when he was not on duty or making rounds. The call from his son was the one that every family throughout that region of the world dreads. Apparently his son had heard through army channels that a young Palestinian man had entered a school in Atsmona, a settlement near Tel Aviv, armed with weapons and grenades and had opened fire on a group of youngsters who were studying there. Eli Picard's younger son, the one who had survived the Sbarro's attack, was there fulfilling his military service, studying the Torah since he was unable to serve in the regular army because his eyesight was bad. Within minutes, Dr.

Picard learned that fifteen people had been killed and more than twenty had been injured. His son was among the wounded. An hour later he learned that his son, suffering from multiple gunshot wounds to his chest, had been rushed in critical condition to the Tel Hashomar Hospital in Tel Aviv. Shortly after Dr. Picard and his wife arrived at the hospital, about an hour's drive from Jerusalem, their nineteen-year-old boy had succumbed to his wounds.

The next day, a videotape was broadcast throughout the Arab world that showed Eyram Picard's murderer celebrating the deed.

In July 2002, I visit the Gaza home of Mahmoud Farhat, the nineteen-year-old Palestinian man who had killed Eli Picard's son and fourteen others during that attack, injuring more than a dozen more. Mahmoud's mother, Um Nidal, explains that the video that had caused such a sensation was in fact made by one of her other sons and showed the last few hours of Mahmoud's life.

On the tape, the future martyr is shown with his mother in the garden of their home. He is pictured with a green band across his forehead featuring the words "Allah Akhbar," back-dropped by green flags and slogans written on the concrete walls of his parents' house. He caresses a Kalashnikov. Um Nidal hugs her son and kisses him as the voice on the tape explains that she is giving him her blessing to go out and kill Jews in the name of Allah. At one point in the video, Mahmoud takes off the green bandanna and places it on his mother's head in a symbol of solidarity with her, not only to

166

show that she is aware of his plan but to demonstrate that she is proud and approves of his decision to die.

The second portion of the video deals with the aftermath of Mahmoud's successful suicide mission. Throngs of people mingle in the courtyard at the entrance to his parents' home in Gaza, spilling over into the garden. The younger men are shooting guns in the air, while the older men are throwing candies. The women are crying, some wailing, wringing their hands and pushing each other out of the way to touch the martyr's mother. There is a frame in the film when Mahmoud's father, obviously weeping, takes the barrel of a shotgun from one of the young militants and lowers it, asking the shooter to refrain from making that celebratory gesture. As the camera moves into the interior of the house, the body of Mahmoud is on the floor of the living room on a stretcher, bound in a white sheet. The wounds on his head and face are wrapped in bloody white bandages.

The excitement reaches a deafening crescendo as the women and men push each other out of the way to touch the body. One woman, the wife of one of Mahmoud's brothers, weeps, her hands covering her face in reaction to the sight of her slain brother-in-law. It is obviously too much for her to bear. One of the most shocking moments on the video is when Um Nidal, clad all in white, the color of mourning in the Arab world, kneels on the floor beside her son. Covering his face and hands with kisses, she finally sits up and raises her arms in a gesture of praise. Her face is covered with her son's blood.

During the course of my visit with Um Nidal, she explains her feelings and her reasons for sending her son Mahmoud, the youngest of her twelve children, to die a martyr's death. "Jihad is a

167

commandment imposed on all of us," Um Nidal begins. "We must save our sons' souls, all the time. What we see every day—massacres, destruction of homes, murder of children and old people—only strengthened my resolve." Um Nidal goes on to explain that when Mahmoud was only seven years old, she hid Imad Aqi, the Al-Qassam commander of the Izz al-Din, the military arm of Hamas, in her house from the Israelis for fourteen months. During that time, other mujahideen would visit to discuss military operations with Aqi. She says that Mahmoud was the only one of her children who was fascinated with the fighter (although Um Nidal's oldest son, Nidal, set out to become a martyr, but was stopped by Israeli soldiers and sentenced to eleven years in prison, where he remains today). "Mahmoud would listen to every word Aqi said," she recalls. "He would carry messages for the other mujahideen, watch the roads for Israeli soldiers, and listen to them planning operations. Mahmoud was Aqi's pupil."

Um Nidal believes it was then that Mahmoud first had the idea to become a martyr. "The atmosphere to which Mahmoud was exposed," she explains, "was full of faith and love. He learned at an early age that a man's faith does not reach perfection unless he attains self-sacrifice."

When Mahmoud was eight years old, Israeli soldiers came to the house in search of Imad Aqi. Um Nidal says her son was not afraid, even when they shot and killed Aqi in the family garden. Mahmoud had covered his mentor's body with his own. "He was prepared to die even then," Um Nidal says. "It was just not his destiny at that moment. That would come later."

According to Um Nidal, before his successful attack at Atsmona her son had tried on numerous occasions to achieve

168

martyrdom. "He would go out to the Al–Muntar Road [in Gaza, not far from a Jewish settlement], taking his gun. When he returned, he would be so disappointed because the opportunity just didn't present itself. He would return with his blood boiling. He would brandish his weapon and tell me that his gun was like a bride. He loved his gun so much. Every time he left to try and make a martyr operation, he would tell me that he couldn't control himself. He only wanted to succeed."

Throughout those years when Mahmoud failed to achieve martyrdom, Um Nidal claims that she would calm her son. "I would tell him that an opportunity would happen and to be patient, plan well, so that he wouldn't act in vain. Act with your mind, not your emotions, I would say to him. Be a man, I told him. My job was to give him psychological training, to be optimistic. His brothers in Hamas trained him to shoot and all the other military actions he needed to know. I was his emotional support."

On the day of the Atsmona attack, Mahmoud came to his mother and told her that this was the day he had been preparing for all his life. It was then, according to Um Nidal, that another son had the idea of making the video and including her in it as an example to other mothers that they should support their sons' actions.

"I never saw Mahmoud happier," Um Nidal says. "After we made the video, he set out for the operation with cold nerves, calm and confident that it would succeed. But still, I was worried that he would be arrested. I prayed for him when he left the house and asked Allah to make his operation a success and give him martyrdom. Then I got a call from his brothers in the Hamas who told me that they had heard from him and he had managed to get inside the settlement. He had cut the barbed-wire fence and killed two giants, Israeli guards. I began to pray from the depths of my heart that Allah should give me ten Israelis for Mahmoud, and Allah granted my request, and his dream came true when he killed more than ten Israelis. I began to utter cries of joy."

Minutes before he was killed, Mahmoud called his mother from his cell phone to tell her that Allah had answered their prayers.

When the operation was over and the Israeli media broadcast the news, Um Nidal and the other members of the family were watching television. At the moment it was announced that the "terrorist had been felled after killing fifteen Israelis and wounding twenty others," Um Nidal happened to be in the kitchen. When she walked back into the living room, her oldest son stood up and embraced her. "Congratulations, Mother," he said. "Your son is a martyr."

Curiously, throughout the entire interview, Um Nidal's husband, the father of Mahmoud, never said a word. He sat quietly next to her on the sofa in their living room. On several occasions it was clear that he was fighting back tears.

During all my visits to other homes of martyrs or failed *shahides* and *shahidas*, without exception, the fathers and brothers are silent, allowing their wives and daughters to justify the deadly actions of their sons. Despite the blatant subjugation of women in this part of the world, it would seem that when it applies to suicide bombings, the women have become the voice of the nation.

Technically, the case of Um Nidal is different from those women who actually take it upon themselves to commit an act of martyrdom in the name of Allah. And yet, by setting an example to other mothers when she sent her son off to die a martyr's death, Um Nidal is considered a pioneer in the woman's role in this Intifada, just as Wafa Idris is considered a heroine of the struggle. Dr. al-Rantisi talked about the responsibility of women, especially mothers, in the struggle to liberate "Islamic land."

During the interview from his home in Gaza, as he cuddled his six-year-old granddaughter on his lap, Dr. al-Rantisi talked about the role of children, the sons and daughters of all good Muslims, who have the obligation to strive for the ultimate reward of becoming a *shahide* or *shahida*. "In the Koran," Dr. al-Rantisi begins, "there is room for women to share in the struggle, and we understood that when our land fell under occupation and enemies invaded Islamic land. Women as men should share in the struggle to defend their land. While Wafa Idris's mother was proud but ignorant of her daughter's intentions, as was Darine Abu Aisha's mother, there are some [mothers] who know in advance that their sons and daughters are about to be *shahides* or *shahidas*. A woman like Um Nidal is burning inside and therefore has the will to defend our people. This woman has a strong Islamic background, and she believes that all men and women, even her own children, should fight against the enemy."

When religious or political leaders within the Palestinian culture expect their mothers to express joy and pride when their sons and daughters commit suicide attacks, they are inadvertently creating a breed of women who are different from other mothers in other parts of the world. They are doing these women an enormous disservice by encouraging something akin to racism against Palestinian mothers who, for the cameras and journalists, are conditioned to contain their feelings of grief and expected to

171

show joy and pride when they learn of a child's death. During all my interviews with Palestinian women who have lost a child in a suicide attack, although their initial reaction did indeed appear to be joy and pride at the fact that Allah had "chosen" their offspring as martyrs, in the end they wept and admitted to feeling anguish and pain. Accusing the religious and political leaders of betrayal might have been the next step in a normal process of grieving or anger, but that would take enormous courage within a society such as this one that punishes its own people for not following all political and religious rules without question.

Um Nidal would appear to be the exception since every sentence she uttered concerning her son's death was steeped in rhetoric. And while it is true that she did not show any apparent display of grief, there is another explanation for her stoicism.

Iyad Sarraj, who has studied this problem every day in his practice, gives the following reasons for Um Nidal's ability to contain her feelings. "When someone dies there is a feeling of loss," Dr. Sarraj begins. "There is no doubt that a mother who offers her son always grieves for him, but then there is a psycho-logical process, a denial of death. Often she believes that her child is not dead because she doesn't want to believe she has lost him forever. She lives for a time, supported by the cultural belief that whoever dies a martyr is not really dead, and this helps her to deny that her child is really gone. But go and see this woman six months later and you will see something called a delayed grief reaction."

During my final meeting with Um Nidal, nine months after her son died, she continued to express her pride in her son. "After the martyrdom operation," she began, "my heart was peaceful about Mahmoud. I hope all my sons die a martyr's death, and I wish this even for myself. After all this, I was honored to have received the body of my son, the pure *shahide*, in order to look upon him one last time and allow all the well-wishers who came to us in large numbers and participated in our joy and in his martyrdom to see him as well."

It is only then, when I ask her a question that forces her to address a basic human instinct, that her attitude changes completely. It is as if I am talking to a different woman.

"You carried this child inside you for nine months," I say, "and then you sent him off to die. Where did you get the courage and the faith?"

She pauses and seems to have trouble breathing. Tears well up in her eyes, and she covers her face with her hands and weeps. Several moments pass before she finally looks up again. She can't answer. But in her silence, Dr. Sarraj's thesis is validated.

CHAPTER FOURTEEN

DR. SARRAJ ACKNOWLEDGES the sway held by autocratic religious and political leaders, since he had his own run-in with the persuasive force of the Palestinian Authority, a supposedly more liberal entity than Hamas.

In 1998, Dr. Iyad Sarraj, along with Haidar Abdel Shafi, a prominent Palestinian lawyer, and several other Palestinian intellectuals, applied to register a new political party, the Movement of Democracy, within the Palestinian Authority. According to Dr. Sarraj, the deputy minister of the interior promised prompt approval if he and Haidar Abdel Shafi would agree to some minor changes in the wording of their application. "I was in charge," Sarraj says, "and quickly agreed to the requested alterations, which were not substantial. Then the deputy minister became difficult to reach. Weeks, then months, of false promises followed before our request was denied. We were told that

174

the denial of our right to form a political party came from the highest office, namely Yasser Arafat."

Eventually, Sarraj was arrested by the Palestinian Authority and imprisoned for several weeks as an example to anyone else who had the idea of creating an alternative political party. For something like this to happen to Iyad Sarraj, an internationally respected doctor, writer, and academic who travels throughout the world making speeches and holding conferences on the Palestinian situation under Israeli occupation, it would appear that no one has a free voice within that culture and society. And, once again, for women the situation is even worse.

Mira Tzoreff, the Israeli academic, believes that women like Um Nidal are in fact not prepared to give their children as martyrs. "I don't agree with the party line of the Hamas," she says. "They are not willing to sacrifice their sons. I think she is absolutely the same mother as we know in other cultures, countries, and religions, but the context is a tragic one; that is to say, the context of being sacrificed by the national leadership, and I don't necessarily mean Arafat, but the nationalistic atmosphere in which these women live makes them look as if they are ready to sacrifice and give up their children, as if there is no bond at all when they pose with them and send them off to die. You know, they are living in a not very democratic surrounding, and the discourse in which we see those videocassettes is a dictated discourse. It is dictated from above and they have to sacrifice their sons because they are promised a better life with their other children if they do that."

Tzoreff is convinced that these mothers have a far different moral response going on inside their hearts. "Occupation is an oppression from the outside, and their own leadership oppresses them from inside," she says. "They can't say what they think and feel. They must have a national explanation, and that is to see Israel and the United States as the ultimate enemy. Encouraging suicide bombings is a strong example of a united force against those two military powers."

Another point that Tzoreff makes is that the Palestinian society is not like Western societies. "This is a reactive national culture, a collective atmosphere," she says. "We are talking about postmodern versus nationalistic, and that makes all the difference. People cannot stand alone or think for themselves."

If Mira Tzoreff and Iyad Sarraj are correct, there is within Palestinian society a *silenced* majority rather than a *silent* one, which is not surprising given the atmosphere that surrounds the mothers, fathers, sons, and daughters who live under an occupying force and an autocratic regime. In a religious atmosphere where Imams and revered spiritual leaders issue edicts in the name of Allah, or announce *fatwas* taken directly from the Koran, their words, coming from God, become law.

In a political atmosphere where one person—Yasser Arafat—has total charge of all financial, banking, social service, educational, and administrative systems, and in a judicial system where lynchings of suspected collaborators are commonplace, a free thinker is a danger and a threat to the dictatorship. A woman who is free spirited and independent is not only a danger and a threat, but also a disgrace.

Shalfic Masalqa is another Palestinian psychiatrist who has spent his career studying the motivation of suicide bombers as well as the acceptance of their deeds by their families. When I visited him at his home in Bet Zafafa, a suburb of Jerusalem, I watched in wonder as his six-year-old daughter played with a neighbor, a six-year-old Jewish child who, Dr. Masalqa informed me, was her closest playmate. For him and apparently for the family of the Jewish child, this was a regular occurrence that each family viewed as completely normal and usual. At the same time, Dr. Masalqa was aware that in any other part of the world, when children of a different race, creed, nationality, and religion play together, it does not become a "human interest" story in the daily newspapers. "Education plays a big part in bridging differences and mitigating hatred," Dr. Masalqa explained. "When we suffer under occupation, we suffer for our Palestinian brothers and sisters, but personally we are not in the line of fire."

It is difficult to imagine what it is like for the average Palestinian who lives under Israeli occupation. As we who live in a democratic society understand, to be caught in a traffic jam for any length of time increases our level of stress. To be forced to wait hours just to pass a checkpoint in order to go to work produces a level of stress that often turns into violent rage. As an Israeli Arab who travels regularly between his home in Bet Zafafa and the city of Ramallah on the West Bank, even Dr. Masalqa is subjected to the rigors of checkpoints and security interrogation. Unlike the average Palestinian, however, Dr. Masalqa is far more fortunate. He is educated, earns a decent living, owns his own home, and is able to provide for his family. In addition, as an Israeli Arab, he has the necessary identity papers and an Israeli passport, which enable him to travel outside of Israel and the Occupied Territories without risk that he will be unable to return.

"First of all, I'm an adult," says Dr. Masalqa. "Humiliation for adolescents takes on far greater proportions and has far more serious repercussions than for an adult. If I get stopped at a checkpoint, the soldiers can't humiliate me because I am secure in who I am. But if a fourteen- or fifteen-year-old boy is humiliated, at that moment, at that very instant, being kicked or being forced to lean on a wall, is the moment a suicide bomber is created. That is what makes the pathology. Add to that the other realities, such as where this youngster is returning to, where he lives, what his day-to-day life is about—without education, his father out of a job and unable to feed everyone, or watching a male relative beaten by soldiers. All that youngster can do is explain his experiences at that moment by the fact that it is the IDF [Israeli Defense Forces] soldiers who have done this to him and to his family. It is much easier to make a projection and say the only reason why I am so badly off is because of the occupation."

Dr. Masalqa agrees with Dr. Sarraj that the overwhelming reason that mothers such as Um Nidal are able to convince themselves that the death of their sons is glorious is the tremendous religious influence on the society. "We use religion when it helps us," he explains, "and in this case religion is used to encourage the denial after the fact, that the child is not really dead but alive in another place. In fact, religion or those who use religion for these purposes describe what happens after death in Paradise and they make it very attractive compared to this life under occupation." He adds that given the circumstances throughout the West Bank and Gaza, choosing martyrdom only demonstrates that the real cause for such an act is based on depression and deprivation.

"To be tempted to go to Paradise means that life on earth is hell," he says. "Would they do it if their life was good? If they had a reasonable environment, education, an ability to live with dignity and earn a living, would anyone choose death?" And yet Dr. Masalqa qualifies his position when he says that someone like Um Nidal must be examined carefully in psychological terms since he believes she is an atypical Palestinian mother.

"When such a case happens," he says, "it is a combination of the personal pathology and the atmosphere, and both aspects meet to create an unusual situation or reaction." He points out that mothers in all countries send their children to war, knowing that they might die. "In this case, however," he continues, "the difference is that it is certain that they will die and there is no hope for return. But I believe that these mothers do not represent all Palestinian mothers. In fact, during the months I spent in the West Bank and Gaza, I met Palestinian mothers who, during the difficult days of the Intifada, kept their children awake all night, playing, studying, reading, talking, watching television, just so they would be exhausted and sleep all day, so there was no chance they would go out and confront soldiers and tanks and get killed or injured. I am afraid of this [other] image to the outside world, as if Palestinian mothers don't care for their children," Dr. Masalqa continues. "But when we find such a mother, we must delve into her childhood traumas that account for her willingness to sacrifice her child."

According to the meager details she offers about her own life, Um Nidal is a devout Muslim and a loving mother and grand-mother. She was born in 1944 in Ramla, where she witnessed the death of her parents in 1948 when the family was forced to flee after the creation of the Israeli state. She came to live with relatives in Gaza when she was five years old and experienced material and personal hardship throughout three wars: in 1956 during the Sinai Campaign, in 1967 during the Six-Day War, and in 1973 during the Yom Kippur War. But perhaps more telling is something she says shortly before our interview ends, while standing on the exact spot in her garden where she recorded the video with her son.

"I have never made a decision on my own. As a girl it was God who took my parents and fate that brought me here to Gaza. My marriage to my husband, a cousin, was arranged by my family. The Israelis made rules for me and my children under which we lived all our lives. My strength came from Allah, be praised. When my son decided to become a *shahide*, his father was against it. I decided to support Mahmoud in his decision and I did it alone, without my husband or the Israelis telling me what to do. When one of my other sons asked me to make the video with Mahmoud before he died, it was a moment when finally I could stand up and speak for myself and be an example for all the other mothers whose lives were similar to mine."

Dr. Eli Picard, whose son was one of the victims of the Atsmona attack, is not bitter. He chooses his words carefully. "When a mother sends her son out to kill other children, one can wonder if there is any hope. Any child of nineteen can be easily influenced. These are poor, desperate kids who are promised a reward of Paradise and seventy-two virgins. Of course, what is terrible is that they take others with them. It is true that you can't transform a person's soul. But where there is no hope, there is no life."

Dr. Iyad Sarraj says, "Think about mothers who are so proud that their daughters and sons become suicide bombers, and what we have is a suicide society. Women are the hope for the future. What will be the next generation of mothers born under

Posters honoring Wafa Idris, the first Palestinian *shahida*, plastered walls around the al-Amari refugee camp in Ramallah in January 2002 after the twenty-six-year-old blew herself up in Jerusalem, killing one Israeli and injuring more than a hundred others.

Mabrook Idris displays a portrait of her daughter.

Minutes before she detonated her explosive belt, twenty-year-old Darine Abu Aisha called her mother to apologize for sneaking out of the house that morning without permission; her cousin introduced her to Hamas recruiters at Al-Najah University in Nablus, where Darine studied English literature.

Ayat al-Akhras and her fiancé just weeks before she killed herself along with seventeen-year-old Rachel Levy and a security guard outside a Jerusalem supermarket

Ayat al-Akhras videotaped by her handlers immediately before she gave her final testimony in March 2002

Andalib Suleiman is recognized as the fourth female martyr of the current Intifada; in the bottom right corner of this poster is a depiction of the al-Aqsa mosque in Jerusalem, a symbol of the Palestinian resistance movement.

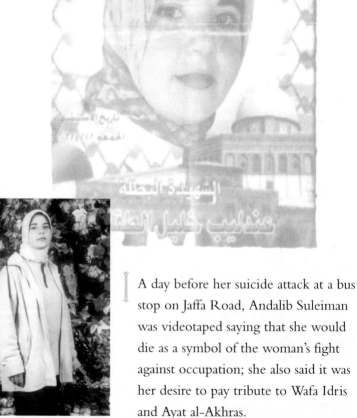

A day before her suicide attack at a bus stop on Jaffa Road, Andalib Suleiman was videotaped saying that she would die as a symbol of the woman's fight against occupation; she also said it was her desire to pay tribute to Wafa Idris and Ayat al-Akhras.

Fifteen-year-old Shireen Rabiya was recruited as a potential suicide bomber by her uncle, who told her that in Paradise she would be considered brilliant and popular; she failed in her assignment, and he is in prison near Tel Aviv.

The author, middle, with two Palestinian women imprisoned for stabbing Israelis—acts of *Jihad Fardi*

Abdul Aziz al-Rantisi, spokesperson for Hamas

Sheik Ahmad Yassin, spiritual head of Hamas

Yasser Arafat delivering his "army of roses" address, January 27, 2002

Zahira Kamal, a Palestinian feminist active in the Women for Peace movement, saw the involvement of women during the first Intifada, in 1987, as "a step forward in creating a democratic society where women are equal and not under the control of religious extremists."

Liat Pearl, spokesperson for the Israeli border police, said that because of the new threat of female suicide bombers, the Israeli government has changed its procedures to be as aware of women carrying bombs as men. "Our men and women are trained to detect the slightest unusual expression, odd behavior, twitching, pacing, anything that is suspicious. It is not possible for someone who is about to blow themselves up to look average or normal."

Israeli border policeman in camouflage, ready to go on patrol. According to Israeli security officials, proactive military and intelligence action to prevent suicide attacks is one aspect of an effective counter-terrorism response, along with a political understanding of the problem that terrorists say justify the attacks, and the public's ability to endure them.

Palestinian children in Jenin in May 2002, near a building partially destroyed by Israeli tanks. Refugee camps across the West Bank have proven to be fertile breeding grounds for suicide bombers, both male and female.

occupation? What will be the atmosphere for the generations to come?"

The question made me remember an incident that occurred in Jenin. During the course of interviewing and filming the mother of a suicide bomber, she held up her grandson, the forty-day-old baby of her own martyred son. "Look at him," she said. "When he grows up, no Jew will be safe from his wrath." When I returned to my hotel in Jerusalem that evening, I couldn't stop thinking that if there had been a way to take that baby out of that atmosphere of death, he would have had a chance for a normal life—or at least a chance to live until his twentieth birthday.

Perhaps Shalfic Masalqa says it best when he states that "extremism in religion or nationalistic or political zeal makes people blind." He offers Yigal Amir, the man who assassinated Prime Minister Rabin, as an example of a Jewish extremist whose ultimate act of murder was the culmination of a lifetime of radical teachings against any conciliation or peace with Palestinians. "The Arab culture is not an individualistic culture, as in the West," Dr. Masalqa explains. "Our mentality is to sacrifice ourselves for the nation. In this society, religion and culture go together. There is no separation. Things that are allowed in the religion pass into the culture. They are not refused. They are taken as gospel, and that is the danger. Society can sometimes use something from the religion for its own purposes and make distortions." And yet he believes that there are two messages for the Israelis in response to this wave of self-sacrifice that costs so many lives on both sides of the struggle.

"The circumstances of occupation are horrible," Dr. Masalqa says. "They produce killing and suicide bombers. When they [the Israelis] change, the Palestinian society will change as well.

Because the circumstances have been so terrible for so many years, and because the psychology of the child is so different than the adult, so much more impressionable, we are left with this tragedy. Only if we allow the peace negotiations to proceed can our children have a chance at a normal life."

During the hours I spent with Um Nidal, her eight-year-old grandson and his six-year-old sister sat cross-legged on the floor of the living room. They were mesmerized by a television program, a cartoon that showed a little boy of about their age confronting Israeli soldiers. With the golden dome of the al-Aqsa mosque behind him, the little cartoon character gathers stones to throw at the soldiers, until finally he is shot and killed. A white flower appears on the screen and one of its petals falls lightly to the ground, symbolic of either a tear for the lost child or the child himself falling away from his friends and family. The next scene is a cemetery where there is a mound of earth covering a fresh grave. One small white flower pushes up through the ground. This time the symbol is of rebirth—the little boy rising from the dead, stronger and more determined than ever to fight his oppressors. As the image of the flower fades, the little cartoon boy appears holding a large rock bigger than he is. The narrator's voice explains that the perfect moment of unity has come to this child, when he has found his place in Paradise next to Allah. After he dies a martyr's death, he has become stronger and more powerful.

Dr. Iyad Sarraj explains that if one analyzes Palestinian history from 1948 up to the first Intifada in 1987, followed by the peace process, which brought more humiliation and despair instead of a solution, it is clear that the children who were exposed to Israeli violence back then have become the suicide bombers of today.

"According to our research," Dr. Sarraj says, "the beatings and killings of their family and friends, the sacking of their homes, all turned these children into something that is inconceivable. The children of today are preoccupied with the question of death and killing, and that is alarming. They are a generation who aspire to become martyrs. If you ask a child of ten what he wants to be when he grows up, he will say that he wants to be a *shahide*. It means that unconsciously he believes that in ten years, when he is twenty, instead of going to university and becoming a doctor or a lawyer, he knows he is going to die."

Rafi Sourani is the director of the Palestinian Center for Human Rights and a respected lawyer in Gaza. Most of his practice deals with Palestinians who bring legal claims against the Israeli government: for the death of a relative or because their homes have been destroyed; to protect their homes if they happen to be related to a suicide bomber; to try to get a permit or a visa to leave the area with the guarantee that they will be allowed to return; or for something as banal as securing a permit to build an extension to their home. Mr. Sourani tells a story about his own eight-year-old twins.

"We live a privileged life in Gaza," he says. "My villa is never bombarded and we have plenty of food and luxuries. My children go to a private school. Imagine my surprise when they came home and asked me to buy them guns. But when I took them to a toy store, they laughed. 'We want real guns, Daddy,' they told me, 'to defend our country. We want to die for Palestine.'"

Sourani shakes his head. "If my children, who have everything, feel this way, can you imagine how easy it is for the children in the refugee camps to strive for martyrdom?"

CHAPTER FIFTEEN

THE PROGRAMMING FOR THIS NOTION of honor and national cause begins early in life and permeates an entire society in a way that makes it easy for eventual recruitment. From kindergarten on, children are taught the Koran by a system called *Da'awa*, which is to repeat what the Imam or teacher reads them directly from the holy book and accept it without interpretation or question. Ironically, the schools themselves are all run under the auspices of the United Nations, which opposes teaching children that the ultimate goal in their lives is to die for a liberated Palestine.

In April 2002, I visited a U.N. school in the Jabaliya refugee camp in Gaza. When I arrived there with my cameraman, I spent an hour talking to the director of the school and his female assistant. From the beginning, the director, Mohammed Abdul, made it clear that he would give the official position of the United Nations when it comes to *shahides* and *shahidas* and then, if I liked, he would give me his personal opinion. "We want peace with the Israelis," he begins, "and obviously we condemn killing of civilians, children and women on either side of the struggle. Here in Jabaliya camp, we encourage the children to study and learn so they can go on to university and have a successful life. But you understand that we are working against all odds when the Israelis close the schools or impose curfews on the people so that life stops." He pauses. "I have seven children," he continues. "Every night when I come home I kiss them all and spend time with each one because I don't know if, tomorrow, I will ever see them again. They could be killed at any moment." Without warning, he begins to weep uncontrollably. His assistant pushes a box of Kleenex toward him and he wipes his eyes. Several minutes of silence pass before he is composed and able to speak again. "I understand why children want to die defending their homeland, and in all good conscience I cannot discourage them. How can I tell them that they can ignore what is happening all around them? How can I guarantee them that their fathers or brothers will not be shot just because they are on the street? The Koran tells us that if we die as martyrs, we will have a better life in Paradise. That is what the children are taught. How can I ask them to live a life under occupation that gives them nothing and then forbid them to talk of achieving martyrdom and living for eternity in Paradise?"

Throughout the West Bank and Gaza, the influence of Hamas and Islamic Jihad is enormous (in addition to their obvious religious base they also supply money for hot meals and warm clothing). According to Nihad Abu Ghosh, a leader of the Democratic Front for the Liberation of Palestine (DFLP) whose organization is Marxist and at the other end of the political spectrum from the ultra-religious Hamas or Islamic Jihad, another reason that Hamas is so popular throughout Palestinian society is that it is not corrupt. "They are clean, which is their big advantage over Arafat and the Palestinian Authority," Abu Ghosh says. "They take very seriously the five pillars of Islam [which are martyrdom, the declaration of faith; *zakat*, charity; *sawm*, fasting for the month of Ramadan; *hajj*, the pilgrimage to Mecca, required by all Muslims who can afford it; and *salah*, ritual prayer five times a day]. There have never been financial scandals with the Hamas. If someone arrives from the United States, for example, with one million dollars from charity, he will empty his pockets and give one million and ten dollars if he happens to have a ten-dollar bill in his pocket. People throughout the Occupied Territories and Gaza trust Hamas because the leaders live among the people. They have direct contact with the people on a daily basis, as opposed to Arafat who is separated from his people."

After the interview with the director of the school in Jabaliya camp, I was then permitted, along with my cameraman, to visit a class of six-year-old girls and a class of twelve-year-olds. The director and his assistant, as well as the female teacher, were present in each classroom. When I entered the classroom of six-year-olds, the children all stood and, in unison, recited a short welcome speech in Arabic. Following, each child, with the encouragement of the teacher, explained what they study: alphabet, reading, writing—the usual subjects for children in the first grade.

When I was permitted to question the class, I initially explained that I wanted to know how they felt living under occupation. Several of the children raised their hands and shared personal experiences. "Tanks, soldiers, shooting," one little girl explained, while another told me about how her "eyes burned from something the Jewish threw in the streets."

Who is afraid? No hands went up.

Why aren't you afraid when you see guns, tanks, and soldiers? All the hands went up. "Because Israeli soldiers are cowards," one child said. "They have tanks and guns. They hide behind their big machines."

How can you defend yourselves? More hands went up. "We pray to Allah to make us strong," a little girl replied as she walked to the front of the room. "They can't hurt us because we pray to Allah."

And finally, after about thirty minutes of questions and answers, I asked the class how many wanted to be martyrs, *shahidas*? All the hands went up, waving excitedly. I chose three little girls, the one who was standing beside me at the front of the room and two others, who, with the encouragement of the teacher, came up as well.

Why do you want to be a martyr? "To have everything in Paradise," one answered. "To kill the Jewish," another added, "and to live near our God." The third little girl waited several seconds before she finally said, "We never die. The Jewish die but we live forever."

My cameraman, Stéphane Rossi, filmed the entire exchange.

Living in the West Bank or in Gaza—surrounded by photographs of those young men and women who had strapped on a bomb and set out to blow themselves up and take as many innocent civilians with them as possible—is a constant reminder to these children that martyrdom is the ultimate achievement: their life's goal and their divine fate if they happen to be lucky enough to be one of the chosen ones Allah selects for this extreme honor.

187

In the summer, Hamas as well as the Islamic Jihad organize camps on the beaches of Gaza and in empty fields throughout the West Bank. If not for the purpose of these outdoor excursions, it would be the only carefree moment these children have in an otherwise tragic existence. But the point of these outings is preplanned and very specific. There, sitting cross-legged in tents in the sand or on the grass, children listen to their counselors recite passages from the Koran that glorify martyrdom, when they are not simulating military assaults or pretending to be suicide bombers. Each child, including the girls, is armed with a plastic Kalashnikov and grenades. Only the most militant and enthusiastic of these campers are rewarded with a mock explosive belt and encouraged to go through the actual training and implementation of a suicide bombing attack. Children realize quickly that the way to win the approval of their teachers is to be the most militant, nationalistic, and religious, even at age six.

The idea of martyrdom follows the children through the rest of their daily lives as well. Early morning cartoon programs, such as the one I watched at Um Nidal's house, depict little boys and girls struggling to reach the al-Aqsa mosque in Jerusalem, being shot and killed by Israeli soldiers and rising up again as stronger and bigger children, prepared to continue the battle for liberation. At six, this kind of play-acting is a game, since the concept of death and dying remains an abstraction. When questioned, however, what these children are very clear about, even if they cannot yet grasp the finality of this kind of violence, is that death offers them a far superior existence in Paradise than a life with an absence of hope.

On December 29, 2002, in Tulkarm in the West Bank, Abdul Karim Salameh, ten years old, was engaged in what has become the most common sport in that part of the world—throwing rocks at Israeli soldiers. Often, the game ends tragically, as it did for Abdul when he was shot in the head. He died instantly. Several days later, his mother, Salman Salameh, received friends and neighbors who came to pay their respects despite the fact that it was difficult to leave their homes because Israeli troops had been occupying Tulkarm since July of that year. From the Israeli side, the justification for the constant curfew was that more than twenty suicide bombers had come from Tulkarm. This was why more than a dozen homes had been destroyed and the army had built a barbed-wire fence around the town, as well as erecting checkpoints on all the roads and patrolling the streets. When Abdul went out to throw stones, the atmosphere was tense. As one Israeli soldier told me, "We had our fingers on the triggers at all times."

Accidents happen, as do deliberate targeted killings. Sometimes children are caught in a crossfire or bullets ricochet into houses, killing their occupants, or soldiers return fire from Palestinian gunmen who take up position behind civilians. There have been many cases where Palestinians who work for foreign news agencies as journalists, translators, or photographers have been killed in the course of a day's work.

The day after Abdul died, his school chums lingered on the spot where he fell, the earth still splattered with his dried blood. His closest friend, Hussein Abu Shanab, tries to explain the events leading up to Abdul's death. "We started to throw stones when we saw the Israeli soldiers coming toward us in a bullet-proof jeep," he begins. "As they passed, we threw more stones, which bounced off the protective plastic of the jeep. We thought they were going away, but suddenly the jeep made a U-turn and came back to where we were. That's when they shot at us. Abdul was the only one who got hurt."

During a visit with Abdul's mother, who was pale and grief stricken and could not stop shaking, she manages to explain that she had always warned her son about throwing stones at armed soldiers. She shrugs. "He said he wanted to be a martyr," Mrs. Salameh says. "All the children say they want to be martyrs. They play with stones. They play Intifada. They don't understand what martyrdom is. They're just kids."

Martyrdom has become the most popular trend that separates the "in" kids from the nerds. Contrary to articles in the press in which journalists have referred to this dangerous "fashion" as parallel to drugs in Western societies and equally as deadly, martyrdom is considered neither a social ill nor criminal activity that ruins young lives.

Continuing my visit at the school in Jabaliya, the director took us to visit a class of twelve-year-old girls. Without exception, all were wearing the *hijab*. This time there was no collective greeting or discussion about their curriculum. Obviously, they knew of our visit in advance and were taking everything very seriously. Only days before, there had been what Palestinians described as a "massacre" by the Israelis in Jenin. The young girls were extremely tense and visibly angry. For the camera, the first twelve-year-old stood up and explained why she wanted to be a *shahida*. "To follow my brother," she said. "And, in honor of Wafa Idris, who proved that women can do as much as men."

Another girl followed. Standing, she explained, "I want to give back to my country everything I can, in gratitude to God. It is only normal that I give the most I can, which is my life, to free my people from occupation."

Finally, a third girl, Tuha Aziz, who looked far older than her years, walked with purpose to the front of the class. Standing next to her, the director, his assistant, and the teacher all smiled and moved aside for her to be in the perfect camera angle. "I will be a martyr," she began, "and I have already talked to the people who will train me. My reasons are obvious: the massacre in Jenin, in Jabaliya, in Nablus, Gaza, and Ramallah. There is no hope for peace because the Jews have no heart. They destroy everything and every Palestinian knows there is no chance to make peace with them."

During Tuha's discourse, she faltered several times and her teacher supplied her with a missing word while the director patted her gently on the back, smiled, and encouraged her to continue.

Did her parents know about her plans to become a *shahida*?

"My parents know and they are proud," she answered. "My parents know about my brothers and sisters too. They are proud of us all because they know it is the only way to conquer the Jews and have a homeland."

The older group of children who attend summer camps, from twelve to sixteen, not only understand that the military training

191

offered there and during after-school recreational programs is to be taken seriously, but they also are very articulate about what is expected of them. Tuha Aziz explained that she was only "waiting for the day when the leaders will consider me old enough to have an explosive belt."

During a visit to the camp in July 2002, Tuha's mother was there. Asked how she felt about the activities that were offered, she said, "I am proud. My little ones are too young to think about being *shahida* because they would get caught before they could commit the act. They have time. My older daughter [Tuha] will be ready soon."

Nihad Abu Ghosh explains that Hamas is not just a religious or political organization within the West Bank and Gaza, but a group that has vast financial resources. "In every city throughout the Occupied Territories," Abu Ghosh says, "Hamas not only has a recreation center that sponsors summer camp and after-school activities, but they also have vocational programs that teach women how to sew and teach men how to be mechanics or work machines, and for both men and women they offer sports lessons."

Among the most important facilities that Hamas has are computer labs, with all the necessary equipment that is too expensive for people to buy on their own. "When a child with no shoes or money comes from Jabaliya camp," Abu Ghosh says, "and you teach him the Internet, or you teach him how to type and print and do all the other functions that will make him equal to every other child in every other country and eventually be able to compete as an adult for a job, you have a vast influence on society. There are three hundred thousand people who benefit directly from Hamas charities in Gaza and the West Bank, even kids from families who have no martyrs."

The most popular television programs for pre-teens and older adolescents are music videos, in the same style as seen on MTV, except that the songs are always about those who have died in suicide bombings. One of the most frequently played is about Wafa Idris, the "flower of womanhood." While the sultry rock star sings about her martyrdom, Wafa is shown on the screen in a series of photographs from her early childhood until shortly before her death when she worked for the Palestinian Red Crescent. After the video ends, Tuha and her friends explain that when they are fifteen they can join the Women for Wafa Idris Martyr's Brigade and commit their acts of *shahida* in their idol's name.

If dying for the nation of Palestine and dying to "sit at Allah's table" in Paradise have become, for some, cherished goals, they are, for most, at least highly admired actions. Throughout the towns and villages, on the walls of the houses and apartments in the refugee camps, all over the hospitals and municipal buildings, schools, and police stations are photographs of every man or woman who has ever committed a suicide attack. For example, covering the walls of Um Nidal's house are posters of martyrs, including her own son, right next to a large photograph of Imad Aqi, her son's mentor. But this kind of glorification of *shahides* and *shahidas* is not limited to public spaces or private homes.

In addition to his position as head of the Palestinian Red Crescent, Dr. Fatri Arafat, Yasser's brother, is president of an association for handicapped children. Included in the wares that the children make and sell to maintain their charity are craft items that have a martyrdom motif. Carpets embroidered with images of

193

martyrs holding Kalashnikovs are popular, as are coasters with the faces of the women who have blown themselves up in the name of Islam. From these handiworks, adults and children alike understand the message of Jihad: to fight until death for an Islamic Palestine. Even at the office of one of Gaza's most prominent feminists, Andalib Audawan, who has made tremendous strides for women's rights within the institution of marriage and divorce, there is a photograph of Andalib Suleiman, a *shahida* who blew herself up at the Mahane Yehuda outdoor market in Jerusalem on April 25, 2002. When I asked why she kept the photograph, Andalib Audawan replied, "Because we share the same name."

There is also an awareness from the time children are old enough to walk that the brothers of those women who have committed suicide bombings are revered. If rock videos have turned Wafa Idris into Britney Spears, the male relatives of every *shahide* or *shahida* also become instant celebrities and immediate heroes on a par with soccer stars and rappers. While the aftermath of the suicide bombing elevates both men and women to superstar status, the reasons for their decision to die differ greatly among men than among women, as do the rewards they receive in Paradise.

During their final video, when they give their reasons for sacrificing themselves as martyrs, men always offer justifications steeped in religious convictions, while in their final videos the main focus of the women's words is their sense of nationalistic pride and the abandonment of Palestinians by their Arab brethren. Based on what several failed women suicide bombers have said, the real reasons that motivate women, as opposed to the rationale that creates male suicide bombers, are subtle and indicative of the second-class status of women in that part of the world.

CHAPTER SIXTEEN

THE UNMARRIED PALESTINIAN WOMAN today lives under a stringent set of social and religious rules: if she is too educated, she is considered abnormal; if she looks at a man, she risks exclusion; if she refuses to marry, she is thought to be out of control; if she sleeps with a man, and especially if she gets pregnant, she disgraces the family and risks death at the hands of her male relatives.

This threat of death is not hollow. The concept of honor is so embedded in Arab culture that, according to Nomi Chazan, honor killings still occur. "Don't make the mistake to assume that honor killings happen only in Gaza or Jenin or in Saudi Arabia," Chazan cautions. "I deal with so many young Arab–Israeli women who fear for their lives at the hands of their fathers or brothers." Andalib Audawan concurs that the threat is real and the fear is warranted. When I ask her for my camera what happens to an unwed mother, she has great difficulty formulating the words. "In our culture," she begins, "when an unmarried girl is pregnant, there are three solutions: either she marries her partner, her father hides her in the house, or . . . "—and here she pauses before concluding—"her male relatives kill her."

In a religious atmosphere in which rules and edicts are handed down under the auspices of the "word of Allah," any notion of women's rights is absolute anathema. What's more, life under occupation has produced two tragic paradigms: that life on earth is merely a preparation for a better life in Paradise, and that a life replete with humiliation and violence is hardly a life at all. Historians and psychologists agree that the second Palestinian generation born under Israeli occupation, particularly women, is doomed to a life of hopelessness, regardless of any future peace process or political resolution. So if these people are forced to live in a society filled with punishment and prohibition, and if they are offered equality and respect only by becoming martyrs, it is not surprising that there is an increasing number of Palestinian women who are opting for the latter alternative.

What has evolved in the past decade, since the failure of the Oslo peace accord, is that Palestinian society, once rich in academic achievements and intellectual prowess, has been hijacked by extreme Islam. Today, women in the West Bank and Gaza, from the moment they are born, are destined to be sacrificed to the extremist views that terrorize not only the West but also those members of their own society who have dreams of creating an independent, democratic, and secular nation. These views, largely influenced by an extremist concept of Islam, push a potential *shahida* to the limit,

196

to where she romanticizes the concept of Paradise and seals her own fate as a martyr. A Palestinian woman's choice to commit suicide, or participate in an act of martyrdom, or send off a son to die in the name of God/country/honor is a misguided and pitiful attempt at liberation.

Andalib Audawan is not optimistic when she summarizes the situation within Palestinian society. "The extreme version of Islam has dominated our society, and I say it with sadness, that it's a tragedy first for us. There are always logical explanations and excuses why our leaders have adopted this policy, to keep their base of power or to get us out from under occupation, but I don't accept this. The simple explanation is that all the extreme groups are using suicide bombers to send a spectacular message, and they are using women because it is the most effective way to send this message. God help us all if we don't stop this insanity now. And yet if men are doing these kind of actions, then it is within the realm of equality that women should be allowed to do them as well."

The fact that women began committing acts of Jihad Fardi, or personal initiative attacks, after they were forbidden to participate with the men during the first Intifada is revealing. According to interviews conducted by Professor Amikam Nachmani from Bar Ilan University, many committed attacks as a sign of their independence, or to escape harsh conditions in their homes. "These are the women," Dr. Nachmani says, "who found themselves still forced, by virtue of the rules of the society, religion, and family, to marry a man whom their parents had chosen. These are the women who decided that they would rather be in prison or die a heroic death like a man rather than be forced into a loveless and unfulfilling marriage. Other women who had problems living within the rules of society also preferred death to a life of humiliation and disgrace in their own culture. In a bizarre way, these women felt secure within the Israeli prison system, knowing that their male relatives could not reach them to kill them because they had disgraced the family."

In an interview that I conducted with a female Palestinian prisoner in an Israeli prison in July 2002, Fatma el Said recounted her reasons for having stabbed two Israeli soldiers at the height of the Intifada in 1987. "It was an act against occupation," el Said explains, "but it was also a way for me to prove to my family that I was as good as my brothers, since they were allowed to go to university and I wasn't."

Zina, who aided the suicide bomber in the Sbarro's attack, is an example of what happens to a woman who breaks with tradition and is subsequently offered a means to rehabilitate herself. Wafa Idris is another. As Wafa said to a friend only days before her suicide, "I have become a burden on my family. They tell me they love me and want me, but I know from their gestures and expressions that they wish I didn't exist." Darine Abu Aisha is yet another—a woman who killed herself because she couldn't face the prospect of an arranged marriage when her goal in life was to continue her education and work in academia. And, of course, there is Um Nidal, considered the quintessential symbol of Muslim motherhood, who sacrificed her son in the name of Allah. Probe deeper, however, and it becomes evident that Um Nidal felt she was finally acting on her own when she made the decision to participate in her son's martyrdom without the permission of her husband.

And yet, contrary to the popular political line, the use of women in the current Intifada has not transformed their role from passive observers to active participants in the struggle against Israeli occupation. Nor has it done anything to elevate their status within their own society. It has merely satisfied the agenda of various opposition groups within the Occupied Territories.

Dr. Nachmani believes that Wafa Idris and the other women who followed her are not pioneers. "The Palestinian leadership decided after the fact that women who committed these actions were the new example of liberated women. They were promised many things, but most of all, when Arafat and the rest of the Arab world realized how the sentiment in the streets supported their actions, suddenly they claimed that they had gained the same respect and admiration throughout the Arab world as the men."

Even in the weeks that followed Wafa Idris's death, despite the sensation her suicide attack caused throughout the Arab world, religious leaders still took into account practical considerations. During one of my visits with Sheik Yassin, he voiced a rather cynical caveat. He proclaimed that while women are "welcome as martyrs," he cautioned that they are less equipped psychologically and physically to carry out a mission than men. "Men are more efficient because they are better at hiding out with the bomb after having crossed the Green Line," he said. "They are stronger psychologically than women, who might not be able to stay hidden and alone in the dark in an orange grove or at the bottom of a garbage dump or anywhere until the moment for the attack arrives."

The sheik gave as an example the suicide bombing attack that occurred on the first night of Passover, March 27, 2002, at the Park Hotel in Netanya, in which a suicide bomber exploded himself and killed twenty-nine Israelis, mostly older people who were celebrating the first Jewish seder. "That was a much greater success," he stated, "than Wafa Idris's attack, which only killed one Israeli man, or Darine Abu Aisha, who only injured several Israeli soldiers." Nonetheless, the sheik went on to say that while he is pleased that women are participating in the struggle, he still believes that "not all women are made to be fighters, and in those cases they have other jobs that are just as important in ridding our land of the invaders."

It is no coincidence that Zina felt particularly honored to have been accepted into Hamas and allowed to aid and abet the Sbarro's pizzeria suicide bomber. She knew then, and she freely admits now from her prison cell, that to her it was a sign that the leaders of Hamas had put aside their prejudices concerning women fighting to liberate Palestine because they considered her so "essential" to the success of the mission.

The violence that prevails today not only produces bloodshed on both sides of the struggle but promotes death equally among males and females. When it comes to dying in the name of Allah, the interpretation of the Koran releases the male suicide bomber from a sense of guilt or bad conscience associated with killing himself and civilians. Now, in the period after Sheik Yassin's special *fatwa* has been issued, religious training has been adjusted to free women as well from the moral restraints that have, in the past, been practiced in the Muslim religion.

A remarkable insight into this situation is seen in a petition drafted by two leading Palestinian intellectuals, Sari Nusseibeh and Hanan Ashrawi, that called for an end to suicide bombings. Apparently a ray of hope, it was distressing nevertheless that the reasons cited were that the bombings only provided the Israelis an excuse to reoccupy the Occupied Territories and the world an excuse to brand the Palestinians—once again—as terrorists. As human rights advocate Rafi Sourani remarks, "Nowhere was there any mention of the immorality of killing innocent civilians on either side of this struggle," while Nomi Chazan observes that there was "something morally missing in their petition."

Ironically, it was an Israeli, the feminist academic Mira Tzoreff, who defended Nusseibeh and Ashrawi's position, saying, "It was a brave step to come out against this. I'm sure they were afraid to say anything more that would have been a condemnation of the leadership."

Without exception, every woman and young girl who attempted to or succeeded in blowing herself up had been marginalized within Palestinian society. Some were divorced, like Wafa Idris; others pregnant out of wedlock, like Zina; while others were being forced into an arranged marriage, like Darine Abu Aisha. In some cases, again like Darine, they were the target of ridicule and exclusion because they were educated and intelligent. Then there is the woman who becomes a *shahida* because she watches a male relative, usually a husband, father, or brother, stripped of his dignity and ostracized because he has been accused of collaborating with the enemy. Given the importance ascribed to honor within Palestinian society, it is no surprise that such a woman might consider it an honor to die for the sake of her family.

Ayat al-Akhras is one more example of a young woman who opted to strap on an explosive belt and end her life.

CHAPTER SEVENTEEN

Ayat al-Akhras grew up in the Dehaishe refugee camp near Bethlehem. Her mother, Khadra Kattous and her father, Mohammed al-Akhras, were both born and raised in another refugee camp in the Gaza Strip, where they had ended up at the end of the 1948 war. After the 1967 war, when Israel occupied the Gaza Strip, Mohammed's family moved to the Dehaishe camp, as did Khadra's. It was there the couple met, in an atmosphere of poverty and despair that has become synonymous with the crudely constructed cinder-block buildings that are found in all the refugee camps throughout the Occupied Territories.

Three years after they met, the couple married and shortly after that, Mohammed began working for an Israeli construction company which was building settlements in an area called Betar Ilit, not far from Bethlehem. With a steady job and decent salary, Mohammed was more fortunate than most of the other Palestinians living in Dehaishe who suffered not only the psycholog-ical but also the financial hardships of living under Israeli occupa-tion. Eventually, Mohammed was able to move his wife and eleven children—four boys and seven girls—into a concrete house that he built in an alley in the refugee camp.

Things were relatively peaceful during the 1970s and early 1980s, until the first Intifada broke out in 1987 and the Dehaisha camp, along with all the other camps and neighborhoods throughout the Occupied Territories, became overrun with militants who confronted the Israeli army. Local youths fought street battles with the occupying army, friends and neighbors grew suspicious of one another's sense of loyalty, or worse, questioned their determination to survive at any cost. Dozens were killed and injured, often lynched by an angry mob that, during the uprising, considered a conciliator to be nothing less than a collaborator.

The oldest child in the al-Akhras family, Samir, was jailed twice for throwing stones at Israeli soldiers. Another son, Fathi, was injured by Israeli bullets, and one daughter suffered a miscar-riage when Israeli tanks rolled into the camp and prevented access to ambulances and hospitals. As the years passed, Ayat, the youngest girl, became consumed by a hatred for Israelis, although for a time she expressed her outrage intellectually. According to friends, she was obsessed by politics, enraged at the apathy of the Arab world, especially those who formed financial alliances with the United States. An outstanding student, the beautiful young girl with long dark hair and intense hazel eyes wanted to become a journalist, as her mother explained, to "communicate to the world about the Palestinian cause." Fiercely opinionated, Ayat always dominated conversations at family gatherings. "She would stick to her arguments even if everybody else argued the opposite," Mrs. al-Akhras says.

203

During a visit to the al-Akhras home in Dehaishe, long after the tragedy, it was apparent that despite her outrage at the Palestinian condition, Ayat was in some respects a typical teenager. On the walls of her small room were photographs and posters of Egyptian and Iraqi movie stars. On one side of the room was a narrow bed where she slept and on the opposite side was a large wooden armoire crammed with sweaters and skirts, shoes, and piles of headscarves, as well as a few possessions that she treasured during her brief life: her Koran and the Protocols of Zion. Observant but not fanatically religious, she wore makeup and dressed in smart Western clothes for school. On religious occasions, such as Ramadan, her head covered, Ayat would accompany her mother and sisters to the Temple Mount in Jerusalem where they would worship at the al-Aqsa mosque. Other than the occasional shopping trip to the outdoor market in Bethlehem, Ayat's world revolved around her school, her friends and family, and her ambition to change the plight of her people.

Shortly after her fifteenth birthday, her parents introduced her to Shadi Abu Laban who also lived in Dehaishe and was the son of a family friend. He was a quiet young man who had been obliged to drop out of school in order to help support his family. Postponing college, he went to work earning a living as a tile layer. Whether or not it was "love at first sight," is irrelevant, but Ayat and Shadi became inseparable. While dating in that culture meant seeing each other always in the presence of a family member, Ayat and Shadi nonetheless took meals together, walked, and spent a great deal of time at either his or her house. When they finally announced their intention to marry, both families were overjoyed. The wedding was set for July 2002 and it was Ayat who suggested that the party be held in the alley and in the street near her house so that that the entire camp could share their happiness and join in the festivities. After her wedding, Ayat planned to enrol at Bethlehem University to finally realize her dream – to study journalism and eventually work as a correspondent for an Arab newspaper in the West Bank. For her, there was nothing more meaningful or important than to report first-hand on the Israeli/Palestinian conflict to mobilize international support for the cause. Her most fervent belief was that without the support of the rest of the Muslim world, there would never be enough pressure on the Israelis and the Americans to force a solution for a Palestinian state.

Shadi Abu Laban, Ayat's fiancé, admits that he was far less politicized than she was, and he claims that often he would try and calm her anger by pointing out that they were among the more fortunate. "But Ayat was never calmed," he says sadly. "When the peace process was going on, she was disgusted by Yasser Arafat's conciliation with the Americans and was furious that the United States was so involved in a conflict that she believed was between Muslims and Jews."

By the time the second Intifada erupted in September 2000, many of the Dehaishe residents took a dim view of Mohammed al-Akhras's job with an Israeli construction company. His privileged position became even more glaring when, during the many curfews imposed on the Dehaishe camp, he was one of the only residents who was allowed out to oversee the various construction projects in the neighboring Jewish settlements. According to Shadi, Ayat was embarrassed and ashamed that as a result of her father's job and contacts she was able to live comfortably and have enough to eat. "People were going hungry," the young man explains, "and even though the family was always very generous to friends and neighbors, Ayat felt that working for the Jews was wrong."

Only months before Ayat's death, a group of local Palestinian leaders, members of the al-Aqsa Martyr's Brigade, appeared at Mohammed's house one evening. Ayat, along with her fiancé and her mother, happened to be in the living room when they arrived. According to Shadi, there were none of the usual niceties; the men refused to sit down and they declined an offer of coffee or green tea. Instead, the spokesman for the group stood flanked by the others and gave Mr. al-Akhras an ultimatum: either he quit his job and stop working "for the Jews" and "assume the hardships of the Intifada like all Palestinians, or suffer the consequences."

Mohammed al-Akhras is a small, muscular man with a shock of white hair, warm brown eyes, and a fearless attitude. To his family, he is a sensitive, loving father at his core, although he is not one to be cowed by emotion or tears. He stands his ground and makes no exceptions when he believes he is right, especially when it comes to not compromising the welfare of his family. Mr. al-Akhras recalls exactly what he told the al-Aqsa men who came to his home to issue the warning. "Politics is one thing and work is something else," he said. "We [he and the Israelis] work together, eat together, live together, like family. I love them like my children and they love me like an older brother. I'm concerned for them [the soldiers who guard the settlements] like I am for my own sons. I taught my children to love others. We hope for life. I never compromised my beliefs for an instant." He shrugs. "And anyway, my job with them goes back almost thirty years. Why would my leaving it now change anything? It was just a question of jealousy, of envy that I was able to support my family."

But not everyone who lived in the Dehaishe refugee camp saw things that way. People began to whisper, and as happens in a small community in dire straits and under constant pressure from an outside occupying force, the facts of Mohammed al-Akhras's relationship with the Israelis became exaggerated. If it began as a Palestinian man who happened to work for an Israeli construction company who should have quit in a gesture of solidarity with his fellow Palestinians, it escalated into a story about a man who was a traitor, a collaborator who had sold out his people in return for a comfortable life. Neighbors who were once close began shunning the family, and on several occasions there was nasty graffiti written on the stone walls of the al-Akhras house.

Mrs. al-Akhras has tears in her eyes when she talks about those trying times, and somewhere in the back of her mind she reluctantly voices the feeling that it was something that gnawed at her daughter, Ayat, perhaps more than her other children. "She adored her father," the woman says, "and at the same time she felt embarrassed. She begged me to talk to him." She shakes her head. "But what could I do? I was only his wife."

Samir, Ayat's twenty-seven-year-old brother, took his father's side. "Things became very difficult for all of us around the camp," Samir says, "and we talked about it at home every night. My mother and my other brothers encouraged my father to quit his job, but I was against it. He always brought us up to be against killing and violence. He is a decent man. He told us that if people want to fight

207

they should fight soldier to soldier, man to man. We suffered like anyone else under occupation, but my father always said that it was the leaders that made the war. Why should innocent Palestinians or Israelis pay the price for the vanity of the leadership?"

According to Samir, despite Ayat's reputation within the family for being the most outspoken, she maintained the respect that was expected of her and never confronted her father. "Looking back," Samir says, "I suppose it was odd that she never offered an opinion on the problems the family was having. I should have noticed something, but I didn't, even though it was strange that she just didn't show any emotion at all. It was as if she kept everything inside because she knew she had the solution to our problems." Mohammed al-Akhras adds, "We didn't sense anything at all, not anything that would indicate what she was planning to do. Had I known she was planning to do such a thing," he says, "I would have locked the door and thrown away the key."

One of the al-Akhras's neighbors, a man named Jamil Qassas who, at thirty-two years old, is one of the leaders of the al-Aqsa Martyr's Brigade in Bethlehem, was particularly bitter about Mohammed al-Akhras's refusal to quit his job. During the first Intifada, Qassas had witnessed his teenage brother shot and killed by Israeli soldiers. Ironically, shortly after Mohammed al-Akhras had been given the ultimatum, Ayat was visiting Qassas's sister at their house when soldiers fired shots through the window, hitting another brother.

"Ayat got hysterical," Qassas recalls. "I picked up my brother, who was bleeding very badly, and ran with him in my arms toward the nearest hospital. Ayat ran with me, sobbing and screaming." He takes a breath. "My brother died in my arms, and Ayat collapsed on the street. At the funeral, Ayat came up to me and said that the death of my brother had changed everything for her. She believed it was a sign from Allah that she had to do something to make her father and the others understand that any contact with the Jews only ended in bloodshed. I knew then that she was destined for great things. She had too much emotion and hatred inside her to just sit quietly while our people were being massacred like that."

The situation for the al-Akhras family became almost unbearable. There were no more trips to the local market because merchants refused to serve them; one of Ayat's sisters maintains that a child of hers was beaten by his classmates at school. "My father is a stubborn man," Riad says.

Although Mohammed al-Akhras refused to give in, he was unable to go to work because his neighbors blocked the entrance to his home. "Not only was there a curfew imposed on us by the Israelis, but there was an army of our friends and neighbors who prevented any of us from going out. Life was hell," Riad says.

Although her family didn't know, Ayat had decided to act. According to a friend who speaks on the condition of anonymity, Ayat approached one of the leaders of the al-Aqsa Martyr's Brigade. "It wasn't very difficult to know where to go in Dehaishe," the young woman says. "Every organization has a storefront recruiting headquarters: Hamas, Islamic Jihad, al-Aqsa. I was probably the only one who suspected what Ayat was planning to do. It wasn't that she was precise or that she told me exactly what the plan was in the beginning, but she told me that she had decided to do something drastic. I knew what she meant. Later on, she told me everything."

One of the reservations that Sheik Yassin expresses about women committing acts of martyrdom is that they are more "unreliable" than men. Not only did he assert that men were more prepared psychologically to remain in a dark, unpleasant hiding place than women, he also cautioned that women had a tendency to reveal their plans more than men.

Amir Levy, who works for the Israeli Foreign Ministry in Jerusalem studying the dispatches and reports issued by the Arab media throughout the Middle East, tells an interesting story. "About two days before Ayat al-Akhras blew herself up in Jerusalem," he says, "a friend of mine who lives in the Dehaishe camp warned me about going to crowded places. He told me that he couldn't be specific but that he knew for certain that someone in the camp was planning a suicide action and I should be careful. Unfortunately, even with this information we were unable to find out more details to prevent the attack."

The same friend of Ayat's who speaks on the condition of anonymity claims that the next conversation she had with her friend was the day before the attack. "She told me that there was only one chance to save her family from disgrace," the young woman explains, "and that was to become a martyr. By then there was talk around the camp that her father was going to be lynched and their home destroyed. There was no way out for the family."

Not only was the family kept virtually prisoner in their own house, but the tension throughout the camp because of the presence of

Israeli tanks, as well as the constant closures and curfews, made the situation even more unbearable for everyone concerned. "We all knew," continues Ayat's friend, "that the next time the Israelis entered the camp with tanks or there was a confrontation when a Palestinian got killed, the al-Akhras family would have paid for it. Ayat knew that too, and she told me that the only way to save her family from disgrace and even death at the hands of an angry crowd was to sacrifice herself. If not, the family was ruined. Ayat was very calm when she told me, and she absolutely understood what she was saying and what that meant. She had witnessed the senseless murder of Qassas's brother who was sitting in his living room watching television when he was shot by an Israeli soldier. But even before that, the anger had already built up in Ayat."

On Friday, March 29, 2002, only months before her wedding day, Ayat al-Akhras snuck out of her house at seven o'clock in the morning. Had the family noticed that she was not stopped by the Palestinian guards who kept vigil over the house, they might have suspected that something was amiss. But no one knew that she had left. According to the same girlfriend, she went directly to the home of one of the leaders of the al-Aqsa Martyr's Brigade, where she recorded a video that would serve as her last will and testament. On the video, Ayat is dressed in the usual symbolic garb, a long dress with her head wrapped in a checkered kaffiyeh. Identifying herself as a member of the al-Aqsa Martyr's Brigade, she affirms her intention to die in an act of martyrdom and, further, she assails Arab leaders for "doing nothing while Palestinian women are fighting to end Israeli occupation."

CHAPTER EIGHTEEN

Suicide bombings are a highly intricate enterprise. They never involve merely the bomber. According to Dr. Ariel Merari, the director of the Political Violence Research Center in Tel Aviv and a leading expert on this phenomenon, in not one instance has a lone Palestinian gotten hold of a bomb and gone off to kill Israelis. Suicide bombings are initiated by tightly run organizations that use at least ten people for each successful attack, and in every attack each person involved knows only his immediate superior and has no information about his coconspirators. "It is highly secretive," Merari explains. "Each person or link has a specific job, and knowledge is imparted on a need-to-know basis only."

The apparatus for the recruitment of suicide bombers operates on two parallel levels: the selection and training of the suicide bomber, and the operational preparation of the attack. On the first track, the potential suicide bomber is usually singled out when he or she joins a political organization as a militant or fighter during basic training. The person who has enlisted or recruited the potential *shahide* or *shahida* also accompanies him or her throughout all the stages of military training as well as the spiritual preparation for the attack. On a parallel level, the groundwork is planned for the physical aspects of the bombing itself. This includes preparing a safe house for the bomber, acquiring and hiding weapons, preparing the explosives according to the method to be used, and finally physically transporting the bomber and the explosives to the target area. And, of course, someone else writes the statement and accompanies the individual when it is time to make a video to memorialize the impending event.

All of these preparations are the primary targets of an Israeli counterintelligence operation. If the bomber can be stopped during these crucial steps, the act can be stopped. If the suicide bomber has already been dispatched to the intended target, security forces try and minimize the physical damage of the attack by keeping the bomber away from enclosed and crowded areas. Unfortunately, in the case of Ibrahim Sarahne, all counter-intelligence operations failed.

In a land where ethnic and religious identity is worn as a badge, being able to distinguish enemy from friend often means the difference between life and death. Ibrahim Sarahne is an example of someone who escapes easy definition or labeling. Nonetheless, he played a crucial role in four successful suicide bombings. In June 2002 he was arrested for complicity in those four terrorist attacks and charged as an accessory to the murder of more than fifty people. In July 2002, I visited with Sarahne in his prison cell in Tel Aviv and he told me his story.

As a Palestinian who lived in the Dehaishe refugee camp and drove a taxi on Israeli streets, Sarahne made it a point to offer immediate assurance to his Jewish passengers that he was bona fide and safe. "A good Arab," he claims his customers called him. "A Palestinian with the proper identity papers who knew enough to behave so he could continue to earn a living." In fact, Sarahne sought to bolster his "acceptable" profile by carrying forged papers that identified him as an Israeli Arab who was a resident of Jerusalem.

He claims that the decision to put his ability to pass Israeli checkpoints to "good use" was made not so much for political, nationalistic, or religious reasons, but rather because he wanted to prove to Prime Minister Ariel Sharon that while he could send Israeli forces across the border into the West Bank and Gaza to kill and injure Palestinians, it was possible to do the same thing on a smaller scale "in the other direction."

According to Sarahne, he offered his services to the al-Aqsa Martyr's Brigade "to help them successfully implement suicide bombings" because they were the most "secular" of all the groups. "God played no part in my decision," Sarahne maintains. "This was about pure force. I don't like to be pushed around."

For the al-Aqsa Martyr's Brigade, Ibrahim Sarahne was a jewel in the lethal crown that made their organization as successful at implementing suicide bombings as their religious counterparts.

214

His best asset was that he was able to fade into the Israeli population while scouting out accessible places for a bomber to attack, choosing those that were heavily populated with civilians. Equally important was that Sarahne, in his taxi with yellow Israeli license plates, could ferry suicide bombers to their target destinations without arousing suspicion.

Three years before his arrest, Sarahne married a Ukrainian Christian named Irena Polichik. Two years later, Irena learned that her husband had apparently neglected to tell her that he also happened to be married to a Palestinian woman who was the mother of his four children. That family lived far from Bethlehem, in a small village in Gaza. Irena Polichik was apparently less disturbed about her husband's double life, however, than she was determined to use her state of unholy matrimony as a way to kill Israeli civilians. Eventually, to facilitate their work together, Sarahne obtained forged identity papers that identified Polichik as a Jewish Russian immigrant named Marina Pinsky. Long after the fact, when both Polichik and Sarahne had been incarcerated, the real Marina Pinsky emerged to deny that she had ever, at any time, engaged in terrorist activities. If she was guilty of anything, it was her failure to report her missing identity papers when she discovered they had been stolen out of her purse months before.

As for Polichik, when asked why she agreed to work with Sarahne, she replies, "I agreed with everything my husband thought. He set out to prove that Palestinians can get into Israel any time they want without any problem, regardless of a curfew." Claiming that religion was not a motivating factor, she also denied that either she or her husband had been paid or forced to provide their services. "I hated them [Israelis]," Polichik admitted, "and I felt no compunction about killing civilians, including women and children. They were part of the army that killed Palestinian civilians. Personally, I hated them because they discriminated against me. They only let me into Israel because I lied and said my mother was Jewish. If I hadn't, I would have been stuck in the Ukraine without any hope of a better life."

Sarahne admits that he not only drove four suicide bombers to their destinations, but he also clocked the times that certain areas in Jerusalem were the most crowded and reported back to the men who planned and implemented the attacks. He boasted that the most successful bombings—the ones with the most victims—were due to his meticulous research. "I took my job very seriously," he said proudly, "and I was always very careful. I was able to get away with it because the authorities never suspected me. I had the right identification and I understood the Israeli mentality. After all, I listened to so many Israelis in the backseat of my cab who claimed to like the good Palestinians, the ones that were grateful for the crumbs and who didn't rebel or make trouble."

Ibrahim Sarahne is the perfect example of what Prime Minister Sharon once described as "mixing banality and brutal purpose—the infrastructure of terror." Given the dramatic results of his actions, Sarahne's matter-of-fact recounting of his role in the attacks is particularly disturbing. When he talked about his secret contacts, simple radio codes, and convoys of innocent-looking vehicles that followed his taxi while carrying potential martyrs, he described them as "all in a day's work." "That's what made these kinds of attacks possible," he explained, "the simplicity of the planning. But after I dropped the bomber off and heard the ambulances and sirens and knew it had gone off as

216

planned, partly because of me, I can't describe the feeling of pure joy that I felt in my heart."

Of the four suicide bombers that Ibrahim Sarahne drove to their final destinations, the first and the last were both women.

For his final terrorist operation, on May 22, 2002, Sarahne took along his Ukrainian wife and their eighteen-month-old daughter in his red Toyota pickup. They followed another car carrying two teenage suicide bombers, a fifteen-year-old girl and her fourteen-year-old companion, toward Tel Aviv. It was Sarahne who picked out the Rishon Letzion site two days earlier, reporting that there were not only dozens of soldiers on their way back to their base passing through the city, but women and children too, who shopped at a nearby mall.

As they approached the checkpoint, the handlers in the lead car communicated with Sarahne by two-way radio using a simple code. The idea was that right before the convoy reached the checkpoint, the bombers would transfer into Sarahne's pickup truck for the rest of the trip toward the target site.

Arine Abu Said, the potential female *shahida*, had been a student in an exchange program with Israeli teenagers and was a member of the Israeli left-wing political group Peace Now. An Israeli Arab, she had learned Hebrew as a little girl and only a year before had attended discussion groups on a kibbutz in the Galilee to "try and find a solution to the conflict." When she learned that her boyfriend, Jad, who was twenty, had been shot and killed by Israeli soldiers during the standoff at the Church of the Nativity in Bethlehem, Arine decided that she wanted to "follow him to Paradise." One of the tragedies here is that long after the fact, Arine learned the truth about Jad. According to

217

one of the men who had recruited her, who spoke from his prison cell, Jad was killed in a "work accident," when the bomb he was carrying exploded prematurely.

Before Jad was killed, he had been an active member of the Tanzim in Bethlehem, and he had introduced Arine to his colleagues. When she announced her intention to become a martyr to vindicate his death, Jad's friends from the Tanzim organized a suicide bombing in which she and a fourteen-year-old boy named Mahmoud would blow themselves up at a bus station in Rishon Letzion. According to Arine, they told her that there were "seven steps to reach Paradise, and if you kill a Jew it counted for one step, and if you committed a suicide act you reached the seventh step without having to pass the other six. . . . They told me I would find Jad waiting for me in Paradise," she explained tearfully from her temporary jail cell in the Russian Compound in Jerusalem.

The plan was that Mahmoud would blow himself up first and, when pandemonium broke out, Arine would then detonate her own explosive belt to ensure the maximum number of casualties. But when she and Mahmoud arrived in Rishon Letzion, they both changed their minds. Arine claims that when she saw women and children, she couldn't bring herself to kill them. "I thought there were going to be only soldiers," she says.

According to Sarahne, after Arine and Mahmoud had transferred into his truck, he noticed that she was extremely agitated. When they finally reached their target, Arine began begging him to let her out of the car. "She kept pleading with me to let her go back home. She threatened that if I didn't let her out she would start screaming and give away the entire plan. Mahmoud was less hysterical although he seemed to go along with her. When I told Arine that there was no way for her to get back, she suggested that she could just hail a taxi. She told me she didn't want to die."

While Arine was resolute in her decision to back out, Sarahne and Polichik convinced Mahmoud to carry out his attack.

Arine confirms Sarahne's version of events. After Mahmoud successfully detonated his explosives and killed himself along with fifteen Israelis, Sarahne and Polichik, with Arine in the backseat, began the drive back to Bethlehem. "All the way back in the car," Arine says, "Irena kept yelling at me and pulling my hair. She spit on me and she called me a brat, a coward, a baby, and a disgrace to all Palestinian women." She pauses. "She was more upset about my backing out than Ibrahim, and in fact he tried to calm her down. She was crazed."

While Sarahne admits that he was disappointed that Arine decided not to die, since she remains his only failure in his career, he expresses joy that Mahmoud managed to kill so many Israelis. "Because of me," Sarahne maintains, "the operation was a success."

That evening, when Arine arrived at the home of her aunt, where she had lived since the death of her parents years before, she knew that it was "only a matter of time" until she was arrested. According to Arine, Nadja, her aunt, screamed at her when she came back, accusing her of lying when she explained her absence by saying that she had visited a friend's new baby. "She thought I had gone out with a boy," Arine says.

When the police finally came to her house to take her away, Nadja cried. "If you had made the right decisions," she told the girl, "you would have a better life." As Arine told the Israeli minister of defense who visited her in jail in an effort to find out why she had changed her mind and what had motivated her in the first place, Arine told him what her aunt had said. "I thought to myself at the time," she said, "that I *did* make the right decision in my life when I decided not to kill myself and lots of innocent people."

Weeks later, Arine's lawyer, Leah Tsemell, an Israeli communist who is renowned for representing Palestinians, made a petition to the court to make an example of Arine. Tsemell's point was that if the Israeli court would make an exception in her case, it would give other potential suicide bombers an incentive to back out before they killed Israeli civilians. However, the court ruled against her petition. Arine was sentenced to twenty years in prison.

Three weeks later, in June 2002, after Arine had confessed and implicated Ibrahim Sarahne and his wife, the pair were finally arrested. It was during his interrogation and during two subsequent interviews that he accorded for this book that he described his most spectacular suicide bombing, involving a seventeen-year-old girl who lived two houses away from him in the Dehaishe refugee camp. According to Sarahne, she had been his first attempt at helping potential *shahides* and *shahidas* to infiltrate Israel in order to kill.

On Thursday, March 28, 2002, Ibrahim Sarahne received instructions for his next attempt over his two-way radio from an al-Aqsa Martyr's Brigade operative, a known recruiter and trainer of women suicide bombers. Sarahne was instructed to pick up Ayat al-Akhras the following morning at a designated meeting place in the Dehaishe camp and drive her to her target destination in Jerusalem.

From his detention cell, Sarahne admits that he knew Ayat only vaguely from around the camp, although when he found out that she was to be his passenger he was not surprised. "Life was hell for her family," Sarahne relates. "It was just a matter of time before one of them exploded, although I admit I was surprised that it was a girl and not one of the brothers." Concerning the site of the attack, Sarahne claims that it was he who chose the target where Ayat would die. It was a grocery store, called Supersol, in the Jerusalem neighborhood of Kiryat Yovel. "I worked there for a while as a packer so I knew when it was crowded, the exact time, and how there was only one security guard who couldn't always check everyone. The best time was on Friday afternoon when the Jews shopped for Shabbat."

The pair crossed an Israeli checkpoint with the bomb in a bag on the floor of the car at Ayat's feet, next to her knapsack. Sarahne says that during the drive he suggested that he just throw the bomb, which would have allowed her to return home. "She refused," Sarahne says. "She said, 'I'm not afraid. I want to kill people.'"

CHAPTER NINETEEN

Although worlds apart in every way, Ayat al-Akhras and Rachel Levy were typical teenagers. The differences between them went beyond the fact that Ayat was Palestinian and Rachel was an Israeli. While the Palestinian was deeply affected by the violence in which she lived, the Israeli did everything to block out the ongoing conflict that caused so many needless deaths.

Avigail Levy, Rachel's mother, is a large woman with dark eyes and long black hair tied back in a ponytail. One of ten children from a family whose roots are in Morocco, she has always been extremely close to her ten siblings and widowed mother. In 1985, however, given the dismal financial situation, Avigail decided to move from Jerusalem to Los Angeles with her husband, Amos, and their three-year-old son, Guy. Her intention was to create an easier life for her family and because she had a sister who owned a small clothing business there,

Avigail had decided to work there and raise her family in America. Two months after they moved to California, Avigail gave birth to a daughter whom she named Rachel. In 1993, after having spent eight years in the United States, a family illness brought the Levys back to Jerusalem and it was there, in 1997, that she gave birth to her third child, a little boy she named Kobi. A year later, her marriage broke up and Avigail took the children to live in a small apartment in Ramat Sharett, a lower-middle-class neighborhood in southern Jerusalem where the buildings are drab concrete hi-rises overlooking one of the main Jerusalem shopping malls.

Long after the fact, Avigail recalls how, of her three children, it was her only daughter, Rachel, who had the most difficulty in adjusting to life in Israel. While Guy, the oldest, had been born in Jerusalem and little Kobi had as well, Rachel had grown accustomed to life in the United States. She had difficulty making new friends and, according to several teenagers who had gone to school with her, she never really adjusted to life in Israel. Her unhappiness reached the point where Rachel even refused to speak Hebrew and would answer her mother in English. Things changed, however, after Avigail sent Rachel to her sister's house in California for a summer vacation. "When she got back to Israel," Avigail says, "she told me that she felt at home here, that this was where she wanted to live."

Avigail was thrilled that her only daughter finally seemed to be adjusting to the rhythms of teenage life. When she talks about her daughter, she has certain very specific memories although she admits that by and large, Rachel was a typical teenage girl who was obsessed by her weight and worked out every day to stay slim. "She never ate properly," Avigail says, "mostly she ate a salad and a diet Pepsi when she went out with her friends." She pauses. "But she never went out unless she was perfectly dressed and showered. She always smelled of perfume and cream. She was perfect, always well groomed." Again she pauses to compose herself before she adds, "Even now I can still smell Rachel in her room, in her closet, in her drawers. Her smell remains. It permeates everything she touched. I can't bear to clean her room or touch her clothes. They are exactly as she left them when she went out on that Friday."

In a café not far from her house, a suicide bomber had blown himself up and killed three people. It was a place where Rachel and her friends liked to go, and even after the suicide bombing there, she refused to change her habits or discuss the possibility that she could have been sitting there when the attack happened. Rachel Levy, like so many other Israeli teenagers, was determined to carry on a normal life in what was a very abnormal atmosphere. According to her mother, she concentrated on school, clothes, writing in her diary and was consumed with the usual films and music that most teenagers enjoyed. When her mother read her diary long after the fact, she found it was filled with poetry about love and death, including passages from the Song of Songs and the Book of Psalms. It was obvious that Pink Floyd and Christina Aguilera were her favorite singers and according to one close girlfriend, the movies she had enjoyed the most were *Pretty Woman* and *Titanic*. As Avigail says about her daughter, "She continued to go to the mall and to the movies. She just refused to change her life." "She wasn't afraid of bombs," another friend, Tali Ganor, agrees. "I used to ask her why she wasn't scared to go out and carry on her life as if nothing was going on, because I know I was. But Rachel always told me that no, she wasn't. She was a fatalist."

Avigail maintains that she never discussed the political situation with her children because it was often so terrifying. "Whenever I had the news on because there was a terrorist attack," Avigail says, "the minute Rachel came home she turned it off. She just didn't want to know."

Nonetheless, Avigail, like all parents, constantly worried about her children when they went out. After each suicide bombing she called her family to make sure everyone was safe, and after she found out that they were, "life went on as usual."

Friday afternoon at the Supersol market was always busy as shoppers rushed up and down the aisles to prepare for the Sabbath. On this particular Friday, it was even more crowded since it was also Passover. Silvan Peretz, who usually worked in the front of the store at the checkout counter, was helping out in the back, wrapping chicken breasts for several customers before the store would close for the weekend. Because of the crowds of pre-holiday shoppers, the security guard who was on duty at the door had trouble checking all the shopping bags and parcels and inspecting purses and knapsacks. At exactly 1:49, Rachel Levy entered the market, her long dark hair falling down her back. At the same moment, Ayat al-Akhras, also with long dark hair falling down her back, walked toward the entrance. Around her waist was a belt containing ten kilograms of explosives lanced with nails and screws.

The girls almost touched each other as they both entered the store at the same moment. But as the guard reached out to stop Ayat, perhaps because her outfit was bulky and made him suspicious, a powerful explosion tore through the supermarket, destroying displays, shattering glass, and sending bodies flying. When the smoke cleared and the agonized screams subsided, the two teenage girls and the guard were dead. Hours later, witnesses would recall that the girl identified as Ayat al-Akhras had noticed two Arab women sitting on the sidewalk selling herbs as she entered the market. She paused and whispered to them. Seconds later, they picked up their wares and ran away.

Five minutes after dropping Ayat off at the supermarket in Jerusalem, Ibrahim Sarahne heard sirens and turned his radio to the Israeli army station. "I was happy that she succeeded," he says, "because that day the Israelis put fifteen hundred police on the street to prevent an attack and they failed." Later on, as he drove back toward Bethlehem, Sarahne noticed that Ayat had left her knapsack in his car. When he arrived at the Dehaishe refugee camp, he dropped it off at her father's house without any explanation.

By the time Avigail called her own mother, everyone knew that there had been a suicide bombing at the market. Her entire family rallied, and within a quarter of an hour her sisters and brothers were mobilized, running from hospital to hospital, searching the neighborhood and finally driving Avigail to the market to look for Rachel. "They wouldn't let me in the market," Avigail recalls, "but they assured me that there were only two bodies. The guard and the woman who had blown herself up."

The wait was excruciating. Rachel was responsible and always called. Now, more than three hours after she had left to buy some fish, seasoning, and rice crackers, there was no word from her. She was missing. An hour later, one of Avigail's sisters and a brother received a call from the police. Without giving any explanation to their distraught sister or other members of the family who were gathered at Avigail's apartment, they rushed out of the house and went directly to the police station. Once there, they were asked to describe the clothing that Rachel had been wearing. When they returned, Avigail was near hysteria. "I realized after watching the news reports and seeing the photograph of the suicide bomber," she says with quiet dignity, "that she resembled my daughter. I knew that somehow they had confused Rachel with the other girl and the body they had was my daughter's."

Eventually the police realized that they too had made a mistake and misidentified the suicide bomber. "I went down to the morgue," Avigail continues calmly. "I didn't have to, but I wanted to see her. They told me she had died instantly." She pauses. "Her face was beautiful, not a mark on it. It was her body that had been destroyed."

Hours later, Avigail learned from several eyewitnesses that Rachel had entered the supermarket at the exact moment that Ayat had walked in wearing an explosive belt. "People told me that when they saw them together, because they looked so much alike, both with dark complexions, long dark hair, that they thought they were two sisters who had gone shopping." Again, she pauses. "The other girl was beautiful too," Avigail says, "just like my Rachel."

★   ★   ★

On Fridays, the al-Akhras family had a ritual. They gathered together at the family home to have lunch. It was unusual that Ayat was late. The family waited and waited and still Ayat did not appear. Mrs. al-Akhras feared the worst. After waiting an hour or more, they finally started lunch without her. At the end of the afternoon, when the family was still gathered around the table, they turned on the television and saw that there had been a suicide bombing in Jerusalem. It wasn't possible that their daughter and sister had been anywhere near there, they reasoned. She had left the house in the morning to go to school, somehow managing to get past the neighbors who tried to block the family from entering or leaving. At any rate, that was what Mrs. al-Akhras and the others had assumed.

When day turned into evening and still there was no word from their daughter, both parents believed that somehow she had gone to Jerusalem without telling them and found herself in the middle of a bombing. But at nine o'clock that night, when they saw Ayat's face on the television screen, they understood that she was the young woman who had strapped on an explosive belt, killing herself and two others and wounding thirty more. Even when a group of militants from the al-Aqsa Martyr's Brigade appeared at the al-Akhras's house, shooting Kalashnikovs in the air and throwing candy at the curious children who had gathered, Mohammed and Khadra al-Akhras still refused to believe it.

More disturbing for them was the celebration that followed. While people flooded into the house to offer their congratulations, some nearly hysterical themselves because they were in the home of an actual martyr, one of Ayat's sisters went prostrate with grief. She had to be carried out of the room by her three brothers.

Ayat's parents were devastated when they learned that their

daughter had died while committing an act of martyrdom. Khadra, her eyes red from weeping, sat on her sofa in her impeccable home in the Dehaishe camp and shook her head. "For months I was planning my daughter's wedding," she says. "Now I can't even plan her funeral since the Israelis won't release my daughter's body." In reality, Ayat's remains were so scattered from the blast that it would take days before Israeli workers could gather all the body parts from the supermarket.

Somehow in the grief-stricken and confused minds of Ayat's parents there was still hope that their daughter had been the victim of mistaken identity or a victim of someone else's attempt to achieve martyrdom. Despite the videotape that she left, in which she was very precise in explaining her reasons for dying and taking with her as many Israelis as possible, there was an unwillingness to believe that Ayat actually committed this act. Mohammed and Khadra claimed that they have never seen the video, although they do have the knapsack that Ibrahim Sarahne dropped off after he'd driven the girl to her death. As she empties its contents, Ayat's mother holds up a copy of the Koran and a chocolate bar and asks me, "Is this what a girl would carry on her way to die?"

Before leaving that evening, I told Mrs. al-Akhras that I intended to see the mother of the Israeli girl who was killed in the bombing. Did she have a message that she wanted me to pass on to her? With tears in her eyes, she finally spoke. "Tell her I feel the same pain as she does. Tell her that a mother is a mother. I loved my daughter the way she loved hers and I suffer for her and for me." And then, suddenly, her tears subsided and her eyes blazed. "But they're the ones who came here from other countries. They are the ones who stole our land. If she had stayed where she belonged this would never have happened to her daughter or to mine."

That same evening, at Avigail Levy's apartment, the distraught woman opened Rachel's diary to read something to me. On her final day of life she had written about love and death. "She questioned what comes after death," Avigail says sadly. "I guess she found out."

Several weeks later, I tried to bring the two mothers together in a neutral place to meet. Khadra al-Akhras was willing, but Avigail Levy was not prepared to confront the mother of her daughter's killer. When I told her what Khadra had said, and asked if she had anything to say in return, Mrs. Levy replied, "I hope she didn't know. But how could she not? I knew every minute where my Rachel was, where she went. This other girl had to be trained for this. She had to be out of the house. Didn't her mother know where she was?" And then came the tears. "They come to a house that didn't do anything to them. They come to my home and they kill me. Rachel was my whole life, my whole life was Rachel."

Meanwhile, Jamil Qassas, Ayat's neighbor whose brother had been shot and killed when Israeli soldiers targeted him through a window, expressed pride. "How many children and innocent people have the Israelis killed?" he asks rhetorically. "This is a natural response. The equation works both ways."

Four months after Ayat's death, in July 2002, Mohammed and Khadra al-Akhras received me in their living room. Mohammed's wife sat next to him. Chain-smoking, he explained that although the al-Aqsa Martyr's Brigade has exonerated him of all suspicion of collaborating with the Israelis, he felt only grief and guilt in his heart when people suggest that Ayat's death was his ticket to respectability. "What's the difference," he asks, tears welling in his eyes. "The Israelis fired me because my daughter is a *shahida*, and now the people here in the camp treat us like heroes. They are angry at us because I refuse to take their money as a reward for being the father of a martyr." He looks contemptuously at one of his sons. "He thinks I should take the money," he says. "Never. To me, it's blood money. Money from the blood of my daughter."

Ayat's older sister prays on a small rug on the floor of Ayat's room. In place of the posters and photographs of movie stars that once adorned the walls is a large photograph of Ayat, the one that is now infamous, tacked up throughout the Dehaishe refugee camp in tribute to her final act of martyrdom

In January 2003, I returned to Israel and the West Bank and Gaza to finish the research for this book. I learned then that the houses of Darine Abu Aisha and Izzedine Masri had been destroyed by the Israeli military.

The al-Akhras family went to the High Court in Jerusalem in an effort to save their home from the same fate. As of this writing, the court has not yet brought down a final decision.

As for Avigail Levy, she exhibited enormous dignity and warmth during every one of my visits to her home, despite the unimaginable pain that she still felt after the death of her only daughter. She told me numerous times that never again could she feel joy or laugh; a part of her had died. I kept thinking that she was obviously in a state of shock and that, one day, she would release all the pent-up anger and pain.

231

Many months later, when Marwan Barghouti, a leader of the Tanzim, was on trial for planning numerous suicide bombings that resulted in the deaths of hundreds of Israelis, the Israeli prosecuting attorney invited some of the victims' families to court. It was then, when Avigail Levy confronted Marwan Barghouti in person, that she finally cracked. It was a heart-breaking scene; she had to be helped from the courtroom, sobbing uncontrollably. "You killed my daughter!" she screamed at Barghouti as he sat passively, seemingly unmoved by her pain.

CHAPTER TWENTY

WHAT MAKES SUICIDE BOMBING SO EFFECTIVE is the pre-meditated death of the bomber, the basis for the success of the attack. Dr. Boaz Ganor from the Counter Terrorism Institute in Tel Aviv says, "It's really very elementary. If the bomber doesn't press the button, there is no attack. The success of the bombing depends on his or her willingness to die."

Suicide bombing is primitive and sophisticated at the same time. It is primitive because from a technological point of view the mechanism is most simple. All you need is a person willing to kill himself, ten kilograms of explosives and nails to commit more damage, a simple understanding of electronics, and the knowledge to use an electric cycle with an on-off shunt. It is sophisticated because, unlike the more conventional operatives who plant bombs and are obliged to gather extensive intelligence to choose a highly populated area so the device goes off at the best time, a suicide bomber will actually see if the target is populated and, if not, can move to a more populated area. And the success rate is almost infallible. Even if the bomber happens to be stopped en route to the target, he can set off the explosives where he is and still kill one or two soldiers or police who have tried to stop him.

The suicide bomber chooses the time and place to execute the explosion so that it causes the maximum damage. In essence, he or she is a "smart bomb" that knows its way, is self-propelled, can choose its target, and leaves no clues behind. One of the most difficult tasks for the terrorist is to plan an escape route and not get caught in order to avoid interrogation. With suicide bombings, no escape route is necessary because the escape is to heaven and interrogation is impossible.

If the mechanics of the operation are relatively simple, however, the reasons for the recruitment and training of the young men and women suicide bombers are far more complicated. When I began this book, it was important to go beyond the technicalities, to explain how a *shahide* or *shahida* starts out as any normal human being who cherishes life before someone turns him or her into a killing machine. Although I circle back to the analogy of a fatal cocktail—religious extremism, the hardships of occupation, and fervid nationalism or patriotism—in the case of women, there is always that additional ingredient that pushes them to die in the name of country, honor, and God.

Dr. Iyad Sarraj claims that male suicide bombers are typically at the "high point of their lives: aware, active, euphoric." During their final videos, when they give their reasons for sacrificing themselves as martyrs, men usually offer justifications steeped in religious convictions.

Dr. Sarraj is troubled by the process that propels a woman to commit a suicide attack. "I believe the women who do this are an exception to the rule. Women are not that full of emotion or violence, and women in our culture are not known to take such an active role. So, I would have to assume that the women who did this are not only an exception but have other psychological symptoms that pushed them to this finality."

The moment when an apparently normal young woman with plans to marry, to continue a university education, or simply to care for her family decides to transform herself into a human bomb is barely imaginable. Yet there are similarities among the lives of these women that point to why some are recruited to be *shahidas*, while others continue to struggle in various ways under the hardships of an occupying force and the dictatorship of a corrupt regime. The most obvious explanation, and one that the leadership of the more militant Palestinian organizations acknowledge, is desperation and hopelessness. Dr. Sarraj is cautious when he offers his opinion. "It is true that the failure of the Oslo peace accord created an atmosphere of such profound disappointment and despair that a large portion of the population believed that they had nothing to lose and nothing to live for. Our nation has become one of anger and defiance. The struggle today is how *not* to become a suicide bomber, because there are long queues of people willing to join the road to heaven."

For women throughout the Occupied Territories, victimization in every aspect of daily life—religion, politics, and the social strictures of their own families and communities—becomes the final ingredient in that fatal cocktail. It is painful enough in life to be left by a husband; or to find yourself the focus of ridicule and disdain because you fell in love with more than one man; or to be considered damaged because you can't have a child; or to be forced to bear the full responsibility for raising a child as a single mother; or because you crave an education unavailable to you; or because tradition forces you to enter into an arranged marriage; or to feel the crushing responsibility of saving a beloved male relative from humiliation or death. But when every life opportunity ends with a closed door, when there are no friends who will offer emotional support, no professional fulfillment that could contribute to a sense of pride and independence, no structure in place within the society to help cope, economically or emotionally, with psychological or financial problems, and above all no assurance that there are second and third chances to begin again, then it becomes a little less mysterious why some of the more vulnerable women could be convinced to end their lives. When you add to these variables the notion that only death brings dignity and offers women another chance, one that is not available on Earth, it becomes almost understandable that they would opt for that alternative to end their suffering.

All men who recruit potential *shahides* and *shahidas* and transform them into human bombs are reprehensible. But in a culture where men enjoy an atmosphere of camaraderie and solidarity, bonded by their gender, pride, and privileged place in Palestinian society, those men who recruit their male friends for this dubious honor are perhaps less venal than those who prey on women. The relationship between the *shahida* and the man or men who seduce, recruit, and train her is different from the inception just because she is a woman. There is no complicity between them; the differences between men and women in a society steeped in

236

fundamentalism and a culture of double standards do not disappear even within that extraordinary concept of martyrdom. Women understand from the beginning that men do not accept them as equals or look upon them as warriors within their ranks until they achieve Paradise and are accepted as such at Allah's table. But by then they are dead. And there are no women who can testify to having had those promises fulfilled in another life.

Men like Sheik Ahmad Yassin, a man of God who invents rewards for women in Paradise that are not written in the Koran, such as promises of beauty if they are plain or a loving husband if they are single, or Yasser Arafat, a Nobel Peace Prize winner, who convinces women that they are his "army of roses" that will crush Israeli tanks, or Dr. Abdul Aziz al-Rantisi, a pediatrician who promises women "satisfaction" in Paradise, a chance to be their own master—these powerful men package the notions of equality, respect, and reverence so artfully that it becomes impossible for the vulnerable, fragile, and naïve girl or distraught young woman not to buy into them. Each of these men seduces women with promises that are easy and attractive for the potential *shahida* to grasp, imagine, and eventually respond to, since the idea of equality touches upon the very core of what they long for.

Alice Chalvi is the founding chairperson of the Women's Network, an advocacy group for women's rights. During the "good" years of the peace process, Chalvi, who is also professor emeritus of English literature at Hebrew University in Jerusalem,

237

had regular meetings with other Israeli feminists and their Palestinian counterparts. "What we had in common," Chalvi says, "was that we were working together for peace and understanding and mutual acceptance. There is still contact between Israeli and Palestinian women, although it's more difficult now for them to move freely across the Green Line."

The use of women as suicide bombers, especially under the guise of equality and liberation, gives Chalvi pause. "If a society prizes above all else the readiness to fight for your country, if that is such a criterion for excellence, then you cannot exclude women just because they are women. It doesn't seem right that women should be excluded from attaining that kind of glory, and one can argue in a perverted way that everything has to be open to women, and if everything includes dying or killing oneself in battle, then that has to be acceptable as well."

Andalib Audawan, the feminist from Gaza, goes beyond the classic notion of gender equality. "I believe that suicide actions are the outcome of despair," she says. "And women are just as desperate as men, so why exclude them from taking these actions just because they are women? There should be no difference and no rules that prevent women from doing the same as men."

Chalvi acknowledges the desperation but is horrified by the lengths that Palestinians will go to demonstrate their misery. "These suicide acts should create a moral polemic within the Palestinian culture as to where the society at large is going. Unfortunately, it has not . . . It seems to me that the degree of Palestinian despair now is so deep that there is a kind of comfort to kill the other side—to do unto us as we have done to them. It's that sense of pride that is so terrible. The Palestinian people

238

must be in such a state of despair to kill themselves or to glory in the deaths of their children. But unfortunately, from the time of Sparta and the Romans, death in battle has been glorified."

The late Ismail Abu Shanab, director of Sheik Yassin's office in Gaza, has a contradictory opinion. "It is not desperation that makes suicide bombers," Abu Shanab says. "It is a matter of creating something, and that something is reflected in the Jihad spirit that is increasing every day. Most of our martyrs are cultured and rich and educated, with master's degrees, so this is not a case of their being desperate. They are not poor. If you say someone is poor, desperate, or frustrated and they commit suicide, this is not Jihad."

Alice Chalvi contends, however, that for women it is different. "Choosing those women and girls as martyrs based on their failure to live up to the standards set by a society governed by militant Islamic edicts that treat women as second-class citizens is immoral," Chalvi says. And yet she maintains that any warfare leads to a "coarsening of the moral fiber. . . . Any society that controls another people has a coarsening effect," she continues. "To have almost absolute power over others means you must be a decent person not to exploit it, and that is rare. It goes against human nature. There were some leaders, however, like de Klerk and Mandela, who were great men because they were prepared to rise above the past and start anew. We need great leaders here."

Suicide bombing is not just a battle tactic but a device of religion that overwhelms the political goals it was meant to serve. In practical terms, the attacks have achieved only delay. If and when the time comes for another peace process to begin, it is unlikely that those militant Islamic groups will go along with any conciliation with Israel but will continue to use suicide bombings as a means to derail it. In response, Israel will continue to deal with suicide bombers on an intelligence, operational, and psychological basis and hold whoever is at the head of the Palestinian Authority responsible for controlling the extremists. At the same time that Prime Minister Ariel Sharon claimed Yasser Arafat was "irrelevant" because he was unable to control the extremists within his society he also held him responsible for suicide attacks. Now the question is whether the newly appointed Palestinian prime minister, Abu Mazen, will be able to control the militants or if he, too, will become "irrelevant." The reality is that the bombs will continue to be in Hamas's and the Islamic Jihad's court.

Adjusting psychologically to the reality of suicide bombers is crucial for Israelis. Just as Sheik Yassin explained that it is advisable not to allow the potential martyr to visit the target area before his or her mission, Israeli counterterrorist experts try to educate the general public before and after an attack. According to Liat Pearl, the spokesperson for the Israeli Border Police, there are three effective counterterrorist responses: an understanding of the politics that terrorists use to justify the attacks, proactive military and intelligence action to prevent them, and the public's ability to endure them. Pearl says, "We try to capture plans for future attacks during systematic raids on Palestinian homes; plant 'birds,' or Palestinians who are willing to elicit information from fellow prisoners in Israeli jails in return for favors or early release and new identities; even collect rolled-up bits up paper with details of attacks that are inserted into tiny Gelusil capsules in the bodies of visitors who, in the normal course of bodily functions, can pass them undetected to prisoners."

Now, with Palestinian girls and young women being used as human bombs because they can pass more easily through checkpoints, Israelis are adjusting to this new and terrible reality.

According to Liat Pearl, since the second Intifada began in September 2000, there have been more than 250 cases in which women were exploited for the liberation of Palestine. Four became martyrs; the others were captured and arrested. Some of those have been released, while the majority are still in Israeli jails. Because of this new threat, the Israeli government has changed its procedures to be as aware of women carrying bombs as men. Where once it was considered unnecessary and cruel, given the modesty code of Arab women, to subject them to body searches, new security measures have been established by the Israeli military and border police to detect any young woman or girl who is carrying a bomb or wearing an explosive belt.

"There is no choice," Pearl explains. "We have to check them because if we look at this problem from the point of view of sensitivity, we will miss them and they will cross over into Tel Aviv or Jerusalem and blow themselves up. But we still realize there is a line between not humiliating them and checking them well. For example, where it is possible, they are checked by women soldiers and police, and, if we can, we take them to a secluded area so they are not humiliated in front of crowds of people. If not, and if the woman is suspicious, or if we have received a warning about a female bomber who is trying to cross into Israel, and if there is no woman soldier or police and no secluded place to search them, we do as much as we need to protect the civilian population."

There are definite guidelines already in place.

"If she appears suspicious," Pearl explains, "because she refuses to cooperate and relinquish the heavy bag she is carrying or identify the bulge under her dress, security goes on high alert. We weigh her honor against saving lives, which is why our rule is not how much we *can* check a woman, or a man for that matter, but how much we *need* to check them given the circumstances. Every case is different."

The border police are trained to look for telling signs. Liat Pearl explains that someone carrying a bomb or wearing an explosive belt might be nervous, perspiring, or unable to look the security guard in the eye. "Our men and women are trained to detect the slightest unusual expression, odd behavior, twitching, pacing, anything that is suspicious. It is not possible for someone who is about to blow themselves up to look average or normal," Pearl maintains.

Security also relies on citizens to report any suspicious-looking individual, although Pearl is careful to explain that if she is too specific about what the border police and soldiers are trained to look for, it will serve as a warning for the "enemy" to train their operatives differently. "One example is Darine Abu Aisha," Pearl says. "From the moment she got out of the car at the Maccabim checkpoint, she walked approximately fifteen meters. When soldiers called out to her to stop, she began running. Obviously, when a security person sees someone running like that, his time is limited to make a decision whether or not to shoot, which is when his training takes over. Darine Abu Aisha walked another six meters before soldiers shot, but at the same moment she detonated the

242

bomb. It was just lucky that she didn't get any closer or she would have killed people. As it was, she severely injured two soldiers."

She continues, "The other problem is that soldiers or police often have no time to clear the area of civilians before they start shooting. We had two border policemen killed because they rushed a suspect and were right next to him when he blew himself up. Our training dictates that we point the gun and tell the suspect to stop and leave his hands away from his body. We do everything possible, keeping a safe distance from the person. That also gives us an opportunity to see if the person is cooperating and is innocent. We don't want to shoot an innocent person, so we give them a chance to stop and raise their hands. Our rule is usually to keep a fifteen-meter [approximately 50 feet] radius from the suspect. That is the limit if someone is carrying a ten-kilogram bomb. Closer, and our people can get injured or killed. Of course, we never know if someone is carrying a ten-kilogram or fifty-kilogram bomb."

On January 4, 2003, Suhad Gadallah, a forty-year-old mother of four from Nablus, strapped a bomb around her waist and headed for Petah Tikvah, an area near Tel Aviv that marks the old 1967 border between Israel and the Occupied Territories. Two Israelis, a young couple, happened to notice that she was holding her stomach and walking slightly bent over. According to the couple, they thought the woman was ill. Approaching her, they asked if they could help. In response, the woman began screaming and crying uncontrollably as she fumbled with the switch that would have detonated the explosive belt that was hidden under her blouse. At that moment, the young man lunged and grabbed Gadallah's arms. "I pinned them behind her back so she couldn't detonate the bomb," he says. "By then, there was a crowd around us and the police came quickly and subdued her, disarmed her, and took her away."

Gadallah was taken to the women's prison in Ramla, where I had an opportunity to talk to her before she was formally charged. The scene was as heartbreaking as it was chilling. Despite the fact she had four children at home, ranging in ages from five to fifteen, and a handicapped husband, she had made the decision to kill herself and take as many Israeli civilians with her as possible.

Why?

"My oldest son, Abdullah, was twenty," she explains, "when he was shot and killed by soldiers. My child is dead. I had no reason to live. I only wanted to avenge his death. I knew Allah would care for my other children and my husband. I didn't tell anyone. My husband didn't know."

In fact, on September 27, 2002, Abdullah Gadallah had been shot and killed by Israeli soldiers as he penetrated the Israeli settlement of Itamar near Nablus, armed with a Kalashnikov and three hand grenades.

While security officials in Israel scramble to find ways to combat the growing threat posed by female suicide bombers, religious leaders, politicians, and women from both sides of the conflict continue to debate the impact that women are having in the struggle against Israeli occupation.

Ghassan Khatieb, a leading Palestinian commentator, says, "Not only will it [the use of women as suicide bombers] make things more difficult for Israeli security, but for security throughout the world."

244

Khatieb believes that women are now setting an example that will "shame" the men into acting. "If the men see that women are prepared to do this, they may be more inclined to get involved."

Dalai Samaleh, a female politician from Nablus, says, "This [suicide bombing] was a reaction from all Palestinian women that this is their war against Israelis and America."

Vera Bakoun, dean at Bethlehem University, agrees. "It is the beginning. Other women will do the same . . . It is our right and our duty to fight in any way that we can and in any way that the men fight. There should be no difference. We are all victims of the same occupying force."

In an interview with Prime Minister Benjamin Netanyahu in July 2002, he told me that when women became involved in this "cult of death," it marked the beginning of the end of any hope for a civilized Palestinian society. "Every totalitarian regime crosses the line of humanity. We saw it in Nazi Germany and Japan and we see it here," Mr. Netanyayu said. "The excuse of desperation and occupation does not justify suicide bombings. When the French were occupied by the Nazis, they did not strap on explosive belts to kill German civilians, women, and children. The Palestinian society has descended beyond the depths of barbary."

During a subsequent interview with Foreign Minister Shimon Peres, while he was part of Prime Minister Sharon's coalition government during his first political mandate, he said, "I used to think that poverty brought terror, but now I believe that it is terror that brings poverty. And when you have terror, the first victims are always women. I want to see our withdrawal from the West Bank and Gaza. I want to see an independent Palestinian state, and we can achieve that, but only if the Palestinians will allow it."

CHAPTER TWENTY-ONE

WHEN A PALESTINIAN WOMAN feels that she cannot control or change her life, when she has no power over her own self-determination, she can become obsessed with her own inner conflict and pain, which is a classic symptom of depression. The pain frustrates the basic needs of the woman because it goes against everything that is normal. To change it she needs love, honor, recognition, success, appreciation, independence, and control over her new life. If she can't get those things, the situation becomes dangerous.

According to Dr. Israel Orbach, a psychology professor at Bar Ilan University near Tel Aviv who specializes in suicidal patients, human beings create dreams and lead their lives according to these dreams. "The dream begins when the individual is born. Each person has his own dream—intuitively, subconsciously internalizing experiences—and then makes the dream a goal to achieve. Hope gives everyone the ability and the desire to continue living. Even if the average individual understands that dreams can be broken, he also knows or wants to assume that there are other dreams that will present themselves to replace them. But if the dream is broken and there is nothing to replace it and give the person hope, then that is where the unbearable suffering begins. When the dream is dead, the dream of life dies, and that is critical, even if an ideal life is an illusion that most people hang on to."

Dr. Orbach maintains that suicide is a long process that begins with a series of failures and disappointments. He goes on to say that when someone cannot build what he wants or what he hopes for, the result is self-guilt and less self-esteem, and out of this process there is pain. In order to escape this pain, the person who is suffering tries to escape his subconscious. He tries to minimize the negative sense of his desire to die by stopping to think or being aware of his surroundings and his inner self. Instead, he tends to look at his life as a series of photos that have no connection with one another.

"There is a lack of equilibrium in the suicide patient that makes the suffering unbearable," Dr. Orbach explains. "He or she has no tool to control the pain and so experiences unbearable suffering in the soul which involves depression, anxiety, fear, and despair. The individual feels he is surrounded by desperate circumstances and responds by an intense, chronic depression. What could make the suicide go quicker, making the patient reach the point of no return, are environmental or cultural reasons that allow the process of self-destruction to accelerate from theory to fact."

One example of this is Darine Abu Aisha. Her best friend and her sister both said that she became nihilistic after constant pressure by her family to abandon her university studies. For her there was no sense to life, no feelings, no meaning, even no negative feelings. Darine became sentimentally apathetic, asleep emotionally. But when that tactic didn't work and the pain didn't go away, the suffering exploded and Darine had to find salvation in another way to eliminate that unbearable pain. And that was death.

Another example is Ayat al-Akhras, who watched her father suffer and anticipated the eventual suffering of her family. Her own source of suffering was aggravated by a feeling of self-loss. Ayat lost her way. She lost the notion of self, and loss has different definitions. It could be material loss, sentimental loss, or spiritual loss, which is very important for Palestinians, the loss of a loved one, or the loss of your self. In the case of Ayat, it was the loss of dignity and respect. She understood that her father had worked so hard to create something within the community and for the family, and Ayat anticipated that eventual loss, which created an empty space within her that provoked radical changes in how she reacted. As a woman and as a daughter, she wanted to be the one to save her father and prove that she was stronger than her brothers. It was telling in her final video that she alluded to the impotence of the powerful Arab nations when they did not come to the aid of the Palestinians.

And yet there are other people who experience sudden loss but who, despite their enormous pain, do not end their lives. Fremet Roth lost her daughter Malki during the Sbarro's bombing. According to her, she is "in constant pain." I asked her how she gets through the day. "I take care of my family," she said in a monotone. "I do what I have to do for my handicapped daughter. I try to write and read but I constantly suffer Malki's loss." Avigail Levy, another mother who lost her daughter, Rachel, to a suicide attack, explained how she manages to survive. "I have a little boy to care for and my mother is old and fragile. I live but I feel that I am living on the fringes of life. I am not really here. I can't feel anything anymore."

Andalib Suleiman Takatka, the fourth female suicide bomber, did not, at least on the surface, suffer from any of the hardships that over time affected her three predecessors, which makes her story perhaps more tragic than the others. Andalib developed a fascination for the female suicide bombers. Curiously, she is also the only one of the four women who was not the subject of lengthy reports in the Israeli media. The reason perhaps is that she had no sensational story. She was just a young woman who was easily swayed and who got caught up in her own fantasy of stardom.

In another society, Andalib might have ended up like countless other young women and girls who fall in with the wrong crowd and become addicted to drugs or involved in prostitution or a life of petty crime. Then again, perhaps if she had lived in another society she might have been rescued by an observant teacher or caring relative and sent to a psychiatrist or counselor for help. But Andalib Suleiman lived in the remote Palestinian village of Beit Fajar, where there is not even a local doctor, let alone a psychiatrist or school counselor.

The entire Takatka clan comes from Beit Fajar. Most of the

families belonging to the clan have intermarried with cousins in order, according to the elders in the family, to preserve their power. "To mix blood," Hussein Takatka says, "is to weaken the strength of the resolve."

Fahti Takatka is one of the older members of the family and considered a *hakim*, or wise man, because of the many family tales of his bravery when confronted by the Israeli military and his daring for having saved the lives of many of the young boys and men who were wounded during the first Intifada. According to Fahti, "There is nothing more beautiful in this world than to die a martyr's death. It is the only thing the Israelis understand because to them, more than any other people, life is the most precious of all treasures."

On April 6, 2001, his two grand-nieces, Iman Takatka, seventeen, and her sister, Samia Takatka, twenty-one, were captured by Israeli security forces as they prepared to carry out a suicide bombing at Jerusalem's Mahane Yehuda market. While Fahti claims that he was unaware of the girls' intentions until after they were caught, he is "overwhelmed with pride" at their daring. "My nephew, their father, came to me and apologized that they had failed. The only sorrow in his heart was that they were now in the hands of the Jews instead of our Prophet."

While there have been numerous men from the Takatka clan who have been killed or arrested by Israeli authorities, and three who have successfully committed suicide bombings, there had never been a woman who achieved that honor. When Iman and Samia tried and failed, they raised the consciousness of the women members of the clan that the time had come to sacrifice themselves on an equal basis to the men.

Andalib Suleiman, a member of the Takatka clan on her mother's side, was a twenty-one-year-old seamstress, a simple woman with "sparkling black eyes" and a cherubic face. Her great-uncle Fahti says that she was "a quiet girl with no particular ambition."

When her cousins were arrested for trying to commit a suicide bombing, Andalib, according to her mother, was admiring and at the same time hurt. "She wondered why they didn't confide in her," she explains. "The girls were very close and we live so near each other. My daughter felt they should have trusted her."

The family of Iman and Samia Takatka was punished severely by Israeli forces. Their house was dynamited, and Andalib, along with her own family and other neighbors, witnessed the devastation. According to Takatka, Andalib's family took the others in to live with them. "When this happened to her cousins, this really affected her," Fahti says. "This was the first time that Andalib reacted to the suffering under occupation. Up until then, she went to work, came home, saw friends occasionally, and always was available to help her sisters and mother. She never went out alone or behaved in any way that wasn't in keeping with our family's traditions and values. But these were her cousins, girls she grew up with and saw all the time. This was her family."

Before her cousins were arrested, other than caring for her siblings' children Andalib's other all-encompassing interest were the movie magazines she bought that were imported from Egypt or Lebanon and portrayed the glamorous photographs and stories of stars who seemed like royalty to her. "She would cut their pictures out and put them all over her walls," her mother says. "When there was a little extra money, for a birthday or something special, all she wanted were movie magazines."

For most Palestinians who can afford them, a television satellite system and a video machine are essential, not only for entertainment during the months when they are under curfew and not allowed out of their homes, but also for keeping in touch with the rest of the Arab world and learning the stories and reactions to news events that were happening in their own towns and villages. According to Mrs. Suleiman, her daughter watched videos whenever she was allowed. Things changed drastically, however, after her cousins were arrested and the Israeli military, even after they destroyed the family home, would make routine visits to Beit Fajar. "They sometimes lined the men up outside or made them sit on the ground for hours without moving," Mrs. Suleiman says. "It was the first time I ever saw Andalib scream. We had to restrain her physically from rushing out there and tearing at the soldiers. She couldn't bear to see her father and brothers humiliated like that."

Before long, Andalib took down the photographs of the movie stars that adorned her walls and put up pictures of martyrs. "She put a picture of Wafa Idris in the middle of her wall, the same picture that is in the main square in Ramallah," her mother says. "Andalib was fascinated with Wafa Idris. She used to say that she wished she had been the first woman to do this."

The turning point in Andalib Suleiman's life came immediately after the death of Ayat al-Akhras. At the suggestion of Fahti Takatka, when the curfew was briefly lifted, all the women in the family made the trip from Beit Fajar to the Dehaishe camp near Bethlehem to pay their respects to the al-Akhras family. It was there at the al-Akhras home that Andalib met a man named Yossef Moughrabi, who was the Tanzim chief in Bethlehem.

One of her sisters remembers the moment clearly. "When Andalib found out who the man was, she walked up to him and told him that she wanted to do the same thing as Wafa Idris, Darine Abu Aisha, and Ayat had done."

In the home of people she barely knew, in a village far from her own, in an atmosphere of grief combined with a macabre celebration, Andalib Suleiman Takatka approached this strange man and offered herself as a sacrifice for the Palestinian cause. Imagine her thrill when she told him she was from Beit Fajar and he replied that he knew her two cousins, the Takatka girls. Her sister recalls that Andalib made it clear that it was a matter of honor that she would succeed where her cousins had failed. In response, Moughrabi merely smiled and moved away to another part of the room. On their way back to Beit Fajar that day, her mother and sisters asked her if she had been serious, to which Andalib replied, "It is up to Allah if he chooses me."

On April 12, 2002, unlike her cousins, Andalib succeeded in blowing herself up at a bus stop on Jaffa Road, right next to the large, open-air Mahane Yehuda market in Jerusalem. Six people were killed—seven including Andalib—and more than forty more were injured.

Shortly after her death, when the prerequisite hoards of people flocked to her parents' house to "celebrate" her martyrdom, her mother was chastised by the other women for mourning Andalib. "There is no joy for me," Mrs. Suleiman wept. "My daughter fell under the evil influence of evil men. If only I had known, we could have helped her."

CHAPTER TWENTY-TWO

IN THE SPRING OF 2002, when Israeli forces entered towns and villages in the West Bank to root out militants under the auspices of Operation Defense Shield, one of the men arrested was Muataz Muhammed Abdallah Himouni. During questioning, Himouni, a resident of Mazruk near Hebron, admitted that he had planned and directed the suicide attack at Jerusalem's Mahane Yehuda market in which Andalib Suleiman Takatka died. According to Himouni, the Tanzim chief Yossef Moughrabi had contacted him, explaining that while paying a condolence call on the al-Akhras family he had met a young girl from the Takatka clan who expressed a desire to follow Ayat al-Akhras's lead.

For the purposes of recruiting Andalib, Himouni decided to establish a Tanzim cell in Beit Fajar. Later on, after her daughter's death, Mrs. Suleiman claims that people told her that her daughter had registered with the al-Aqsa Martyr's Brigade in Hebron as a potential suicide bomber. "Up until she died," the woman says, "I had no idea she was leading a double life. I had no idea that she was really serious."

Himouni was put into contact with a man named Taleb Amr, known more frequently by his nom de guerre, Abu Ali. Ali, another Tanzim military activist, was in charge of supplying the weapons and explosive belt for Andalib. From his prison cell, Himouni says, "Abu Ali put me in touch with Marwan Saloum, a senior Tanzim operative who was the one who was in charge of training Andalib."

Long after the attack, Marwan Saloum was killed by Israeli soldiers in Hebron. Details of Andalib's eventual recruitment and training, therefore, are provided by Himouni, who is the only person currently in custody who has admitted to his involvement in the bombing. According to Himouni, Marwan Saloum put the girl through a bizarre training course that began with his questioning her as to the seriousness of her intentions. "He asked her if she was sure she wanted to be a *shahida*, and she said she was. He asked her to give him three reasons, and she told him that she wanted to avenge all the killings of women and children by the Israelis, to prove to the Arab world that women were braver and stronger than their best fighters, and to show all the Palestinians that the Takatka clan was fierce and resolute in resisting the occupation." He pauses. "She also wanted the assurance that after she died, she would be famous all over the Arab world."

Himouni goes on to explain that once a girl is chosen, she is given psychological tests and lectured on the rewards she will receive in Paradise. "What the leaders are looking for in a martyr is a woman or girl who is precise, determined, stable, and ready

255

to act," he explains. "When it comes to women, we try even harder to make sure they are serious and prepared for everything so there is no chance they will back down. We try to make sure that the reasons they give, and what we have learned about them, guarantees a successful mission."

Thus, without exception, each female martyr is chosen very carefully, screened by the leadership through information gathered from teachers, family, friends, and neighbors, often unknowingly but always efficiently.

According to Andalib's mother, she learned afterward from friends of her daughter's that Saloum took a long time to accept Andalib. "Her friends told me that she kept asking him when he would make up his mind, and he told her maybe in a week, a month, or a year," Mrs. Suleiman explains. "The most important thing as far as he was concerned was that she was psychologically prepared."

Himouni claims that he was ordered by Saloum to make an in-depth investigation of Andalib's life: her friends, activities, past acquaintances, hobbies, likes, and dislikes. During the week before she died, when Andalib was being put through her training, one of her friends claims that she was approached by several men checking on Andalib's sincerity and stability. "I didn't know the men," the friend explains, "but I knew they were from the Tanzim. They wanted to know if Andalib could be trusted—if she had any Israeli friends or if her parents associated with Israelis. They asked a lot of intimate questions about her and were very hard [tough] about getting the answers. They told me that I better tell the truth or I would be sorry. When I told Andalib that I had been questioned, she seemed happy. She said that meant they were taking her seriously."

Hamouni confirms the story and explains, "It was routine to make sure that there was no possibility that she was planted by the Shin Bet to lead them to the Tanzim cell." Hamouni goes on to say that when Saloum was certain that the girl was sincere and had been completely honest with him, he put her through one of the ultimate tests. "He came for her at her parents' home late one night and drove her to a secluded area in Beit Fajar," Himouni says. "There he told her to dig a grave. When she had finished, he instructed her to lie down in the grave. He wanted her to get used to the idea of her own death. She passed the test without any problem."

A day before the attack, Himouni filmed Andalib with a handheld video camera. Dressed in black and holding a Koran, she recited the words that had been written for her, claiming to be a member of the al-Aqsa Martyr's Brigade and explaining that she was about to die as a symbol of the woman's fight against occupation. She also said that it was her desire to finish the work that had been started by her two cousins, and to honor the memory of Wafa Idris, Darine Abu Aisha, and Ayat al-Akhras. After the videotape was made, Himouni instructed a female cousin of his to oversee Andalib's "purification." "She bathed and said her prayers and fasted," Himouni explains.

Hours before she set off to commit the attack, Andalib met with Himouni and Saloum to learn how to activate the bomb. Rather than wearing an explosive belt, it was decided that she would carry a black handbag that contained three plastic pipes filled with explosives and nails connected to a battery.

On the day of the attack, a Friday, Andalib was driven to Abu Dis, where she took a taxi to Jerusalem. According to Himouni, he had ordered Andalib to go either to Jaffa Road or to the Mahane Yehuda market, whichever of the two sites was more crowded. Andalib Suleiman opted for the Mahane Yehuda market. There she exploded the bomb in her purse. Six people died, and dozens were injured.

During an interview with Mrs. Suleiman after her daughter's death, she reflects upon the reasons that could have driven Andalib to commit such a violent and horrific act. "My daughter was aimless," she says softly. "She was pretty but not particularly bright, which is why we wanted her to marry as soon as possible. We were always afraid that she would be talked into doing something immoral, that a young man would take advantage of her. I am proud that she never did that." She pauses to wipe a tear from her eye. "We never thought she would do something like this, kill herself in the name of Allah. We never thought she could imagine such a thing."

Andalib's actions and her professed reasons for joining the ranks of the heroines of the Palestinian cause add a frightening aspect to the usual explanation of why women undertake suicide missions. Clearly it is too simplistic to assume that it was only her suffering under occupation that accounted for her horrific decision. Andalib had developed a fascination for suicide bombers. She believed that dying as a *shahida* would transform her into an instant superstar. In fact, she succeeded in killing more people than the other three women martyrs.

Just before sundown, as Sabbath approaches, the price of fresh vegetables and fruit drops at the Mahane Yehuda market. Along with the elderly retirees and ultra-religious Jews who went to the market late in the day on April 12, 2002, to shop were three Chinese men who had come to Israel as construction workers to earn money to send back to their families in China. Rachel Adatto-Levy, one of the doctors on duty and the deputy medical director of the Shaare Zedek Medical Center in Jerusalem where the wounded were brought, was deeply affected by the plight of the Chinese men. "Two of them died," Dr. Adatto-Levy says, "and the third man was very badly injured. He lost a hand. It was very tragic. Here were three people who came to Israel to work because they are so poor and couldn't support their families, people who had nothing to do with our political situation in this part of the world, and two are dead and the third will go back to China without his hand."

During a visit to the surviving man's hospital room, where he sits in a wheelchair, covered with wounds from the nails that exploded into his body, I find that he is baffled as to why this happened to him. He has no opinion about the Israeli–Palestinian conflict, no personal knowledge of the desperation or humiliation on the side of the Palestinians or the fear and horror on the part of the Israelis that had cost him his hand and undoubtedly the ability to work as a laborer. He is cared for in the hospital at the expense of the state of Israel until he is well enough to be repatriated to the small town in northern China where his family awaits his return. They are as confused as he is concerning the war of terror that rages in the Middle East. He'd never even heard of Andalib Suleiman or her story.

Many of the other injured who survived were so mutilated from the explosion that they will never be able to lead normal lives again. A sixty-six-year-old man lost one leg and the use of the other, while a young woman of thirty who was visiting from Chicago, Illinois, received the brunt of the blast in her face.

When she had instinctively covered her face with her hands, she also sustained severe wounds that cost her six fingers. Two others who were severely injured in the attack later took their own lives.

CHAPTER TWENTY-THREE

BETWEEN JANUARY 2002 AND JANUARY 2003, according to Liat Pearl, there were thirty-eight women who intended to carry out suicide attacks but were arrested by Israeli security forces either en route to their targets or before they could actually strap on the explosive belts. After their arrest, two of those women admitted to having committed an act of murder prior to making the final decision to become a *shahida*.

On January 17, 2002, Amna'a Mouna, a journalist and Fatah activist from Ramallah, using the pseudonym "Sally," began a correspondence in an online chat room with an Israeli teenager named Ofir Rahum. Six months later, on July 20, the boy finally agreed to meet her at the central bus station in Jerusalem, based on her promise that she would take him to her apartment for sex. Mouna picked up Ofir in a car and drove him instead to a deserted area between Jerusalem and Ramallah. There, two male accomplices, also members of Fatah, met them and killed the boy with eighteen rounds fired from two Kalashnikovs into his face, head, and chest.

Two weeks later, on August 3, Amna'a Mouna was stopped by Israeli border police on her way to the Israeli settlement of Ofra. She was carrying two pistols and three hand grenades. During her interrogation she admitted that she intended to carry out a suicide act at Ofra, and, under intense questioning, also eventually admitted to the murder of Ofir Rahum. Psychology tests revealed that Mouna suffers from paranoid schizophrenia. Incarcerated in a women's prison near Tel Aviv, she was put briefly in solitary confinement. When she was released into the general prison population, prison authorities maintain that Mouna was designated the "leader" of the inmates, not only because of the fear she instills in the other prisoners but also because the Fatah leadership believes she can control them better than any other prisoner.

On August 11, 2002, one day after the Israeli Defense Forces withdrew from the town of Tulkarm, Shefa'a Alkudsi, another Tanzim operative, a twenty-six-year-old divorced mother of a six-year-old girl, was arrested in her parents' apartment. Under questioning, she admitted that she had planned to carry out a suicide attack disguised as a pregnant woman. She also admitted to having shot and killed at random an Israeli motorist who was driving near Maale Adumim, an Israeli settlement near Jerusalem. Friends of Shefa'a from East Jerusalem claim that she had a penchant for torturing animals and on one occasion had skinned alive a neighbor's cat. According to those same friends, Alkudsi had had a series of disastrous love affairs, one with a married professor at Bir Zeit University. When her lover rebuffed her, she stabbed him with a pair of scissors.

Another example of a failed *shahida* is Shireen Rabiya. Shireen is a fifteen-year-old girl who had problems both at home and at school. She was recruited by her own uncle, with the complicity of her school principal. The uncle, who was interviewed for this book from his prison cell near Tel Aviv, admitted that while training Shireen as a suicide bomber he had convinced her that in Paradise she would be brilliant and popular in school. "Her life on earth was worthless," he said during that interview, "and there was no doubt in my mind that she would have a more rewarding existence in the afterlife."

Israeli security forces captured Shireen before she had time to be fitted for an explosive belt. Because of her age and the fact that she was not caught with weapons, they took her into custody, accompanied by her father, and kept her for questioning for only two days and two nights. After her release, I visited the family in their home in Bethlehem. Judging by the furnishings and good condition of the house, it was apparent that Mr. Rabiya was able to provide for his family. In addition to a small convenience store he owns, he also has a chicken farm and, at least outwardly, appears affable and serene, not particularly angry or resentful.

During my visit to the Rabiya household, the Church of the Nativity in Bethlehem was under siege, and the Israeli army had closed off all the surrounding towns and villages. Mrs. Rabiya, a plump and pleasant woman who was more animated than her husband, was the one family member who talked about the hardships the family suffered under occupation. At the very beginning of my visit with Shireen and her family, her mother pointed to the pile of

263

rubble next to the three-story building in which the family now lived. "My husband built this house with his own hands," she explained, "and after years of problems with the Israeli authorities concerning a building permit, they finally appeared one night and destroyed the entire house. They also slaughtered all our animals."

According to Mrs. Rabiya, the family lived in a tent on the site of the debris for years, until finally they were able to construct a building next door where all sixteen children, including their own families, live. Mrs. Rabiya claims that Shireen was too young to remember the anguish that the family endured. "She is the youngest and was sheltered. She never suffered or wanted for anything." She also expressed outrage at her sister's husband, who had attempted to recruit the youngest of her sixteen children.

In another culture, Shireen Rabiya, a beautiful, long-legged girl with all the attributes and grace of a fashion model, might have found her niche as just that. In her culture, however, living in a society where a girl is teased when she is too attractive and has to be conscious and aware of her every gesture or word, Shireen found herself without friends.

The atmosphere around Shireen's house and the attitude of her parents when they discussed and allowed her to discuss the reasons that she decided to become a *shahida* were telling. Shireen shrugs. "I don't know," she says when asked. "It sounded like fun. It sounded exciting and so many others had done it or tried that I thought, why not me?" Shireen also explained that her uncle had promised her that she would never again be teased or excluded when she found her place at "Allah's table."

Did she realize that becoming a *shahida* would mean she would die?

"Of course," she says calmly.

And then what?

"Paradise. I would be in Paradise and live happily ever after." But when I repeat the question, insisting that being dead meant she would never see her family again, and ask if she really, deep in her heart, believed she would end up in Paradise, she finally replies, "No."

What did she think would happen after she died?

She giggles and says, "That they would put me in a plastic garbage bag and that would be it."

Her father and her mother both laugh, as if their daughter had been caught playing a harmless prank.

Clad in bell-bottom jeans and a tight T-shirt, it is apparent that Shireen takes pride in her appearance. I ask her to show me her room and suggest that for the camera she sit in front of her dressing table; she complies. Without prompting, she combs her hair and applies makeup. "It [being a *shahida*] was a bad idea," she finally says, and giggles again.

Back in the living room, Mrs. Rabiya speaks at length about her brother-in-law, Shireen's uncle. "He had no right to involve my daughter," she says. "He has children of his own. The only reason he picked on Shireen was because she is the only one who is not married. I have sixteen children. Shireen is the youngest. I would have preferred that one of my sons was a *shahide*, not a daughter."

Mrs. Rabiya went on to say that it was the "duty" of every Muslim to try and become a *shahide*, but not a girl and certainly not a girl who hadn't yet given birth. "If one of my sons had done this," she says, "I would have been proud. It would have

265

been normal, but my youngest daughter . . . And certainly not someone who would be certain to be caught. That makes the whole attempt without meaning or purpose."

There is a contradiction here. Mira Tzoreff, the professor at Ben Gurion University who specializes on the condition of Arab women, points out that "there are still constraints among the religious Muslims about keeping a daughter at home. To sacrifice a son brings enormous honor."

Dr. Israel Orbach demurs. "It is still not normal," he says. "We learn to preserve our bodies and our souls through touch, especially between mother and child. Based on scientific evidence, growing up with the idea of sending a message to a child that he should die is something that goes against nature."

Mrs. Rabiya goes on to explain that while she and her husband did not punish Shireen, they decided after the ordeal that she should be married as quickly as possible. As she cuddled one of her little nieces, Shireen agreed. "Of course I want to get married and have children," she says. "That's always what I wanted to do with my life. I never wanted to die. Things just happened so quickly that I never realized what I was doing when I agreed to the plan my uncle suggested."

According to Shireen, she met her uncle by chance on the street. "When you see a relative," she explains, "you naturally talk to him. We started to talk and he asked me how I was doing at school, if I was happy, if there were problems at home. I told him that my parents were strict with me, they wouldn't let me dress the way I liked, and that my friends at school teased me because I was taller and thinner than they were. I had no girlfriends, and he agreed that it was difficult for me."

A week later, the uncle appeared at Shireen's school and, accompanied by the principal, went to her class to summon her into the hall. It was there, according to Shireen, that her uncle first proposed the idea of her becoming a *shahida*. In the presence of the principal, he explained to Shireen that she would be fitted with an explosive belt and would be taken somewhere in Jerusalem where she would blow herself up. After that, she would awake to find herself in Paradise. According to Shireen, the idea sounded plausible and exciting. "I never thought about doing it for the Palestinian state," she says. "He never mentioned anything like that. I only thought about Paradise and that I could do anything I liked and that everyone would like me."

There are children even younger than Shireen Rabiya who are confronting Israeli soldiers and attempting suicide attacks. In February 2003, two boys, aged thirteen and eight, tried to infiltrate the Netzarim settlement near Gaza. Both were shot and killed by Israeli settlers.

Dr. Iyad Sarraj claims that because of the failure of adults to achieve a Palestinian state or make things better for their offspring, their children are becoming increasingly insolent toward teachers and family members. "They are calling adults by their first names," Dr. Sarraj says, "which is a sign of disrespect. They should always refer to women as Um and the name of the oldest child, or to men as Abu before the name of the oldest child. What they are really saying is that you, the adults, are doing nothing, so we, the children, will take charge."

Dr. Israel Orbach believes that children who attempt terrorist acts do so because they think they are immortal. "When you are a child," he says, "you don't consider the possibility of dying. It is just not within the realm of conscious thought."

Another reason why the age of Palestinian fighters is getting younger is because with the closures and curfews there is no school. Children roam the streets, aimless and available to fall under the influence of older youth who might set a bad example. Dr. Amikam Nachmani, professor at Bar Ilan University, compares this new wave of child violence to the last days of the Third Reich. "During the last days of Berlin," Dr. Nachmani says, "the Hitler Youth fought like lions. They were the last line of fighters, and they were more desperate and more daring because the notion of death was still an abstraction. The Allied forces never saw such fierce resistance. In the end, decades later, if you watch interviews with some of the survivors of the Hitler Youth, you will see they are bitter. They say now that their leaders sent them off to die."

Rafi Sourani, the Palestinian lawyer and advocate for human rights, believes that children commit acts of violence out of vengeance, desperation, and "the disintegration of Palestinian society." These same factors have a particularly powerful effect on Palestinian women.

Israeli curfews and closures that prevent younger students from going to school also affect college-age students. Married women, because of the closures and curfews, are spending more time at home with husbands who are out of work, frustrated, and angry.

According to Zahira Kamal, the feminist from Gaza, there are more incidents of domestic violence. "Men are taking out their frustrations on the women," Kamal says. "And the birthrate has increased because there are more women getting married at a much younger age. Education is no longer an option."

As we have seen, when Yasser Arafat called for his "army of roses" to participate in the struggle against occupation in January 2002, he might not have imagined the success of his words. Now, given the increasing influence of Hamas and Islamic Jihad throughout the West Bank and Gaza, he seems to be carefully rethinking his policy regarding women and the Intifada. According to Mohammed Dahalan, Arafat is now telling women that they should stay home and have babies. "He specifically talks about the demographic role of women more than he encourages them to give their blood for Palestine," Mr. Dahalan explains.

The Palestinian feminist Andalib Audawan claims that Arafat has once again adapted his thinking to gain popularity in the street. "Because of the backlash from the men against the excessive role of women, which threatens their own status, they are making their women pregnant."

From a religious perspective, Dr. al-Rantisi, the spokesman for Hamas, recently told me that while women are still welcome as *shahidas*, the *fatwa* has been adjusted. They must have produced one son and one daughter before they can blow themselves up. "After she fulfills her demographic role," Dr. al-Rantisi explains, "then she can participate in armed struggle."

A fatal cocktail of circumstances, a cult of death, an absence of hope for future generations—these are the realities that result from intractable religious and ideological forces on both sides of

269

the struggle. The reasons for a woman or young girl's involvement, however, remain a separate issue—one that has its genesis in history, its justification in the Koran, and its realities in the ambitions of political and religious leaders.

CHAPTER TWENTY-FOUR

RUNNING A TERRORIST ORGANIZATION TODAY is like running a business. Those who work within the Fatah, al-Aqsa Martyr's Brigade, or the Tanzim receive close to $1 billion a year in donations (a quarter from the European Union and a third from the Arab League). In addition, there are hundreds of millions of dollars in revenues generated by various Palestinian government monopolies that sell consumer goods, from flour to cigarettes. These funds are often said to be corrupt as they support militant groups that carry out terrorist attacks against Israel. Hamas and Islamic Jihad get money from Syria, Iran, Iraq, and Saudi Arabia, often under the guise of charity organizations that support widows and orphans. Upon close inspection, the majority of those widows and orphans are the families of suicide bombers. But who actually receives the money in the Occupied Territories and Gaza?

271

According to a senior Israeli intelligence official, the money passes from "hand to hand and through banks . . . The fastest way is that women usually smuggle it across borders. In the last six months we have caught twenty-five women and six men who have tried to enter the West Bank from Jordan or Gaza from Egypt. All of them carried more than ten thousand dollars concealed on their bodies."

In addition to illegal means, Yasser Arafat has his own legitimate funding sources, most from the European Community but also, during the Oslo days, from Israel, a practice that has been discontinued since the breakdown of the peace process.

Now, with the appointment in April 2003 of Abu Mazen as prime minister of the Palestinian Authority, Arafat has to deal with an official who will be leading an increasingly independent parliament that has proved its willingness to stand up to him. In fact, that independence began when international pressure for reforms forced Arafat to accept Salam Fayyad as finance minister during the summer of 2002, which diminished Arafat's control over Palestinian finances.

Under Fayyad, a former International Monetary Fund (IMF) official, the books are allegedly more open. American officials, however, claim that there still is not enough transparency, and that parts of the government that control funds remain under Arafat's power.

Arnold Roth, who lost his daughter Malki in the Sbarro's bombing, has made it a point to attend meetings with various officials from the European Community, as well as the IMF, in an effort to prove that monies sent to the Palestinian Authority end up financing terror operations.

According to Mr. Roth, Thomas Dawson, the director of the

External Relations Department of the IMF, made a statement that was ultimately contradicted by a Palestinian official of the same organization. "The IMF does not monitor foreign assistance to the Palestinian Authority," Mr. Dawson said. "It simply provides the EU [European Union] with information about broad developments related to its budget. It does not monitor or control every item in the budget."

However, in a September 2, 2002, cover article in the online edition of the IMF's official publication, the *IMF Survey*, George T. Abed, director of the IMF's Middle East department, claimed that "because of the IMF's mandate," donors to the Palestinian Authority rely on the IMF to develop the framework for the Palestinian economy. "In other words," Mr. Roth asserts, "the IMF and Mr. Abed are there to ensure that the Palestinian Authority gives the IMF funds for the purposes intended, such as wages and other normal spending for any civil society. But then Mr. Abed goes on to explain that because the budget is nearly $1 billion, 'there has, no doubt, been some abuse' of funds."

It is at this point in the conversation that Arnold Roth becomes emotional. "When the IMF's director for the Middle East states that he obviously cannot control the spending by the various Palestinian agencies," he says, "because that part of the budget control remains between the various Palestinian agencies, I assume that somewhere along the line, money was given for terrorism and that money coming from the IMF indirectly is responsible for the death of my daughter."

Mr. Roth goes on to point out that the article identifies Mr. Abed as a Palestinian and a Jordanian national. "Here is a Palestinian speaking as the voice of the IMF, contradicting in

September 2002 what the European Commission's deputy director general for external relations and director in charge of political issues, who reports directly to Commissioner Chris Patten, said on December 17, 2002, that 'money transfers from the European Commission to the Palestinian Authority are made under the IMF's supervision, and this ought to put the concerns of worried Israelis to rest.'" He takes a breath. "That does not put me at rest at all and I'll tell you why. I was at a meeting in Strasbourg and I listened to and even spoke directly to Chris Patten and to Louis Michel, the current head of the European Parliament, who is a Belgian national. The whole operation consists of people who blame each other for a shocking lack of transparency."

During the course of his meeting with the members of the European Parliament, Mr. Roth made the claim that there's a chain of events leading from the European Community to the Palestinian Authority to terrorist acts such as the Sbarro's bombing that took the life of his daughter. "In my mind," Mr. Roth continues, "there are serious problems with the way Palestinians spend the EU money, and that's a problem which the EU should deal with without attempting to pass the blame on to the IMF."

What is clear is that the European Union is the biggest financial supporter of the Palestinian Authority, although since July 2002 the transfer of funds has been under much closer scrutiny, since sensitive documents were captured by Israeli forces during the raid on Yasser Arafat's headquarters in Ramallah.

In January 2003, the European Parliament took a vote to launch a complete investigation. According to Arnold Roth, every right-wing European member of the Parliament voted in favor of the motion, although they received only 120 votes and needed 167 for the motion to pass.

There are many ways to deal with grief. Arnold Roth has made this investigation his life's work.

CHAPTER TWENTY-FIVE

IF THE PALESTINIAN QUEST for independence began as a revolutionary movement whose objective was the creation of an autonomous Palestinian state, suicide bombings have turned the conflict into a disease that is afflicting an entire generation with a consuming desire to die. By promising a glory-filled journey from earth to Paradise to escape the indignity and humiliation of Israeli occupation, politically motivated Palestinian leaders misuse and misdirect the despair and hopelessness of their people against the prospect for peace and eventually against all hope.

When ambition motivates religious and political leaders to encourage this cult of death in order to achieve their own goals, the result is the ultimate abandonment of limits as we understand them with the democratic mind and, even more tragic, the victimization of the Palestinian people by both their occupiers and their own leaders. Perhaps the most immoral of these leaders is Yasser Arafat, who has been lauded by the world as a "man of peace," a symbol of a revolution who, more than anyone else, has held the fate of the Palestinian people in his hands since the inception of their struggle. And yet, for his own political survival, he too has sent the deadly message that suicide bombings are the decisive weapon in a war that pits Israel's longing for security against the Palestinians' longing for statehood. The world expected more of Mr. Arafat and yet he, like the extreme religious leaders, has transformed the religious justification for martyrdom into a social and cultural mandate for the female members of the society. It is a dangerous game that will not assure Mr. Arafat a revered place in the annals of history.

Since the beginning of the Intifada, the most prevalent question in Israel and throughout the Occupied Territories has been whether Yasser Arafat is able to confront and control Hamas to succeed in making peace with Israel. According to Shalom Harrari, the former Israeli intelligence officer, Hamas is the biggest opposition party. "It is a complicated question," Mr. Harrari begins, "because Fatah is still strong, not because of its structure but because it is technically the authority. But it is no secret that Arafat has lost control, and proof of that is seen in all the symbols of death that permeate Palestinian society. There is a doomsday mentality."

In all the universities, teachers, guards, students, and employees are all under the control of Hamas or the Islamic Jihad. And, because of their vast influence and their charitable infusions into Palestinian society, they, more than any other political entity, can indoctrinate the people into believing that the most revered and crucial contribution to the cause is to die for Palestine. "They may not have as big an infrastructure as the Palestinian Authority," Shalom Harrari says, "but they have plenty of money to mount and pay for these suicide attacks. As much money as they need from Syria and Iran."

According to Mohammed Dahalan, now minister of security under Abu Mazen's new Parliament, Arafat knows that the worst thing for the Palestinians is a civil war within their ranks. "Arafat told Hamas this," Mr. Dahalan says, "and explained that if they didn't stop suicide bombings, he would be forced to confront them and there would be a divided Palestinian community, which would weaken our position and our mutual goals vis-à-vis Israel."

If one is to believe Mr. Dahalan's analysis, then why did Arafat's al-Fatah commit a suicide attack in Tel Aviv on January 5, 2003, which killed more than twenty-nine people? After the explosion, it was the al-Aqsa Martyr's Brigade, the military arm of the Fatah organization, that claimed credit for the bombing.

Despite the constant double messages that Mr. Arafat gives to his own people and to the Israelis, Europeans, and Americans, and notwithstanding the corruption that is rampant within the Palestinian Authority, there are important voices throughout the West Bank and Gaza that remain optimistic even if they feel sadness and frustration over the current state of affairs. Dr. Iyad Sarraj is one example of those who harbor hope. "I believe in life," he says, "and I believe people believe in life. The problem is that these [Palestinian] children have no childhood. They are not living. If you change the environment, you change the children. Arafat came eight years ago and did nothing to make life better. Gaza is worse. On so many levels, it is worse. On the other hand, Sharon's policy is to kill hope within the Palestinian population. The result is a moral corruption on both sides of the struggle. While Sharon crushes hope, Arafat doesn't serve as an example to the people, by encouraging men and now women to die, and that is the real moral corruption and failure." And therein lies the dilemma.

One of the reasons other moderate Palestinians and Israelis harbor hope is that Arafat, under pressure from Israel and the United States, finally appointed, through an election within his cabinet, Mahmoud Abbas, commonly known as Abu Mazen, to serve as prime minister. Arafat, however, claims that appointing a prime minister was only in response to recent Palestinian opinion polls. In August 2002, 69 percent of Palestinians polled by the Palestinian Authority showed support for a prime minister, while in November 2002 the level of support rose to 73 percent. The party line within the PA is that creating a prime minister was part of the promised Palestinian "reform process intended to create a better government through a division and balance of power at the senior level of the Palestinian Authority executive branch."

Immediately after the announcement was made, there was cynicism throughout the Palestinian Authority, Israel, and the United States about whether Arafat would allow Abu Mazen to exercise any authority. Another concern was that extremist groups would not adhere to the new rules proposed by President George W. Bush's "road map." Would Hamas and Islamic Jihad stop using suicide bombers and other terror tactics? Even within the Palestinian Authority and the PLO, the actual laws that stipulate a prime minister's power were at best confusing.

According to the bylaws of the Palestinian Authority, the appointment of the prime minister "does not directly relate to negotiations with Israel because the prime minister is a position within the Palestinian Authority, whereas negotiations with Israel are conducted by the Palestinian Liberation Organization." Curiously, the rules also state that "negotiations with Israel are led by the PLO's Negotiations Affairs Department, headed by Mahmoud Abbas, operating under the authority of PLO Chairman Yasser Arafat," and it would seem, barring any unforeseen developments within the structure of the two entities, that Abu Mazen would have concurrent duties within both organizations. If there are complications, they could arise because of the differences under law of those two entities.

The Palestinian Authority was set up as a temporary administrative body (intended to serve only during the interim period prior to the establishment of a Palestinian state) established by the Oslo Accords in 1994. The purpose of the PA was to govern those areas of "Occupied Palestinian Territories from which Israeli occupation forces withdraw [currently 17.2 percent of the Occupied West Bank and approximately 80 percent of the Occupied Gaza Strip]." According to the PA, Yasser Arafat was democratically elected president of the Palestinian Authority on January 20, 1996. As of this date, Abu Mazen has not held a position within the PA.

The Palestinian Liberation Organization, established in 1964, is the Palestinian government in exile and, according to its rules, "carries out the state functions of the Palestinian people, including negotiations with Israel." As part of the Oslo Accords, the government of Israel recognized the PLO as the "representative of the Palestinian people and to commence negotiations with the PLO." What might account for the optimism throughout the area is that while Yasser Arafat is the "chairman of the PLO," Abu Mazen is secretary-general of the PLO

Executive Committee and, as mentioned above, heads up the PLO's Negotiations Affairs Department.

As it turned out, the problem of interpreting the bylaws of each entity was less problematic than either Mr. Arafat's willingness to relinquish some of his power or the extremist groups' willingness to relinquish terror. Abu Mazen's popularity is limited to within Arafat's inner circle and the Israeli government. And Hamas and Islamic Jihad have not changed their position concerning any comprehensive peace accord with Israel, nor do they consider acquiescing to Israeli and American demands for a new Palestinian negotiating partner a positive move. Suicide bombings continue. In fact, the Iraq war has been cited as an additional reason for impending martyrdom. The Islamic Jihad suicide bomber who blew himself up in Netanya, Israel, on March 30, 2003, said in his final, videotaped statement: "We make no difference between the Israeli occupation of our land and the American invasion of Iraq."

If his words seem like harmless rhetoric, there is an underlying message that must be heard. As a result of what has become a conflict between political and religious ideologies within Palestinian society, as well as within Israeli society, there are now too many variables obstructing what was once an automatic equation for peace: the dismantling of settlements, which would bring about an eventual cessation of violence and suicide attacks; or an Israeli withdrawal to the 1967 borders with the guarantee of safe borders and the automatic creation of an independent Palestinian state.

On April 24, 2003, after a ten-day stalemate when Arafat and Abu Mazen finally agreed on a compromise cabinet for the governing Palestinian Authority, a suicide bomber blew himself up at Kfar Saba, north of Tel Aviv, in a train station during rush hour, just across the border from the West Bank. Killing himself and an Israeli guard, the bomber seriously wounded thirteen Israelis. Credit for the blast was taken jointly by Hamas and Islamic Jihad, which drove home the challenge facing the new Palestinian prime minister, who will be expected to rein in militants as part of a peace initiative.

One of the issues that provoked the ten-day stalemate was Arafat's resistance in accepting Mohammed Dahalan, his former security chief who had resigned and who, subsequently, Arafat and his close collaborators considered to be favored by the United States and Israel as someone willing to crack down on militant Palestinian groups. On the day of the suicide attack, in spite of a tentative agreement, it remained uncertain if the fragile balance of power between Arafat and Mazen would lead to less or more Palestinian instability. What caused many to be restrained in their optimism is Arafat's penchant for embracing terrorist activities not only to further the Palestinian cause but to help secure his political survival.

Suicide bombings may have politicized the Palestinians but they have had the effect of depoliticizing the Israelis. In the past, in Israel there were very definite party lines that separated the Likud and a variety of ultra-religious parties from Labor and other left-wing groups. Every action or reaction taken by the Israeli government in conjunction with the military always evoked dissenting opinion on either side of the political spectrum. While the right-wing and ultra-Orthodox groups applauded the construction of more settlements throughout the Occupied Territories, in keeping with the Zionist dream of a "greater Israel," the Labor and left-wing parties were opposed to them, at least in theory, as an "impediment" to the peace process. Wholesale killing of Palestinians, collective punishment, destruction of homes, zealous and humiliating border checks, and strong-armed tactics that included raiding villages during the night to root out suspected militants and terrorists were actions that resulted in not only world sentiment running against Israel, but also bitter debate in the Knesset and on the streets when the Israeli population came out en masse either for or against these practices.

As the country approached elections in January 2003, the Israeli public, for the first time in decades, were less interested in the political platforms of either the main parties, Labor and Likud, or the newly formed Shinui party, which positioned itself as a secular alternative that adopted the best of both the left- and the right-wing's visions for the elusive peace process. In fact, the one point that all parties seemed to agree on was that any chance of a peace accord as outlined in the past was impossible, and in its stead the idea of building a fence to separate Israel from the West Bank appeared to be the most viable solution.

After Prime Minister Ariel Sharon was reelected, the idea of free passage between Gaza and the West Bank and Israel became something that the majority of Israelis also agreed might never happen again. According to Dr. Boaz Ganor, most people no longer talk about peace. "The road map to peace has become irrelevant," Dr. Ganor says. "Peace has cultural connotations and sociological connotations and something that is dictated by an agreement that does not embody the sentiment on the street. As a result, it may never be realized again, at least in the far future, which includes the concepts of two states with open borders. Suicide bombers changed the face of peace forever."

*   *   *

A fence separating Israelis and Palestinians—already under construction at certain borders—is not simply a physical structure but also an abstract concept that could create even more problems than before. "How can Palestinians live behind a fence," Saeb Erakat, the chief negotiator for the Palestinian Authority, wonders, "and be able to cross into Israel to work? If your neighbor has a bad life, he is bound to make your life bad. The problem with the Sharon government is they don't care whether Arafat is head of the PA, or Attila the Hun. They refuse to negotiate with us. They claim, on one hand, that Arafat is irrelevant, and on the other that he is responsible for all the suicide attacks. Which is it? The Israelis can't have it both ways."

If Palestinian society has become a culture of death, where life has little meaning and the preferred reaction to humiliation, violence, and occupation is a willingness to die, then Israeli society has become a culture of fear permeated with a psychology of shock. Both sides have rightly lost confidence in their leaders. Both are skeptical about the prospect of peace.

In many ways the opportunity for peace has passed for both sides: for the Israelis, since the assassination of Yitzhak Rabin and the subsequent ascent to power of the right-wing Likud party, which formed a coalition with the ultra-religious parties; and, for the Palestinians, since Yasser Arafat made a conscious choice that terror had always gotten him more than negotiation. Added to his woes was that even after he adopted a terror strategy, he still lost control as a politician, when Islamic extremists gained control of public sentiment on the streets.

There is no doubt that given the current situation, the Palestinian people suffer from an absence of hope and desperation because they are humiliated and treated less than democratically in a society that claims to be the only democracy in that part of the world.

There used to be a joke in Israel: "Ask five Israelis their opinion on politics and you'll get six different answers." If Palestinian society has been united in a culture of death, Israeli society has been united in a psychology of fear, and that fear has united a people once separated by politics.

A cabdriver from Herziliya who served in the Israeli army during the Lebanon War, and who subsequently demonstrated against that unpopular war while he was still a soldier, says, "Protect the people, that's the only thing that matters. How the government does it is not important. Just save Israeli lives."

Roni Shaked, a journalist from *Yediot Ahranot*, the centrist daily newspaper, maintains, "We want a divorce. We've been sleeping in the same bed with the Palestinians for years without having sex. The time has come to have separate bedrooms."

Ask a mother who once marched for peace in the good old days, or a shopkeeper who used to travel to the West Bank to visit his Palestinian friends, or the man who owns the Memento Café in Jerusalem, which was destroyed when a suicide bomber blew himself up at the door and killed dozens of Israelis and injured dozens more and they will all say the same thing. "Whatever it takes to save lives, that's the policy that should be taken. The depth of the Palestinians' hatred for us has gone beyond repair."

It is this unanimous fear that has fostered support for such extreme right-wing Messianic leaders as former general Effie Eytam, who is now a minister in Sharon's government on the extreme religious right. "The Palestinians need land and we don't have that land to give them," General Eytam told me quite seriously during an interview. "We have to tell them the truth. The only solution to their problem is the Sinai Desert. We [Israelis and other Arab nations] should get together and give the Palestinians the Sinai so they have room to live. It is the only solution where our land is no longer an issue."

With sentiments such as those expressed by General Eytam and many others who hold similar views, it is understandable that the Palestinian people feel hopeless and desperate. The immorality comes into the picture when their own leaders offer them death as the only viable solution.

Throughout history, Israelis and Palestinians have been inextricably linked in life and in death. Because of the deadly trend of suicide attacks that has captured the Palestinian culture and the deadly retaliatory response that has seized Israeli society, the worst of both people has become the dominating factor in Israel and throughout the West Bank and Gaza. While survival has become the prevailing political agenda on the lips of both Israelis and Palestinians, the concept of that survival defines the difference between the two people. Survival for the Israelis means living to preserve their land, while survival for the Palestinians means dying to strengthen others to continue the struggle for statehood.

From the moment that religious and political entities in Israel united, they guaranteed an automatic barrier to any reliable attempt to breathe life into a moribund peace process. As long as occupation is an intricate part of Israel, not only is the peace process dead but their own democracy is at risk of dying.

From the moment that religious and political entities within the West Bank and Gaza clashed for control of the population, it was only a question of time before the very religious and cultural glue that held the Palestinian people together for centuries would be used to destroy what is a normal instinct for survival in any culture or civilization. Evoking the name of Allah or making videotapes that cite desperation, humiliation, frustration, and hopelessness to explain why Palestinians have chosen to die and take with them others who just happened to be in the vicinity of their explosive belts is still murder. There is no excuse that will ever console those grieving families and friends on both sides of the conflict who have lost loved ones, and no defense appropriate for those women who have been duped into believing that, finally, by dying and becoming a *shahida* they are equal to men.

The most frequent question asked of me from both sides when I am working in that part of the world is if I am pro-Palestinian or pro-Israeli. It is always posed as an either/or question, and those who want to know are usually not prepared to accept equivocations. Even among journalists themselves, those who work in the region develop reputations about their sympathies for either one side or the other.

In the context of the present Intifada, with Israeli reoccupation of land that had been turned over to Palestinians and the use of human bombs by Palestinians in what is clearly Israel proper, it has become even more difficult to explain my feelings about this conflict. The either/or responses belong to the extremists on both sides, whether it is General Effie Eytam, who believes the Palestinians should accept the Sinai Desert as their homeland, or Dr. Abdul Aziz al-Rantisi, who is determined to turn all the land into an Islamic state. If I say that I am against occupation and all the humiliating details that it entails,

I am identified as pro-Palestinian by both Palestinians and Israelis. If I maintain that I am against suicide bombings, I am identified as pro-Israeli by both Israelis and Palestinians.

Palestinians believe that Israel should sit down and negotiate with the Palestinian Authority under Yasser Arafat a comprehensive peace plan that identifies definite borders for a Palestinian state and allows for self-autonomy, regardless of whether or not Arafat can control the radical factions that will continue to commit acts of violence; this is considered a moderate position.

Israelis, for their part, insist on the cessation of all terrorist attacks and a guarantee that Mr. Arafat can control the radical factions of his society; this, too, is the moderate position.

The only way to appease both sides, then, might be to embrace the most radical position in either camp. Curiously, even the moderate Palestinians who are violently against the policies of Ariel Sharon also voice their mistrust of someone like Shimon Peres, who has been the voice of conciliation and moderation since long before the peace process began. I have heard so many Palestinian intellectuals say that they would prefer to sit down and negotiate with people from the extreme right wing in Israel or the Likud party than to listen to empty promises and liberal rhetoric from those on the left or the Labor and Meretz parties. At the same time, the intellectuals inevitably point out, "If the Israelis succeed in getting rid of Arafat, they will only find themselves facing a Palestinian leader from Hamas or Islamic Jihad, which would be far worse."

Since the beginning of this Intifada I have become increasingly convinced that it is better to negotiate a lasting peace with an Israeli leader from the right wing, who might be inclined to give less politically but who could push for the safety of his own people. At the same time I have come to believe that a Palestinian leader who is clear about his religious and political beliefs is the best alternative, even if that leader happens to come from Hamas or Islamic Jihad. At least the world would know where he stands.

Arafat's doublespeak is a huge impediment to peace and a tragedy for both the Palestinian and Israeli people. It misleads the European community and the United States and is responsible for the spilling of blood throughout the region. Leaders on both sides have the responsibility to state their positions clearly in language that doesn't change, whether they are addressing their own people or the international community. Meanwhile, the only hope for peace is in the gray area of possible solutions—a far better color than the blood red of continuing violence.

AFTERWORD

As soon as the war in Iraq began, a "solidarity tent" was erected in the middle of Gaza City. Arranged beneath a large canvas were desks and chairs displaying banners of support for Saddam Hussein and the Iraqi people. At any time during the day or evening, university or high school students were either on duty in the tent or milling around to show their solidarity. Placards and bumper stickers scattered around proclaimed anti-American and anti-British slogans and depicted unflattering effigies of George W. Bush and Tony Blair along with photographs of dead or maimed Iraqi civilians.

Abdullah Horani, the head of the Iraqi branch of the Palestinian Liberation Organization, had come to Gaza in 1998 after spending many years in Syria and in Lebanon. As the self-appointed leader of the movement to mobilize Palestinians in support of Saddam Hussein, it was Horani who organized a special antiwar program for residents in Gaza. Each day there was something different planned. Usually on Mondays he called for an Iraqi flag to be displayed in every Palestinian window. Tuesdays, Wednesdays, and Thursdays were designated as "Take the tears out of Baghdad" days; residents were given random phone numbers of Iraqi citizens whom they could direct-dial from Gaza to offer their comfort and solidarity. There were no special days or times for burning the American flag, he told me. "That is a spontaneous emotion that is not organized," he said. "People here are angry. They are fed up and want to show their feelings for Mr. Bush and for Mr. Sharon. Occupation is occupation, regardless of where it is or which country is the invader."

There was something that I found particularly disturbing during the anti-American rallies in Gaza during the Iraq war. While the men were chanting "Death to America! Death to Bush!" the women were adding their own refrain: "We will sacrifice our blood and soul for you, Saddam!"

The words had a familiar ring. When I mentioned to Mr. Horani that a crowd of women had chanted the same thing to Yasser Arafat during his "army of roses" speech in January 2002, only hours before Wafa Idris blew herself up in Jerusalem, he told me that the world would be seeing more and more women committing suicide attacks. And in fact, not long after, on April 2, 2003, two Iraqi women blew themselves up near Basra in Iraq. "You should be happy," he said. "They killed two American soldiers. Their target was the military, not civilians."

I spoke with Abdullah Horani again after the war was over. He had dismantled the tent and seemed weary. "No one wins in this conflict," he said thoughtfully. "Here in Gaza or in Ramallah, people have no jobs, no money. They are constantly humiliated by the Israelis." He smiled. "The only winners are the people who manufacture the American flags. Every time we burn one, they make more money to send their families away to a safe place." He shrugged. "Probably in America."

What he did not add was the usual justification, which I've heard so many times from the leaders of Hamas, the PLO, and Islamic Jihad, that in a society that lacks high-tech weapons, the best response against the enemy is a human bomb, especially in the defense of one's country.

The dilemma that confronts all civilized nations is a moral one. In the context of a declared state of war, either we condone suicide bombings as the weapon of the technologically challenged, or we condemn those regimes that train and encourage human beings to transform themselves into bombs and kill themselves while killing others. Before we can make that choice, however, we are immediately confronted by another moral dilemma. The Palestinians consider that they are in a state of war with Israel, which for them means that they have the right to defend themselves against their "invaders" or "occupiers." Saeb Erakat, the chief negotiator for the PLO, told me during an interview in his office in Jericho that while "Israelis systematically target Palestinian civilians, the PLO has categorically condemned terrorist attacks against Israeli civilians." And herein lies the dilemma.

What is the definition of a "civilian" in Israel, Gaza, and the West Bank? Since each Palestinian faction holds a different view of what the final borders should be for a Palestinian state, there are several different possible definitions for "civilian." For the PLO, it could be an Israeli resident of Jerusalem or any of the settlements within the West Bank and Gaza, while for Hamas and Islamic Jihad it could be an Israeli mother or child who lives in Tel Aviv, Netanya, or Holon. In all three possible cases it would seem that no Israeli civilian is safe in cafés, on highways, on buses, or in the streets, since all are considered by one group or another as invaders or military surrogates. Which brings us to the next question: When is war justified, and when is guerrilla or covert warfare defined as legitimate resistance and not as terrorism?

Again, a moral dilemma, although in every war there are civilian casualties and guerrilla or covert operations that work in tandem with the regular or conventional military. And in every war there are some who define it as justifiable and others who consider it criminal.

It was because of these moral dilemmas that I decided to write this book, but also because the most immoral act that has become a trend is the utilization and victimization of women who are recruited, trained, and sent off to die with explosive belts strapped around their waists and kill others under the guise of equality or the promise of rehabilitating a family member or cleansing their own reputations. In the end, the burden of immorality lies with those cynical leaders who first marginalize their women, setting impossible conditions for them to lead happy lives and then send them off to die by promising them equality and a better life in Paradise. And, while training young men as suicide bombers is equally immoral, they, more than women, have the benefit of more attractive options during life and, therefore, make that choice more freely.

Suicide bombings give voice to the desperate. They also provide the desperate with a powerful weapon that makes the battlefield more equal since the concept of death and deity in Christianity and

293

Judaism is different than it is in the Islamic faith. And yet, without that fatal cocktail of poverty and desperation living under an occupying force and a regime that has not, until now, encouraged democracy or transparency and a nationalistic fervor that rewards the families of martyrs coupled with an unwavering religious belief that life on earth is merely a preparation for eternal life in Paradise, there is no winner in this conflict.

The problem with war in the twenty-first century is that it is either so sophisticated and high-tech that it becomes almost banal, or it is so crude and primitive that its aftermath causes everyone, even those far from the explosive belts or bomb-laden cars or trucks, to sustain lasting traumas. The tragedy today is not in our inability to define terrorism or guerrilla warfare or even in the morality or justification of war itself, but rather in our inability to rid the world of leaders who kill soldiers and civilians in the name of God. If focusing on military targets makes suicide bombers more moral than a regular army that kills civilians, then leaders, regardless of where they are from, who claim to be guided by God or religion, regardless of which one, are equally evil. Inevitably, it is always the people who die and rarely those divinely inspired politicians or leaders who suffer the consequences of their own visions.

In all cases, the language of justification is the ultimate insult to all the Israeli and Palestinian victims of this atrocious new weapon.

It is difficult to finish a book on this subject without constantly wanting to add another name and another story to this ongoing tragedy. When I arrived in Jerusalem days after Hiba Daraghmeh, the fifth Palestinian woman suicide bomber, killed herself and three others and wounded dozens in Afula on May 19, 2003, it was impossible for me not to want to learn her story, to understand what circumstances pushed her to that horrific finality. The reports in the press about her were eerily familiar: a brilliant student of English literature who had turned down several marriage proposals because she wanted to study, and then an incident at an Israeli checkpoint where soldiers allegedly forced her to remove her veil. It was the same life plan and humiliation as Darine Abu Aisha, the fourth suicide bomber who blew herself up at the Maccabim checkpoint near Jerusalem, had strived for and suffered.

But then, after every suicide bombing a variety of contradictory and often untrue stories about the martyr circulate on both sides of the conflict. As for Hiba Daraghmeh, she was a student of English literature, although unlike Darine and the other three Palestinian women who blew themselves up, she was extremely religious. Hiba didn't just cover her head with a *hijab* and wear a *jilbab*, she covered her entire body in black, including her hands, which she covered in black gloves. All that showed of Hiba were her eyes. As for being humiliated by Israeli soldiers, there are always reports of humiliation at checkpoints, some of which are undoubtedly true, although soldiers ripping off Palestinian women's headscarves is something I have never witnessed.

What struck me as odd from the beginning was that her faith and her modesty seemed to border on obsession. According to her friends and her parents, she would not even eat in the university cafeteria in the presence of the other students. She hid herself

295

in another room so she could lift her veil in private, or she went to her aunt's house to eat. According to one of her friends, no one had seen the young woman without her gown and head covering. They had never even seen her hands. Yet, when she set off to blow herself up, she chose to disguise herself as an Israeli woman, wearing jeans and a T-shirt, for her final trip to Paradise.

During a visit with Hiba's mother, Fatmah Daraghmeh, at her home in Tubas on the West Bank, she began by expressing fierce pride about her daughter before she dissolved in tears, lamenting her child's decision and mourning her death—as has been the case with every mother of a suicide bomber. When she finally talked about Hiba's life, she began by saying, "She was the daughter I never knew." According to Mrs. Daraghmeh, the closeness and intimacy she had with Hiba from infancy ended abruptly. At fourteen, according to her mother, the girl had been raped by a mentally retarded uncle. There was no pregnancy. There was no collective punishment by the family because Mrs. Daraghmeh decided not to tell anyone. She waited and she prayed and when there were no physical repercussions from the rape, she told her daughter that God had granted them both another chance. It was then, at fourteen, that Hiba took to covering herself so that she was unrecognizable. Mrs. Daraghmeh recalls that she could never touch her child's skin since the girl would not even allow her own mother to see her uncovered.

Within weeks of the trauma, the uncle was found dead on an abandoned road near his home. There was no autopsy. There were no signs of violence. The death was attributed to natural causes. Mrs. Daraghmeh refuses to say anything more about her brother's death except that it was another sign from God that her child had another chance. But what she does say in great detail is that before the rape, her daughter was an outgoing, beautiful, charming girl who dressed in modern clothes and had aspirations to marry some day and have children. After the age of fourteen, she hid herself away and concentrated on her studies. "More and more, she became religious," Hiba's mother says. "More and more, she read the Koran, and more and more, she became distant from me." She cries. "I believed it was my punishment for keeping our secret. And now I believe her death is my punishment as well."

The fact that Islamic Jihad took credit for Hiba's act is not particularly surprising or relevant. It was their turn to claim a woman; al-Aqsa and Hamas had claimed Hiba's four predecessors. To prove that point, immediately after her death yet another sheik, Yusef Al Qaradawi from Qatar, reiterated what Sheik Yassine and countless others have said, that a woman could reach Paradise by committing a suicide bombing.

On December 13, 2003, American forces near Tikrit pulled Saddam Hussein from a hole in the ground on property that contained a small hut which had been one of his hiding places since coalition forces deposed him. The reaction throughout the world ranged from unabashed jubilation to measured satisfaction. For once, President George W. Bush had the good sense to exhibit a cautionary sense of victory, warning the world that "the capture of Saddam Hussein does not mean the end of violence in Iraq. We still face terrorists who would rather go on killing the innocent than accept the rise of liberty in the heart of the Middle East."

Ironically, the first television station to report the event was not CNN or the BBC but rather al-Jezeera, the most watched channel across the Arab world. Their airing of the capture and the disturbing images of a bedraggled Saddam Hussein submitting to an examination of his mouth and head by an American medic, were presented in such a way as to demean the so-called victory in the eyes of the Iraqi people and the Arab world. Al-Jezeera understood better than any other Western media outlet how humiliation is the most crucial driving force in every Arab psyche. The humiliation of an Arab, even a secular Arab such as Saddam Hussein, even a man who brutalized his own people, by Western forces for all the world to see, provoked resentment even among those who had directly suffered from his cruelty. Al-Jezeera knew that to depict the man who had been a symbol of resistance and arrogance to America and American military forces in such a demeaning and humiliating manner would clearly evoke fear from other Arab leaders that they could be next; or fury from the people that a symbol of resistance had fallen in such disgrace at the hands of the most hated imperial power—America.

It was, therefore, no surprise that Palestinians in Gaza and Nablus and even in less radical West Bank cities, took to the streets in opposition of Saddam's capture. They marched in outrage and grief, shot AK–47s in the air, burned American flags and threatened violent reprisal. Abdul Aziz Rantisi, the spokesman for Hamas in Gaza, appeared before the media and made a statement that was both bitter and menacing. "What the United States did (capturing Saddam Hussein) is ugly and despicable. It is an insult to all Arabs and an insult to Muslims…[The United States] will pay a very high price for the mistake."

It was not the first time that Palestinians had taken sides with Saddam against the United States. It happened during the first

Gulf War when Yasser Arafat became Saddam's poodle, dubbed "little Saladin," by the Iraqi tyrant and lauded as the leader who would finally give the Palestinians their rightful place in the Middle East. Each time an Iraqi scud missile landed in Israel, Palestinians went wild with joy, even on those occasions when the scuds misfired and landed on occupied Palestinian land. In the end, of course, Saddam was forced out of Kuwait and the Gulf States cut off funding for the beleaguered Palestinian Authority. More damaging for Arafat was that thousands of Palestinian workers who had been living comfortably in Kuwait were ultimately expelled and ended up without passports or identity cards in Gaza, doubly displaced and destitute and resenting Arafat for their humiliating plight. But even then, despite Arafat's penchant for aligning himself with the losing side, his decision to support Saddam was a choice not without logic. After all, Saddam Hussein had always stood up for the Palestinian cause. In fact, he was one of the primary contributors to the families of suicide bombers and gave many more millions as well to fund the current Intifada. What is baffling now, however, is Mr. Arafat's total and complete silence concerning the capture of Saddam Hussein.

One might misconstrue that silence to mean that Mr. Arafat had finally learned a lesson after having found himself on the losing side of all solutions or conflicts that might have improved the lives of his people. This time around, the Palestinian leader has not lauded Saddam nor condemned the United States. And yet, his silence is deafening, loud enough to be heard throughout the world as a sign that he has still not learned how to make the transition from terrorist to statesman. His silence only proves—once again—that he is a leader who resists the notion of supporting his own Prime Minister or joining the mainstream to become a valid partner for

299

peace that could result in the beginning of a process that would eventually lead to a comprehensive accord for his people. Or, perhaps Mr. Arafat is a coward, afraid to send a signal to his people that an era has passed, an epoch of brutality, oppression and glaring inequity between the opulent lifestyle of a dictator and the indescribable misery of the people. Up until now, the only road map that Mr. Arafat has supported is the one that leads his people, jobless or employed, religious or secular, educated or illiterate, into the clutches of those men willing to sacrifice them as the most effective weapon to slaughter their enemy. And, the latest female suicide bomber, Hanadi Jaradat, is just one more tragic example of this horrific trend.

Until she blew herself up at Maxim's restaurant in Haifa on the eve of Yom Kippur, on October 4, 2003 at exactly 2.35 in the afternoon, taking with her nineteen Israelis and Israeli Arabs, and injuring more than sixty others, Hanadi Jaradat was one of the lucky ones. She was lucky because she was one of the few privileged Palestinians living under Israeli occupation. A lawyer who had studied in Jordan, she came from an educated family (several of whom had also been sent abroad to study) who lived above the usual poverty line and was about to begin her law practice in a brand new office in Jenin. What makes this suicide bombing so terrifying is not that Jaradat was a woman, but that she was proof that the culture of death permeating Palestinian society is no longer limited to the poor or desperate. Jaradat enjoyed a life of promise where she was in a position to help others and, against all odds, succeed.

When Jaradat returned from Jordan to her father's house in Jenin, she found herself living in an atmosphere of militant Islam that viewed women as second-class citizens. A woman who is free spirited and independent is not only a danger and a threat to rigid cultural and religious rules, but also a disgrace to her family. Jaradat's father had spent years in an Israeli prison in the 1970s and was a member of the Islamic Jihad, as were all her male relatives. In fact, her cousin, Salah Jaradat, was the commander of the Islamic Jihad in Jenin.

Last May, Jaradat, along with her cousin, Salah, and her brother, Fahdi, were sitting in a café in Jenin when Israeli security agents disguised as Arabs confronted them. Parked not more than five feet away was a bomb-laden car that Fahdi was supposed to drive and explode in Haifa the following day. Without preamble, the Israeli agents shot and killed Salah and Fahdi. Later they would explain to their superiors that the "beautiful girl" who had been with them got away. Jaradat may have gotten away from the Israelis, but she ran directly into the arms of Yasser Obeidi, one of the most wanted men in the West Bank. Obeidi, a twenty-nine-year-old married man and the father of two young children, was the military commander of the Islamic Jihad in Jenin.

For the next two months, Hanadi lived with Obeidi and his family in Zboda, a village not far from Jenin. According to neighbors and friends, Jaradat vowed revenge for the deaths of her cousin and brother and began fasting and praying that Allah would accept her as a martyr. Obeidi seduced, recruited and trained Jaradat until she was ready for her mission. He became her lover, mentor and one-way ticket to Paradise where he promised that they would find eternal happiness together as man and wife. She was to go first and he would follow. Jaradat's voyage to eternity ended at that seaside restaurant in Haifa when, dressed in a mini skirt and carrying a knapsack filled with ten kilos of dynamite, she detonated the bomb.

The relationship between Jaradat and Obeidi was doomed from the inception. There was no complicity between them since in a society steeped in fundamentalism, double standards don't disappear even within the concept of martyrdom. Hanadi Jaradat was in love with a married man who duped her into believing that by dying a martyr's death, she would achieve equality, exact revenge and find fulfillment as a woman. Tragically, her relationship with her handler is not unusual in the context of the five other women who blew themselves up in the name of liberating Palestine.

Within hours of the attack, Israeli forces blew up her family home in Jenin as well as Yasser Obeidi's house in Zboda. In fact, when they entered the house, they told Obeidi's wife that regardless of where she went, they would follow her and destroy whatever house in which she took refuge.

Not surprisingly, there are now conflicting stories about how and why Jaradat decided to end her life. On the Palestinian side, people say that she had been determined to avenge the deaths of her cousin and brother at the hands of Israeli soldiers who had targeted him, along with other suspected members of the Islamic Jihad. On the Israeli side, intelligence sources claim that she was depressed because at twenty-nine she had no prospects for marriage; allegedly she intimidated men because of her good looks and education. There are also conflicting stories concerning the route she took from Jenin to Haifa. On the Palestinian side, they say that she managed to penetrate the wall with the help of an Israeli Arab. On the Israeli side, the official word is that she slipped into Israel with the help of an operative from the Islamic Jihad at a spot where construction of the security fence had not yet been completed. The two versions are very telling, not so much because they recount the last hours of Jaradat's life or even the motive for her horrific act, but because they attempt to justify the cause and effect of this on-going conflict from both perspectives. From the Palestinian side, walls are useless in keeping out the hatred and vengeance that fills the hearts and minds of the people. From the Israeli side, an unfinished portion of the wall enabled a bomber to carry out a deadly mission—only more reason that the wall must be completed. From the Palestinian side, even an Israeli Arab who purportedly lives better than most, has the same instinct to help kill his occupiers. From the Israeli side, a member of the Islamic Jihad, the usual radical terrorists who reject any negotiated peace accord, led the bomber to her target.

As usual, there are also conflicting opinions about how to stop this deadly violence on both sides of the Green Line. Expelling Yasser Arafat from the Occupied Territories, assassinating him or simply rendering him impotent are not viable solutions. Nor is building a wall to physically separate Israelis from Palestinians. Nor will a unilateral retreat by the Israelis ensure a democratic Palestinian state where there is an absence of violence, vengeance or financial irregularities. The truth is that neither the disappearance of Arafat nor the construction of a wall can protect either side from the hatred, fear, and suspicion that has been embedded in both people for generations. And, in the context of reality, not without a substantial change in the mindset of the Palestinians will their leaders ever relinquish the strangle hold they have on them.

The Palestinian people need a new symbol of liberation to replace Mr. Arafat. More crucial is that Palestinians themselves need a new image—one that will replace the starving children in refugee camps, angry adolescents deprived of an education, able men and women without the means to support their families, and even Palestinians who prefer to die in the prime of their lives rather than realize their personal and professional dreams.

The people whose stories have been told in this book are either dead or imprisoned. The families of the victims continue to suffer equally from their losses, whether their relatives were the actual bombers or simply bystanders who just happened to be in the vicinity of the explosives. The tragedy and the cynicism and the horrific waste of life, however, continues and will undoubtedly go on for an indeterminable amount of time. Surely there will be another woman—or man—who succeeds in penetrating Israeli security to blow herself up at some point during this latest ceasefire.

In November, 2003, there was a glimmer of hope when a group of Israelis and Palestinians met in Geneva to try and open up a moribund peace initiative. The problem was that Yossi Bellin, an Israeli, and Yaser Abed Rabbo, a Palestinian, had no authority to represent either side officially. Nonetheless, the agreement that they signed called for Israel to pull back to the 1967 borders, relinquish half of Jerusalem and turn over authority of the Temple Mount to the Palestinians, in return for the Palestinians relinquishing the "right of return" for their refugees. While the agreement that was signed in Geneva on November 7, 2003, had no official consequences, it clearly raised the consciousness of both sides to realize that there were still Palestinians and Israelis who were willing to make compromises to find a solution to the on-going bloodshed. In fact, of the two protagonists, it was Yaser Abed Rabbo who exhibited extraordinary courage since he took the initiative to act without the sanction and blessing of Yasser Arafat, after Abu Mazen, the first Palestinian Prime Minister appointed by Arafat had resigned.

As for Abu Mazen, he was an honest man who genuinely wanted to lead the Palestinian people to a better life. Proof of his honest intentions could be that he finally resigned under pressure from Mr. Arafat who refused to allow him to function autonomously to achieve his goals. Currently, Abu Ala has taken on the thankless job of Prime Minister although it is debatable how much effect he has and will have on controlling the extremist elements in his society or restraining Mr. Arafat. In an interview with Abu Ala by telephone from his office in Ramallah after Saddam Hussein's capture, he finally broke the silence from the Palestinian camp, even if his remarks were ambiguous at best and non-committal at worst. "This is the problem of the Iraqi people, not other people," he said. "I just hope that some good change will come about for all oppressed and occupied people of the world."

All Palestinians suffer under a harsh and humiliating Israeli occupation. But even if world pressure succeeds in ending that occupation, how will the Palestinian people free themselves from that fatal cocktail of religious doctrine that promises the bomber eternal life, nationalistic fervor, and economic deprivation? The tragedy is that these reasons are no longer even sufficient to justify this senseless phenomenon. Desperation must now be redefined to include the hopelessness of Palestinians like Hanadi Jaradat who have no leadership to encourage, validate, and applaud their accomplishments and ambition.

For those of us who are pessimists concerning any solid agreement, the reasons for our negativity are certainly justified. As long as the Palestinian leadership believes that, in sacrificing their

305

own, they will eventually break the will of the Israeli government, the violence will go on. After all, the Palestinian Authority in the Occupied Territories owes its presence there to the first Intifada which began in 1987. The collapse of the Oslo Accords, however, is not only due to the on-going violent revolt of the Palestinians, but also to the intransigence of the Israelis to withdraw, as provided for in Oslo, to make room for a Palestinian State.

Currently, in Israel, elections are won and lost on the basis of resisting the creation of a Palestinian State under the guise of protecting the people from terrorist attacks. In the West Bank and Gaza, the popularity and survival of Palestinian leaders is contingent upon stirring up religious fervor to demolish the Jewish State. The reality, of course, is that financial gain and political power are the underlying motives for both Israeli and Palestinian leaders. And, as usual, the ultimate victims of that ambition are the people who will continue to die in senseless attacks. Sadly, it has become much more than merely preserving Holy Land, but rather guaranteeing the survival of future generations. The economy on both sides of the Green Line is abysmal, fear and hatred are rampant, and an obsession with death and dying has entered into the lexicon of all children.

Solutions are elusive in this conflict. The media has no interest in a peaceful Middle East, since harmony and tranquility do not make for sensational reporting. The politics of non-violent resistance is as fruitless in that area of the world as trying to build a foundation in the quicksand surface of the moon. The only hope is to place the responsibility with the international community who have the financial power to force both sides to accept the reality that both will exist. Perhaps even more crucial is for the international community to encourage the Israelis and the

Palestinians to revolt not against each other, but rather against the betrayal of their respective leaders who are the only winners in this horrific situation.

ACKNOWLEDGMENTS

MY GRATITUDE TO all those on both sides of the Green Line, throughout the West Bank, Gaza, and Israel, who were so generous with their time when it came to talking to me and sharing their experiences. Thanks to those academics, psychiatrists, and military personnel who helped me understand all the various aspects of this struggle, including the more painful life-and-death realities that occur every day. Most important to this book and to my documentary film were the families who, despite their grief, were able to tell their stories, and those of their family members who died, with such poignancy and dignity.

ACKNOWLEDGEMENTS

INDEX

311

314

315

317